SUCCESS BY DESIGN

SEVENTH EDITION

Gabby McCutchen | Erin Riney

hayden-mcneil
Macmillan Learning

Printed in the United States of America

10 9 8 7 6 5 4 3 2 1

ISBN 978-1-5339-7330-6

Macmillan Learning
120 Broadway
New York, NY 10271
www.macmillanlearning.com

Our products are in compliance with the European Union's (EU) General Product Safety Regulation (GPSR). If you have any safety concerns about our products, please contact our EU authorized representative:

Macmillan Publishers International Limited
1st Floor, The Liffey Trust Centre
117-126 Sheriff Street Upper
Dublin 1
D01 YC43

MCCUTCHEN 7330-6 F25

Macmillan Sustainability

Hayden-McNeil/Macmillan Learning Curriculum Solutions is proud to be a part of the larger sustainability initiative of Macmillan, our parent company. Macmillan had a goal to reduce its carbon emissions by 65% by 2020 from our 2010 baseline and achieved at least a two-thirds reduction in emissions during this period. Additionally, paper purchased must adhere to the Macmillan USA Paper Sourcing and Use Policy. To learn more about the status of our sustainability initiatives please visit: http://sustainability.macmillan.com.

FSB Professional/Shutterstock.com

Table of Contents

Shutterstock.com

Introduction: Getting a Good Start

Congratulations on enrolling in ACA! This class will help you prepare for academic success at your college and beyond. *Success by Design* has been written to accompany what you learn from the class through the inclusion of content and practice activities customized for North Carolina community college students.

Success by Design and your college success course will provide a useful structure to learn more about yourself, your college, and learning strategies. While you likely already have some knowledge of these topics, it is often difficult to prioritize the reflection and research necessary to further develop your awareness and skills on your own. *Success by Design* and your ACA class will provide you with expert instruction in academic and career goal discernment, learning strategies, and college culture to take your knowledge to the next level.

Many NC community colleges require ACA for degrees or diplomas because college success classes like ACA have proven to be very important to student persistence and success, as national research tells us. In fact, data from within our state indicates that students taking and passing ACA with at least a C are more likely to return to the college the next semester. And that's exactly what your college's faculty, staff, and administrators want to see—students coming back semester after semester to earn the credits necessary for a college credential. Succeeding in this class will lay a foundation for success in future courses.

As you prepare for academic success this semester, have a look at the Table of Contents and note the concepts you will be discussing through this class. Flip through the book to see how you might augment your knowledge and become prepared to meet college expectations. Notice, too, the large margins, which provide plenty of room for you to take notes easily, and the end of chapter questions, which will review important chapter concepts. You'll also find helpful tracking sheets to personalize your learning and strategies as well as troubleshooting tables, sidebars, and bolded terms with critical information and tips. Throughout *Success by Design*, you'll find useful information and strategies that you can start to apply immediately to guarantee your college success.

Begin planning for your success today!

Unit 1

COLLEGE CULTURE

To fully understand how to participate in the scholarly community of a specific institution of higher education, you have to understand the culture of the institution. College culture includes more than just knowing where different offices are on campus. You must be able to speak the language, observe the cultural norms, and navigate the systems. Many students experience "culture shock" in their first semester because college is so different from what they experienced in high school or because it has been a long time since they've been in a classroom environment. The chapters in this unit will help prevent you from suffering from "culture shock" at your community college.

You can learn a lot about the culture of a particular college or university by reading its mission statement. The North Carolina Community College System mission statement is excerpted below from its website (nccommunitycolleges.edu, accessed November 22, 2024):

"The mission of the North Carolina Community College System is to elevate North Carolina's future by delivering a diverse, highly skilled talent pipeline aligned to the labor market, supporting economic mobility that creates transformational generational change, and setting the national standard for innovation in higher education and workforce development by providing:

- Education, training and retraining for the workforce including basic skills and literacy education, occupational and pre-baccalaureate programs.
- Support for economic development through services to and in partnership with business and industry and in collaboration with the University of North Carolina System and private colleges and universities.

STUDENT NOTES

- Services to communities and individuals which improve the quality of life."

Look for your college's mission on its website or in the college catalog to learn more about the college's values and how it perceives its role in your community. You'll likely find some of the same concepts (for example, supporting student success, providing a qualified workforce, offering a variety of levels of instruction to adults) as you see in the system-wide mission above.

CHAPTER 1: Orientation to Higher Education
In order to move successfully through a culture, you must know how systems are organized and what behaviors are appropriate and inappropriate. It should be obvious to you by now that you can't assume that successful navigation of high school will automatically prepare you for the college environment. This chapter highlights many of the expectations that most community colleges have of their students.

CHAPTER 2: The College Experience
As you become familiar with your different roles as a college student, you may seek help from the college in fulfilling those expectations. Chapter 2 describes many of the most valuable resources on campus for new college students as well as tips for using them effectively.

CHAPTER 3: Wellness in College
In addition to being fluent in the culture of higher education, your academic success is also correlated with your personal wellness strategies. Chapter 3 presents strategies for leveraging your mindset, sleep, nutrition, and exercise for your academic success. It also explores techniques for minimizing common traps like stress and multitasking. And your long-term financial health depends upon your current financial health and planning.

Important Learning Outcomes for Unit 1

- Explain the rights and responsibilities of a college student and an advisee.
- Identify essential college policies and procedures, including academic integrity, avoiding plagiarism, calculating a GPA, and maintaining satisfactory academic progress for financial aid eligibility and/or good academic standing.
- Identify essential college resources, including financial aid, advising, registration, tutoring, library services, computer labs, and counseling services; and recognize the importance of these resources on student success.

Unit 1: College Culture Tracking Sheet

STUDENT NOTES

As you read Unit 1, record the individual elements of your personal college culture in the table below. This will be a helpful record to track your personalized preferences and plans.

Advisor Contact Information	Student Clubs or Organizations That Interest You

College Wellness Goal	Two College Departments or Services to Explore Further

Cumulative GPA Goal	Program GPA Goal

STUDENT NOTES

Robert Kneschke/Shutterstock.com

UNIT 1

Chapter 1

Orientation to Higher Education

Before you read this chapter, reflect on the following:

1. *What do you already know about student roles and responsibilities? Think about your high school experiences. What were your responsibilities and what were your teachers' or your parents'? How might that differ in college?*
2. *How many of the 100+ North Carolina colleges and universities can you name?*
3. *What do you need to learn about student responsibilities? Why?*

These questions will help you plan your learning, an important part of metacognition.

Higher education has its own culture, with norms that often differ from other contexts, including high school. You need to learn the language, expectations, and processes of this new environment. Unfortunately, this important orientation is often not clearly or thoroughly relayed to new students; nevertheless, you are expected to abide by and operate within these norms. If you're a first-generation college student (meaning you're the first in your family to attend college) or otherwise find yourself without a successful college graduate to guide you in the process, it's common to feel overwhelmed or confused when navigating college procedures, resources, and expectations both in and out of the classroom. Chapter 1 will provide much of this critical background to help you understand your new context as a college student. Understanding these concepts will help you make sense of the various interactions you have with college faculty, staff, and other students.

STUDENT NOTES

An institution is any community college, university, or place of higher education.

The Structure of Higher Education

When someone says they are going to college, they can mean a lot of different things. In the United States, there is a wide variety of institutions of higher education, including universities, colleges, and community colleges. In general, **universities** are post-secondary (that is, school after high school) institutions that award bachelor's degrees, master's degrees, and doctoral degrees. Universities tend to be large and offer a wide variety of majors and programs. **Colleges**, on the other hand, are usually smaller and focus on bachelor's degrees. There are exceptions to these general descriptions, and universities and colleges can change their designation with the approval of their accrediting organizations. **Community colleges**, like universities and colleges, offer post-secondary programs and can vary in size, but they almost exclusively offer associate degrees, diplomas, and certificates. Another important characteristic of institutions of higher education is whether the school is public or private. **Public universities, colleges, and community colleges** receive state funding, and the majority of enrolled students are from in-state. Public institutions typically have two different tuition rates—a lower tuition rate for students who qualify for in-state status and a higher tuition rate for students who qualify for out-of-state status. Public institutions cost considerably less than private institutions, and they typically have higher acceptance rates. The 16 universities in the University of North Carolina system are all public universities:

- Appalachian State University
- East Carolina University
- Elizabeth City State University
- Fayetteville State University
- North Carolina A&T State University
- North Carolina Central University
- North Carolina State University
- UNC Asheville
- UNC Chapel Hill
- UNC Charlotte
- UNC Greensboro
- UNC Pembroke
- UNC School of the Arts
- UNC Wilmington
- Western Carolina University
- Winston-Salem State University

Note that all community colleges are public institutions. In North Carolina, there are 58 community colleges:

- Alamance Community College
- Asheville-Buncombe Technical Community College
- Beaufort County Community College
- Bladen Community College
- Blue Ridge Community College
- Brunswick Community College
- Caldwell Community College and Technical Institute
- Cape Fear Community College
- Carteret Community College
- Catawba Valley Community College
- Central Carolina Community College
- Central Piedmont Community College
- Cleveland Community College
- Coastal Carolina Community College
- College of The Albemarle
- Craven Community College
- Davidson-Davie Community College
- Durham Technical Community College
- Edgecombe Community College
- Fayetteville Technical Community College
- Forsyth Technical Community College
- Gaston College
- Guildford Technical Community College
- Halifax Community College
- Haywood Community College
- Isothermal Community College
- James Sprunt Community College
- Johnston Community College
- Lenoir Community College
- Martin Community College
- Mayland Community College
- McDowell Technical Community College
- Mitchell Community College
- Montgomery Community College
- Nash Community College
- Pamlico Community College
- Piedmont Community College
- Pitt Community College
- Randolph Community College
- Richmond Community College
- Roanoke-Chowan Community College
- Robeson Community College
- Rockingham Community College
- Rowan-Cabarrus Community College

STUDENT NOTES

What 2–3 community colleges are nearest you? Community colleges offer different credentials, and it may be advantageous to attend a community college farther away.

STUDENT NOTES

- Sampson Community College
- Sandhills Community College
- South Piedmont Community College
- Southeastern Community College
- Southwestern Community College
- Stanly Community College
- Surry Community College
- Tri-County Community College
- Vance-Granville Community College
- Wake Technical Community College
- Wayne Community College
- Western Piedmont Community College
- Wilkes Community College
- Wilson Community College

Private universities and colleges, on the other hand, depend on private donations and tuition, and their students may be more diverse in the states that they come from. Private institutions cost considerably more than public institutions, charge the same rate of tuition to all of their students regardless of whether they have in-state or out-of-state status, and can be more selective in which students they admit. While tuition and fees at private universities and colleges are considerably higher than tuition and fees at public institutions, many private schools offer generous merit and need-based financial aid packages for eligible students. There are 36 private universities and colleges in North Carolina:

- Barton College
- Bennett College
- Belmont Abbey College
- Brevard College
- Cabarrus College of Health Sciences
- Campbell University
- Catawba College
- Chowan University
- Davidson College
- Duke University
- Elon University
- Gardner-Webb University
- Greensboro College
- Guilford College
- High Point University
- Johnson C. Smith University
- Lees-McRae College
- Lenoir-Rhyne University
- Livingstone College
- Louisburg College
- Mars Hill University
- Meredith College
- Methodist University
- Montreat College

- University of Mount Olive
- NC Wesleyan College
- Pfeiffer University
- Queens University of Charlotte
- St. Andrews University
- Saint Augustine's University
- Salem College
- Shaw University
- Wake Forest University
- Warren Wilson College
- William Peace University
- Wingate University

STUDENT NOTES

North Carolina has the second highest number of HBCUs in the country. Ten of the state's public and private colleges and universities are designated Historically Black Colleges and Universities, commonly called **HBCUs**, which were established to serve African American and Black students at a point in American history in which African American and Black students were denied entry to traditionally White institutions of higher education. Several of the state's HBCUs are noteworthy, including Bennett College, which is one of only two women's-only HBCUs in the United States; North Carolina A&T State University, which is the largest HBCU in the country; and Shaw University, the first HBCU in the southern United States. North Carolina's HBCUs include the following:

- Bennett College
- Elizabeth City State University
- Fayetteville State University
- Johnson C. Smith University
- Livingstone College
- North Carolina A&T State University
- North Carolina Central University
- St. Augustine's University
- Shaw University
- Winston-Salem State University

Although none are located in North Carolina, many other Minority-Serving Institutions (MSIs) exist in the US, including Hispanic-Serving Institutions, which can be found in over half of US states; Tribal Colleges and Universities, which are mostly in the Rocky Mountain, Northern Rockies, and Southwest regions of the US; and Asian American and Native American Pacific Islander-Serving Institutions, which are predominantly on the West Coast and in major metropolitan areas.

In addition to a variety of types of universities and colleges, there are also several different types of post-secondary credentials that students can earn. Community colleges award associate degrees, diplomas, and certificates, and you can learn a lot about these credentials in Chapter 5 of *Success by Design*. These credentials require the least number of credits and time in colleges and can lead to high-paying jobs and/or seamless transfer to senior institutions. **Associate degrees** require a minimum of 60 credit hours and take approximately two years of full-time enrollment to complete. Universities and colleges all offer **bachelor's degrees**, which typically require 120 credits to complete and include some general education courses and some major or program courses. Most students finish bachelor's degrees in 4 or 5 years if enrolled full time. There are lots of different kinds of

A credential is a certificate, diploma, or degree.

STUDENT NOTES

bachelor's degrees, including Bachelor of Arts (BA) and Bachelor of Science (BS). Associate degrees and bachelor's degrees are undergraduate credentials, and students enrolled in these programs are often called undergraduates, or undergrads.

After graduating with a bachelor's degree, some students continue their education in pursuit of a graduate degree like a master's degree or doctoral degree. **Master's degrees** typically require two additional years of study beyond the bachelor's degree and allow students to further specialize in a field of study. College graduates can also pursue **doctoral degrees**, which can require extensive research, study, and testing that can take 4–9 years. Students can earn doctoral degrees in a variety of different disciplines, such as a JD or doctor of jurisprudence for law, MD or medical doctor, or PhD or doctor of philosophy. Some professions require master's degrees or doctoral degrees. And most professions that require advanced degrees offer higher salaries than those professions that require a college degree (which typically pay better than professions that require only a high school diploma).

Community College Students

arek_malang/Shutterstock.com

There are 1,167 community colleges across the United States and a little over 10 million people enrolled in community colleges according to the American Association of Community Colleges. Community college students made up 41% of all US undergraduates according to recent statistics, so you are in good company in choosing to enroll at your local community college. Nationwide, community college students are more likely to be female than male, enroll part-time while they are working, and receive some kind of financial aid. The average age of community college students nationwide and here in North Carolina is 27.

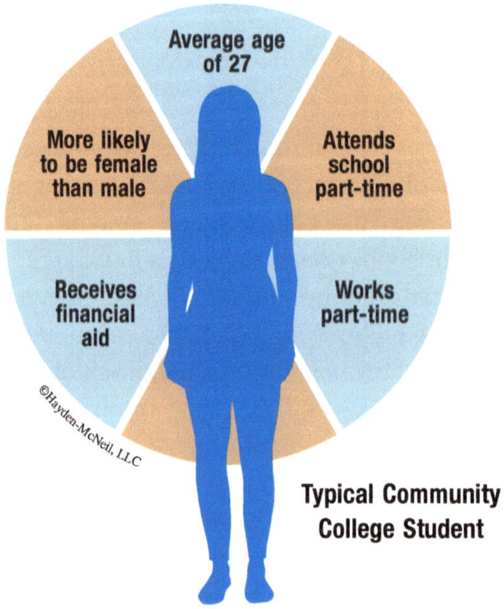

STUDENT NOTES

Look around any community college classroom, and you are likely to find a diverse group of people. Some of the diversity is obvious like students of different races, ethnicities, cultural backgrounds, and ages. But some of the diversity is harder to observe. Some community college students enroll right after high school graduation, while others wait several years to enroll for the first time or return to community college after a previous attempt that was unsuccessful. And still others choose to take community college classes while they are still in high school. In North Carolina, eligible high school students can participate in **Career and College Promise** programs that allow them to enroll concurrently in high school and community college classes. Some students who participate in Career and College Promise programs graduate with a high school diploma and an associate degree at the same time. Community college students may also already have college degrees and are returning to college to learn a new skill or prepare for a different career.

Within the diverse community college classroom, you will have the opportunity to engage people with not only different life experiences but also different ideas and ways of being in the world. One of the benefits of going to college is interacting with these different ideas that might challenge your thinking and understanding of the world. Engaged college students look for opportunities to interact with people who have different ideas in order to strengthen their ideas and develop new ways of understanding the world. These meaningful interactions can take place in the classroom and in co-curricular programs. See Chapter 2 for examples of clubs, organizations, and other co-curricular programs that are available at many community colleges.

Course Types

Students choose to attend community colleges for a great variety of reasons: to earn a credential to transfer to a university, to become licensed in their fields, for personal interest or growth, to learn English, and many more. To meet the needs of all students, community colleges offer two different types of courses: curriculum and non-curriculum courses.

Curriculum courses award college credit toward a certificate, diploma, or degree. If you are taking ACA, you are a curriculum student, and all courses on your Plan of Study (see Chapter 5) are curriculum or credit courses. The programs that are described in Chapter 5 are all curriculum programs. As a curriculum student, you have more resources available to you than most non-curriculum students. See Chapter 2 for information about academic and personal supports offered by the college. Although some of the information in this textbook will apply to non-curriculum students, the information is intended specifically to help curriculum students.

STUDENT NOTES

Locate your college's continuing education courses on your college website. Which would be of interest to you now or when you graduate?

Diego Cervo/Shutterstock.com

Community colleges also offer **non-curriculum courses**, which are classes for personal growth or skills-building and are usually offered through three departments. **Continuing Education** courses are offered by the college to promote lifelong learners who engage in learning to better themselves not only for their careers but also for personal enrichment. Individuals choose to take these classes for self-interest (such as sewing, upholstery, yoga, or sign language classes), licensing or certification (such as vehicle emission inspection, CNA, or personal trainer certification), job training (such as Career Readiness Certificate or Job Skills programs), or to improve basic skills to become more marketable (such as computer or interviewing skills classes).

Non-curriculum classes can also include **College and Career Readiness** and **English as a Second Language (ESL)** classes, through which individuals may obtain a high school diploma, high school equivalency like GED or **HiSET**, or English-language skills before enrolling in curriculum courses. College credit is rarely awarded through Continuing Education, College and Career Readiness, or ESL classes, although individuals in those programs may work toward a completion goal, such as certification or an adult high school diploma.

While these classes will not directly advance you toward your selected curriculum credential by awarding you curriculum credit, some Continuing Education classes may be of interest to you now. For example, if you are unfamiliar with computers or do not feel confident in your abilities to use word-processing software, you may elect to take a keyboarding class or Microsoft Office Word course to prepare you for curriculum courses.

Expectations of College Students

Entering college can be a surprisingly difficult adjustment for some students, whether they are coming right out of high school or whether they have been in the workforce for some time. Considering the differences between high school and college students' roles and responsibilities provides a good starting point for understanding expectations of college students.

In high school, the teacher is frequently in charge of students' learning. The high school teacher often provides regular opportunities for students to check their understanding with graded homework and chapter tests or quizzes. The high school teacher also gives regular reminders of upcoming deadlines and tests and may devote significant time in class to helping students prepare for assignments and tests. Also, high schools often have strict policies (for example, government-mandated attendance until the age of 16), but there are important variations in the policies (for example, a differentiation between excused and unexcused absences).

STUDENT NOTES

In college, on the other hand, learning is often self-directed. College instructors facilitate fewer in-class opportunities for students to check their understanding. College students may take fewer tests, and the individual test grades will count significantly more toward their overall grade in the class. For example, you may take only four tests in one class, and each test may cover up to five textbook chapters and several weeks of classroom instruction. Likewise, college homework is rarely graded; college instructors often just assume that students see the value of the homework and that students have completed it before class. Completing college homework is often part of the maintenance studying you will learn about in Chapter 11. The payoff for doing homework in college comes when you are well prepared for class, you are learning the material at the pace set by the instructor, and you do well on your tests. Finally, college policies can also seem strict, and they are applied to all students with fewer exceptions (for example, excused absences in college are very rare).

Daisy Daisy/Shutterstock.com

These differences exist because the purpose and approach to college education varies from that of a high school education. Understanding the perspectives of higher education faculty, staff, and administrators will help orient you to your new roles and responsibilities.

For example, let's take the purpose of college. If someone asks you why you're enrolled at a community college, you might answer that you're here to get a promotion or to receive a credential that will allow you to begin working in a field; while true, it's important to understand that higher education isn't just job training. If you ask most administrators or instructors, they'll tell you that the goal of higher education is also to produce better thinkers who are skilled not only in their trade but also in communication, problem solving, cultural competency, leadership, and sound judgment. They are interested in producing lifelong learners who can adapt and be prepared not only for the tasks ahead of them, but also be ready for unforeseen challenges down the road. The emphasis on producing better critical thinkers is the reason you take classes that aren't just in your field—composition courses teach sound logic and communication, and philosophy courses teach the basis for ethical decision making. The goal of higher education is complex, but understanding your instructors' and administrators' perspective on a college education may provide you with insight into their motivations, approaches, and decisions.

To cultivate skilled critical thinkers, colleges shift the depth of learning and locus of responsibility. Specifically, college instructors expect students to actively participate in and out of the classroom. This includes contributing to the day's lesson by thoughtfully completing the assigned readings and homework before class. Your college instructors expect that you are spending two

STUDENT NOTES

hours outside of class for every one hour in class. This level of dedication to your education cannot be met if you throw together homework assignments at the last minute or skim textbook chapters that you should have read more carefully. Students who understand the level of preparation expected of them have a clear advantage over students who aren't aware of their responsibilities. For example, students sometimes expect their instructors to provide an overview of reading assignments and homework during class. Many college instructors will not provide such an overview; instead they will use class time to build upon the concepts introduced in the reading assignments and homework. When you prepare appropriately for class, you can then completely participate in discussions and group activities. This participation will help you pay attention during class and will help you understand the course content.

The following chart, adapted from **Bloom's Taxonomy,** provides a visual representation of your instructor's expectations for your class preparation. The bottom two levels of the pyramid represent the lowest levels of learning. Being able to recall the information and to summarize the main idea are minimum expectations of preparation in college. Your instructors will ask you to utilize higher order learning, such as applying your new knowledge or analyzing and evaluating it during class. The highest level would require you to create something new based on the information you prepared for class. If you haven't done the prep work, you can see how class might be confusing or frustrating. Most students don't realize that what they are being asked to do in college is much more difficult than what was probably expected of them in high school. See Chapter 9 for details about how to effectively complete college reading assignments utilizing the Bloom's Taxonomy framework.

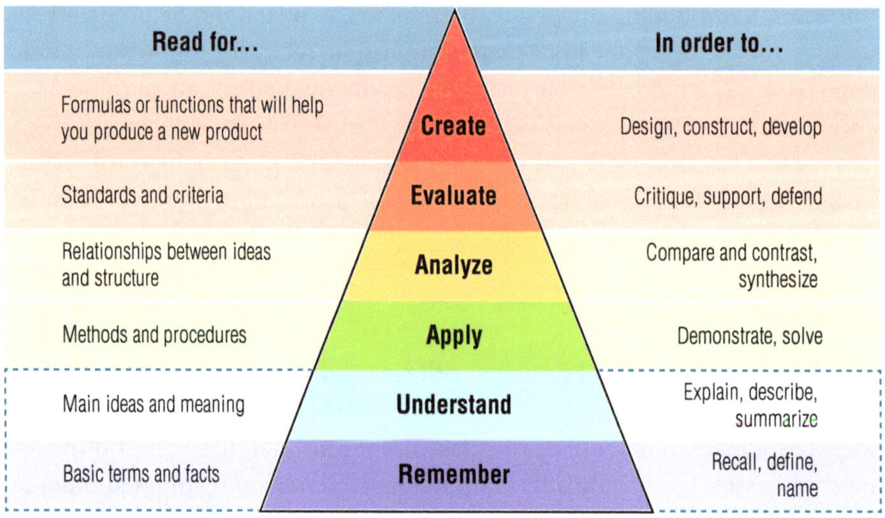

Minimal expectation for college reading assignments

STUDENT NOTES

Similar to expecting a higher level of engagement and thinking, another common expectation of college students is that you are now responsible for your own education. You should monitor your own learning and seek help when you need it. Monitoring your own learning is an important part of metacognition. College instructors rarely give weekly quizzes to check students' comprehension of the small details of the class. Instead, college instructors expect students to keep up with the class instruction by completing homework and by actively participating in class. In addition to paying attention and taking notes, successful college students also ask their instructors to clarify and/or elaborate on confusing concepts. You should also know how you learn best and then find the resources that will help you succeed in each of your classes. For example, if you have a strong preference for a visual learning style and like to see pictures, images, and color, and your instructor uses lecture exclusively, then you should ask your instructor about visual resources you can use to enhance your classroom learning. See Chapter 4 for more examples of how to make your learning style preferences work for you by adapting to a variety of learning environments and teaching styles.

It is appropriate to have certain expectations of your college instructors, too. You can expect your college instructors to be well prepared for class, to start and end class on time (using the full period of instruction each week), and to fully explain the course learning outcomes and each assignment's learning outcomes. Notice the emphasis on the reciprocity of the expectations of college students and faculty. For example, students are expected to arrive on time, and faculty are expected to begin class on time. Students are expected to seek help when they need it, and faculty are expected to be available to students outside of class.

Your college instructors are experts in their fields and dedicated educators. They take their responsibilities very seriously, and they have high expectations of you as an adult learner. If you adequately demonstrate your dedication to your education through regular attendance, participation in class, and using out-of-class resources (including office hours and tutorial services), then your instructors will do their best to help you succeed in their classes.

Academic Integrity

Institutions of higher education value academic honesty. When many college students consider academic honesty, they think specifically of plagiarism, which is only one important part of academic honesty. **Plagiarism** is the presentation of someone else's words or ideas as your own. It is possible to plagiarize purposefully or accidentally, and both are infractions of your college's Academic Integrity Policy. Therefore, college students must educate themselves about their college's Academic Integrity Policy and strategies to avoid plagiarism.

STUDENT NOTES

FIVE STRATEGIES FOR AVOIDING PLAGIARISM:

1. When conducting research, make photocopies or printouts of information you want to include in your paper.
2. Use quotation marks around phrases or sentences that you copy word for word from someone else's work.
3. Follow the citation guidelines as required by your instructor (for example, MLA or APA).
4. Don't forget to cite paraphrased material in addition to quoted material.
5. Ask an expert for help. Your instructor, a tutor, or a librarian can help you figure out what you should cite and then how to do so.

In research papers and class discussions, college students are expected to synthesize what they learn from published articles and books and then make some new points based on the previously published ideas. On assessments and tests, college students are expected to demonstrate their understanding of course content. When students plagiarize or cheat, they violate the college's Academic Integrity Policy, and (just as important) they fail to demonstrate their own learning or understanding of the course material.

Students frequently encounter the temptation to plagiarize when they procrastinate on assignments or feel overwhelmed by the expectations of a class or of a specific assignment. Technology, including but not limited to using AI (Artificial Intelligence) or finding essays and tests online, makes plagiarism very easy for students; at the same time, technology makes it easy for instructors to detect plagiarism.

While some students plagiarize material on purpose, others do so unintentionally because they do not know how to appropriately incorporate other people's ideas and writings into their own papers. Be careful to avoid plagiarism when you quote, paraphrase, and summarize someone else's ideas or words. The best way to avoid plagiarism is by using in-text documentation and a Works Cited or Bibliography page at the end of your paper. Your college English classes will give you many opportunities to practice these writing strategies. Even though you will learn and practice these skills in English classes, your other college instructors will expect you to avoid plagiarism in their classes, too. No matter what program or class you are in, college students are expected to maintain some common standards of academic honesty, including not plagiarizing in writing assignments.

Most Academic Integrity Policies include examples of actions that violate the college's standards in addition to plagiarism. For example, potential violations of a college's Academic Integrity Policy include copying a classmate's homework, using papers from online paper mills, and working with another person on a take-home test. For the college's Violation Procedure and most current information on the Academic Integrity Policy, see the college website. You may also find your individual instructor's application of the Academic Integrity Policy for their class on the class syllabus.

Transcripts

While students may be familiar with transcripts from high school experiences, the importance of your transcript increases in college. Therefore, it's important that students understand exactly what a transcript is and how others will read it. Your **transcript** is the official record of all the classes you enroll in and the grades you earned in those classes at a specific college or university (see page 20 for an example of a transcript). The transcript is usually

STUDENT NOTES

organized by semester with a list of the classes you are taking for that term, the credit hours for those classes, and the grades you earned. Note that if you attend multiple colleges, then you will have multiple transcripts. The transcript is specific to a particular college or university. Also note that if you previously enrolled at the college and stopped attending classes after one or two unsuccessful semesters, those unsuccessful semesters stay on your transcript.

Most colleges and universities report every class that a student attempts (even if it is for the second or third time) on the transcript. Your term GPA and cumulative GPA as well as any special distinctions will also be listed. Special transcript distinctions might include term-specific information like academic honors (for example, President's List, Dean's List, or eligibility for Phi Theta Kappa). Transcript distinctions are also provided at the course-level to indicate transferable courses (see Chapter 5 for more information about UGETC courses and the importance of this designation), honors courses, or service-learning courses.

Your transcript sends a powerful message to future institutions of higher learning and to future employers about exactly what kind of college student you were. They request your transcript because it is a summary of your past behaviors and achievements and is a quick way to judge your candidacy. If you transfer to another community college or a university, then you will request that your college transcript be sent to the new institution. And more and more employers are asking for college transcripts as part of either the application or onboarding process for new employees. Remember, transcripts show all courses ever taken, so if you had a previous attempt at college that did not go well, this will show up on your transcript and you should be prepared to explain it in an admissions essay or job interview. Therefore, it is important to earn as high a grade as possible in every class you register for, regardless of whether the class is a pre-requisite for your program or a class that is required by your Plan of Study. And it is important to monitor your transcript and the impact one semester's grades can have on your overall record.

ESB Basic/Shutterstock.com

Conclusion

Students beginning college are entering into a unique context. Students who strive to understand the culture of higher education and their roles within it will benefit from their informed perspective. Not only will they be able to understand how their work at the community college fits within higher education, but they will also be able to avoid potential pitfalls, such as plagiarism, and be prepared to succeed since they know their roles and responsibilities within their own educations.

STUDENT NOTES

REVIEW QUESTIONS

Chapter 1
Orientation to Higher Education

These questions will help you monitor and evaluate your learning, two important parts of metacognition.

1. Match the terms with the correct information. More than one answer may apply and answers may be used more than once.

    1. Associate degree
    2. Bachelor's degree
    3. Master's degree
    4. Doctoral degree
    5. 2-year college
    6. 4-year college or university

    a. Typically takes 2 to 3 years to complete
    b. Typically takes 4 to 5 years to complete
    c. Often takes 4–9 years to complete
    d. Examples include JD (law school), MD (med school), or PhD
    e. Can be public or private
    f. Offers Associate degrees, diplomas, and certificates
    g. Offers Bachelor's degrees
    h. Can only be pursued after students receive a Bachelor's degree
    i. Usually requires 60 credit hours
    j. Usually requires 120 credit hours

2. Locate your college's mission on your college's website or in your student handbook. Is it what you expected? How does the college's selected mission help you understand your roles and responsibilities in the eyes of the college?

3. Skim back over the Expectations of College Students section. What are two things that you learned that you didn't realize before reading this chapter? How will knowing this information help you in college?

4. Evaluate this student's transcript.

   a. Pretend you're a potential future employer. What questions do you have for this student?

   b. Pretend you're a potential transfer school admissions counselor. Would you admit this student? Keep in mind that you may have limits on the number of students you can admit and that you are looking for students who will persist to graduation at your university.

Sample Transcript

Page: 1 of 1

Date: December 2 2024
Name: Studante, Susanah I.

SSN: XXX-XX-
Birth Date: 10 12 2006
ID: 0998765

Issued to:
Susanah Isa Studante
1234 Home Address Road
Raleigh NC 27713

Curriculum:

Course	Title/Comments	Grd	Repeat	Hrs Att	Hrs Cmpl	Grade Points	Course Dates
	Fall 2023						
ACA-122*A	College Transfer Success	F		1.00	1.00	0.00	08/14/23-12/13/23
CIS-110*	Intro to Computers	D		3.00	3.00	3.00	08/14/23-12/13/23
ENG-111*U	Writing and Inquiry	W		3.00	0.00	0.00	08/14/23-12/13/23
	Term Totals:			7.00	3.00	3.00	GPA = 1.33
	Cumulative Totals:			7.00	3.00	3.00	GPA = 1.33
Academic Standing: Academic Warning							
	Spring 2024						
ACA-122*A	College Transfer Success	A	Y	1.00	1.00	4.00	01/08/24-05/08/24
CIS-110*	Intro to Computers	B	Y	3.00	3.00	9.00	01/08/24-05/08/24
ENG-111*U	Writing and Inquiry	B	Y	3.00	3.00	9.00	01/08/24-05/08/24
MAT-143*U	Quantitative Literacy	B		3.00	3.00	9.00	01/08/24-05/08/24
	Term Totals:			10.00	10.00	31.00	GPA = 3.1
	Cumulative Totals:			17.00	13.00	34.00	GPA = 2.0
Academic Standing: Good Standing							

AA/UT-Arts
Program Total: Completed Cred: = GPA =
Note:
The courses with *U are Universal General Education Transfer Component courses.
The courses with *A are CAA courses.

END OF TRANSCRIPT

5. Janice has been in the workforce for a while and is excited about finally beginning her college journey. However, she's experiencing some challenges in her first semester of college. In particular, she's been frustrated in her chemistry class because she feels like the instructor doesn't explain the concepts well enough for students to understand them. To Janice, it seems like the instructor glosses over topics quickly and then moves into demonstrations or lab assignments. What does Janice need to understand about expectations of college students? How will this help her?

6. Samantha is in ENG 112 (Writing/Research in the Disciplines) this semester. She has always done well in English classes, and so far has an A in ENG 112. However, her first research paper is due in two days, and she hasn't started it yet. While she was researching her topic, she found a paper on the internet that a student at another college had written. It almost meets the requirements of her assignment, and with only a few small changes, she could turn it in as her own. Samantha wouldn't ordinarily do this kind of thing, but she's in a hurry, and she thinks if she makes enough changes to the paper, then she won't get caught. What college policies and procedures does Samantha need to understand to help her make this decision? What advice would you give her?

7. Read the circled part of the original text below from the Occupational Outlook Handbook. Then read the following sentences and decide which sentences are plagiarized. Assume that the student who wrote the sentences had never heard of respiratory therapy before reading this webpage.

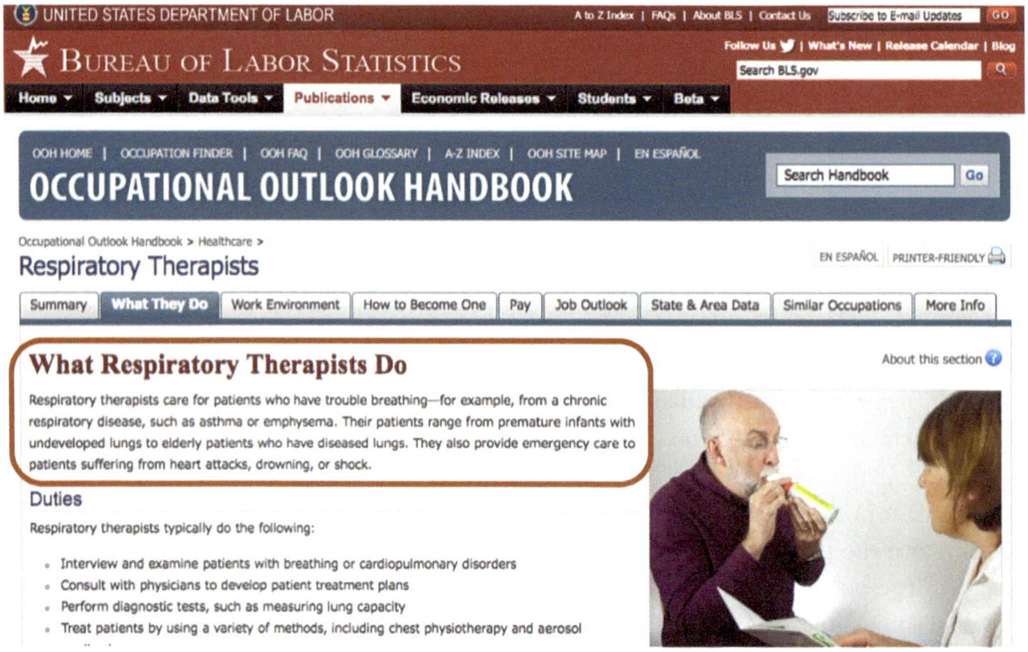

a. Respiratory therapists care for patients who have trouble breathing—for example, from a chronic respiratory disease, such as asthma or emphysema.

b. According to the Occupational Outlook Handbook, respiratory therapists care for patients who have trouble breathing—for example, from a chronic respiratory disease, such as asthma or emphysema ("Respiratory Therapists," What They Do).

c. According to the Occupational Outlook Handbook, "respiratory therapists care for patients who have trouble breathing—for example, from a chronic respiratory disease, such as asthma or emphysema" ("Respiratory Therapists," What They Do).

d. Respiratory therapists provide direct care for patients with breathing disorders.

e. According to the Occupational Outlook Handbook, respiratory therapists provide direct care for patients with breathing disorders.

f. Respiratory therapists provide direct care for patients with breathing disorders ("Respiratory Therapists," What They Do).

Discussion Questions

Plagiarism is not always intentional. Sometimes students incorrectly cite sources or improperly integrate source materials into their assignments. Still, it is a critical issue of academic integrity. Have you experienced challenges with proper use of outside sources? What aspects of citing sources do you find unclear? What steps can you take to make sure to give proper credit to borrowed information?

sirtravelalot/Shutterstock.com

UNIT 1

Chapter 2

The College Experience

Before you read this chapter, reflect on the following:

1. *What campus resources have you already utilized?*
2. *Why do colleges offer these activities and services?*
3. *What kinds of resources might be helpful to you in the future? How would you know if you need them?*

These questions will help you plan your learning, an important part of metacognition.

Chapter 1 approached higher education with a broad lens; Chapter 2 will narrow the focus to what you can expect at your local community college and how you can track your academic progress. Successful college students also know how to navigate and effectively use their campus resources, including the class syllabus, attendance policies, and student services offices. This chapter will introduce you to some of the most useful campus resources for new college students and will also provide you with helpful tips on how to best use resources available to you. Keep in mind that these resources are available on most community college campuses, but you can always check your campus website, talk to your instructors or advisor, or contact the appropriate department to learn more about your school's specific options. The Contact List at the end of the chapter can help you keep track of your college's specific resources and their points of contact.

STUDENT NOTES

Class Schedules

North Carolina community colleges offer classes at a variety of times and in a variety of different formats. Many in-person college classes meet two days a week (for example, Mondays and Wednesdays or Tuesdays and Thursdays) for at least one hour each day. You may also find classes that meet three days a week (for example, Mondays, Wednesdays, and Fridays) for a little shorter time each day. Rarer are the classes that meet only one day a week. The length of class meetings is determined by the number of contact hours associated with a class and the number of days per week that it meets. Many general education classes are scheduled for mornings, afternoons, and evenings. Some **weekend classes** are even scheduled for Saturdays.

Depending on the academic program, some program classes are offered only during the day or only in the evening. As you explore the many programs available to you at your college, look for terms like "day program" or "evening program" on the Plan of Study to determine when classes within that program are scheduled (see Chapter 5 for more information about the Plan of Study). You may find that you can complete a program more quickly if you take day classes. Or you may be able to fit your education around your work schedule if you participate in an evening program. Some programs do not give you an option, though, so you will have to take the courses at the pace and in the sequence in which they are required to be completed.

At most NC community colleges, the fall and spring semesters are 16 weeks long. To help students move more quickly through their coursework, some classes are scheduled as **8-week** classes (sometimes called compressed semesters), which meet for half of the regular term (eight weeks in 16-week fall and spring semesters). These classes cover the same content as the full semester classes, and they meet more frequently (sometimes four days a week). If a class is part of a sequence and it is offered in 8 weeks, then you may be able to complete a two-semester sequence in one semester. For example, SPA 111 (Elementary Spanish I) and SPA 112 (Elementary Spanish II) may be offered in the same semester. If you register for these classes, then you will take SPA 111 in the first eight weeks of the semester and SPA 112 in the second eight weeks of the semester (provided that you pass SPA 111, of course). If you register for an 8-week class, you should plan to be very busy with homework, textbook reading, class meetings, test preparation, and assignments for eight weeks. Taking 8-week classes or compressed semesters requires careful planning to account for the faster pace.

arek_malang/Shutterstock.com

The **summer terms** vary from college to college, but most often they are eight or ten weeks long. This means that summer classes more closely resemble the fast pace of the 8-week schedule than a 16-week fall or spring semester class. When you register for summer classes, anticipate more time

STUDENT NOTES

in the classroom each week and shorter turnaround times between tests and graded assignment deadlines. For example, if you take a psychology class in a fall semester, then you might have tests every four weeks and papers due every three weeks. If you take the same psychology class in the summer, then you might have tests every other week and only a week and a half between paper deadlines. One good strategy for summer enrollment is to take two classes that you expect to be very interesting and/or very easy to you. Another strategy is to take one class that you expect to be challenging, so you can give that one class all of your attention and focus. Whatever approach you take to summer enrollment, expect your summer instructors to use a more fast-paced approach to instruction and sequence of deadlines.

Instructional Delivery Methods

A large number of college courses are offered in the traditional face-to-face format described above. These are the classes that meet for several hours each week on campus.

In an effort to offer greater flexibility to students, many community colleges have increased their offering of **online courses**. Online courses use the college's learning management system (such as Canvas, Blackboard, or Moodle) for all instructional purposes. Online students log in to the learning management system weekly to complete online assignments, take quizzes and tests, participate on discussion boards, and work through online activities. Most online courses are asynchronous, which means that students can do the work for the course at any time during the week. The instructor and students do not have to be online at the same time. Some online courses are synchronous with regularly scheduled online class meetings. In these classes, the instructor and students log on to a video platform at the same time. Whether they are asynchronous or synchronous, most online classes are not self-paced. Students must work through the course content at the same pace with weekly deadlines to organize their learning.

Online classes offer great flexibility for students with irregular work schedules or other time challenges. But many students report that their online classes seem harder than their traditional, face-to-face classes because they don't have regularly scheduled opportunities to meet with the instructor if they have questions and because online classes require excellent time-management skills. Online classes can also require more time than a face-to-face class might require. Instead of attending class three hours per week and doing five to six hours of homework and class prep, the same class in an online format might require a student to spend 9–12 hours per week reading lecture notes, online resources, and discussion board posts, not to mention preparing assignments and studying course content.

STUDENT NOTES

FIVE STRATEGIES FOR SUCCESS IN ONLINE, HYBRID, AND BLENDED CLASSES:

1. Consider whether your skills and learning style preferences are a good match for online learning. Are you a self-motivated, independent learner with sufficient time management and computer skills?
2. Stay in contact with your instructor. If you have a question about an assignment or course content, email or call your instructor with your questions.
3. Don't wait until the last minute to begin your assignments. If you have technological problems or need help from the instructor, it may be too late to get that help.
4. Schedule time to work on your online class at the same day and time each week.
5. Don't get behind. It is even harder to catch up in an online class.

If you enroll in an online course, pace yourself. Most online instructors make the weekly activities and assignments available on the same day each week. Check in with the online class on this day every week, so you can see how much work there is and gauge how long it will take you to complete it. Also, get comfortable with the class website early. Different instructors expect students to submit work in different ways (for example, via email, assignments, view/complete, or a digital dropbox). Make sure you know how to use all of the features of the class site before your first assignments are due. Finally, maintain your academic integrity. If your instructor stipulates that you not use your textbook or other materials during a test, then don't. Focus on your learning process, and the good grades will come. Consider, too, the additional strategies in the margin of this page to help you plan for success in an online learning environment.

Kzenon/Shutterstock.com

If you are unsure about whether online classes are right for you, consider taking a hybrid or blended course first. A **hybrid or blended course** features a combination of weekly face-to-face class meetings and weekly online activities and assignments. Keep in mind that the online activities and assignments are not homework for the class meetings; rather, they are part of the class instruction. You will have significantly more work to do outside of class in a hybrid or blended course, but you will have greater time flexibility because many hybrid and blended classes meet face-to-face only once a week. A hybrid or blended course will give you a sense of the online demands of an online course but will also provide you with regular opportunities to meet with your instructor and your classmates.

Self-paced courses are another instructional format, although they are very rare. **Self-paced courses** provide an outline of course expectations, learning objectives, and requirements that the student achieves at his own pace throughout the semester. Often an instructor is available to assist the student with questions, but much of the content is learned independently through a textbook, videos, or online component. Some disciplines, such

STUDENT NOTES

as math, are better suited to self-paced instruction than others. One of the biggest benefits of this learning method includes the ability for students to learn at their own pace, slowing down to spend additional time on concepts they struggle with or advancing quickly through information they already know.

Many science, math, foreign language, and career and technical education classes include a lab component. **Labs** give students the opportunity to apply the theories and concepts they learn in the classroom. Labs provide much-needed hands-on practice with new skills and concepts. Depending on the class, your lab may be taught by the same instructor, and your classmates may be the same classmates you see in the lecture or classroom component of the course. Other classes have lab components taught by a different instructor, and only some of your classmates may be in your same lab. However your lab is organized, prepare for labs in the same deliberate, thoughtful way you prepare for class (for example, reviewing your notes ahead of time and preparing lists of questions you want to ask your instructor).

In addition to class time and lab time, many students pursuing careers in health fields can expect to spend time in clinical settings. During **clinicals**, students practice their newly learned skills in a variety of real-world settings under the supervision of an instructor or preceptor. Clinicals give students further opportunities for hands-on practice of the concepts and skills they have learned. Students can also see a variety of departments, workplaces, and specializations that they can pursue after graduation. Many clinical experiences require additional preparation, such as a criminal background check, CPR training, and documentation of specific immunizations. When students begin their clinical rotations, they can expect to spend a significant number of hours in the real-world setting. Clinicals can seem like part-time employment (unpaid, of course) in terms of the number of hours required each week.

Another common type of off-campus learning environment that community college students may experience is **work-based learning** (sometimes called cooperative education or co-op). Most students in career and technical programs participate in some form of work-based learning experience. Like clinicals, work-based learning classes provide students with real-world practice of the skills and concepts they have studied in the classroom. Also, like clinicals, work-based learning classes can require a substantial time commitment from students. Work-based learning classes are a great opportunity to practice essential skills, such as punctuality and appropriate workplace language. Some students have leveraged their work-based learning experiences into full-time employment by demonstrating to the company providing the work-based learning experience that they are well qualified for the position

STUDENT NOTES

and demonstrate strong work habits. Even if the work-based learning doesn't lead to employment, the experience can often provide the hands-on experience that many employers seek and that you can list on your résumé.

Like clinicals and work-based learning experiences, service-learning classes offer students the opportunity to apply their knowledge in a real-world setting. **Service-learning** includes a volunteer or community service experience that directly supports the learning outcomes of the course and meets a demonstrated need in the community. Unlike required service hours in high school, service learning is a structured service experience with the service clearly corresponding to the material learned in class. If your class has a service-learning component, then your instructor will discuss your service options and expectations and likely guide you through a reflective writing or discussion experience to both prepare for the service learning and then reflect on your experiences.

Finally, some colleges also offer **honors classes** for students who want to participate in advanced learning experiences. Courses designated as honors classes each semester often require independent study components (often an honors project) that are designed in collaboration with the instructor and/or an honors program coordinator or committee. The benefits of taking honors classes include collaborating more closely with instructors, conducting research or improving your depth of understanding on a topic of interest to you, challenging yourself to prepare for future advanced courses, and participating in a program that will impress senior institutions when you apply for transfer. Check your college's website to see if honors classes are offered and the requirements for participation.

Whatever schedule, instructional delivery method, or course format you choose, be sure to select your classes because they are right for you and not because they are the only classes available when you register. Also, keep in mind that online classes are usually very popular and are often the first classes to fill, so if you want to take a class online, you need to register as early as possible. Talk to your advisor about your readiness for these different instructional delivery methods.

How to Use a Syllabus

STUDENT NOTES

The class **syllabus** is the most important handout your instructor will give you all semester. Think of the syllabus as both a plan and a contract of sorts. The syllabus lays out the instructor's approach and intentions for the course as well as the expectations that you will be held to and that your instructor will uphold. Your instructor will likely discuss the syllabus on the first day of class, but you should read the syllabus very carefully after class, so you'll know exactly what to expect in a specific class. Each instructor organizes the information in her syllabus differently, but you can typically find the following very useful information in every college syllabus: instructor contact information, class policies, and an outline of instruction.

The class syllabus will list your **instructor's contact information**, including her telephone number, email address, office location, and office hours. Your instructor will likely have an office on campus but not necessarily in the same building as your classroom. If your instructor is a part-time college employee, then she may not have an office on campus; however, you should still be able to call or email the instructor for out-of-class assistance. All full-time instructors and many part-time instructors dedicate a specific amount of time each week to working with students outside of class. This time is called **office hours**, and it is your opportunity to connect with your instructors beyond the classroom. Most instructors prefer for students to make an appointment to see them even during office hours. Sometimes instructors are meeting with other students or have to be called away from the office unexpectedly, so an appointment will help guarantee that your instructor is in the office and available to you during a convenient time.

FIVE REASONS TO VISIT YOUR INSTRUCTOR DURING OFFICE HOURS:

1. You have a question about concepts presented during class.
2. You have a question about content in your textbook.
3. You don't understand an assignment or know how to get started.
4. You want feedback on a paper or assignment you are working on.
5. You don't know how to prepare for an upcoming test.

Your syllabus will also include **important class policies**—for example, the attendance, withdrawal, late work, and grading policies. The attendance policy will indicate whether or not you will receive a grade for your attendance in the class and how your instructor counts absences and tardies. The withdrawal policy will indicate the last date to withdraw from the class and earn a grade of W. It will also tell you whether the instructor will withdraw students from the class and under what circumstances. Different instructors have different policies about late work; these policies will be clearly identified in the syllabus. For example, some instructors don't accept late work at all while others accept late work but deduct points from the grade for every day that the assignment is late. Finally, the syllabus will also detail how grades in the class are calculated and what grades you can possibly earn. Most syllabi include a list of the major graded assignments and the point values or percentages that the assignments will count toward the final course grade. (See Grades starting on page 32 for more information.)

STUDENT NOTES

FIVE WAYS TO MAKE EVERY CLASS MEETING COUNT:

1. Read the textbook and other assigned materials before class, so you will be prepared for the lecture, discussion, and activities. See Chapter 9 for more on reading strategies.
2. Review your notes from the previous class meetings. See Chapter 10 for tips on making the most of your class notes.
3. Arrive early and get your notebook, pen, textbook, and other materials out before class begins.
4. Make a list of any questions that you have from the textbook or previous notes, and use the minutes before class begins to ask your instructor these questions.
5. Go to class even if you are late. It is better to miss half of a class meeting than to miss an entire class meeting.

Each class syllabus also includes an **outline of instruction**, or schedule of class meetings, with varying levels of detail. At the very least, most instructors include a schedule of what content or textbook chapters will be covered in each class meeting. Many instructors also identify when tests and assignments are due. And some instructors also list the homework that is due for each class meeting. This outline of instruction is incredibly useful to students who are taking multiple classes. If you write down all of your test days and assignment due dates in your weekly planner at the beginning of the semester, then you can easily plan for these deadlines and not be surprised when your instructor mentions the test that will take place in the next class meeting.

Keep your syllabus in a safe place like at the very beginning of your class notebook or binder. You should refer to it often as you track your progress in the class. Depending on your instructor's teaching style, she may not remind you of upcoming assignment deadlines or tests. It is your responsibility to come to class prepared to submit work or complete assessments according to the outline of instruction that your instructor provides on the syllabus.

Shutterstock.com

The Importance of Attendance in College

Your class attendance is a critical part of the learning process in college. Class meetings are your regular opportunities to learn from your instructor and to demonstrate your learning to your instructor. If you must be absent from class, be strategic about when you are absent. For instance, some college students assume that nothing really happens on the first day of class, but this is often an incorrect assumption. On the first day of class, you not only receive the class syllabus and meet your instructor, but you also can get vital information about how the class is organized and what expectations your instructor has of you. Many college instructors also begin teaching the course content on the first day of class, so if you are absent on the first day, then you can find yourself behind in class before you really get started.

STUDENT NOTES

Prioritizing your attendance for class meetings right before a test is especially important. While few college instructors will dedicate an entire class meeting to preparing for an upcoming test, many instructors will give you guidance on what content to expect to see covered on the test and what kinds of test questions to expect. Instructors may also give you last-minute directions or resources that will help you with an assignment that is due in the next class meeting. Then, of course, you should avoid being absent on the day of the test. Not all college instructors allow for make-up tests, and even if they do, making up a test outside of class can be difficult to schedule. If you must be absent on the day that an assignment is due, then plan to submit your assignment ahead of time or email it to your instructor if possible. Finally, plan to be in class right after the test or assignment deadline or when the instructor returns the graded test or assignment. Your instructor may review the commonly missed test questions, which is a great opportunity to learn from your mistakes and to start to prepare for any upcoming mid-term or final exams. Learning in college is cumulative, which means that concepts build in complexity and difficulty in a single class or course of study, so if you don't understand the concepts on the first test in a class, then you might struggle to understand all future class concepts. If you are absent on the day that your instructor returns the graded tests or assignments, then you miss a chance to learn from your mistakes.

Also, keep in mind that some college instructors give students a grade for their attendance (check your class syllabus to find out if this is true for your instructors). Typically, developmental education and other introductory or pre-requisite classes are most likely to include students' attendance into the overall grade calculation. Even if your instructors do not give you a grade for your attendance, it is possible to fail a class due to poor attendance.

Student-Initiated Withdrawals

Most community colleges allow students to withdraw from classes until some designated point in the term. A **withdrawal** is an official college process often requiring a form; withdrawing indicates you do not plan to complete the class. After withdrawing, you no longer attend the course and will receive a W as your grade. If you must miss several class meetings in one semester, consult with your instructor to find out how the absences will affect your grade. Depending on the quantity and timing of the absences, it might be in your best interest to withdraw from the class and receive a grade of W for the class. Just keep in mind that at most community colleges, W grades do impact your financial aid status but do not impact your GPA. Also, note that many community colleges restrict the number of times a student can register for the same course. Specifically, at some colleges you cannot register for the same course more than three times without special permission from the Dean.

If you plan to transfer to a university, consider the message your transcript sends when you have a lot of W grades. Your advisor, success coach, or instructor can help you weigh these factors to determine whether the W is the best option for you.

STUDENT NOTES

Before you withdraw from any class, be sure to talk to your instructor and a financial aid counselor or advisor (if you are receiving financial aid). Also, note the last day to withdraw from your classes on your class syllabi. If you choose to withdraw from a class, then you must do so by a certain date depending on the length of the class. Look for the most up-to-date information about your college's withdrawal policies on the college website.

Faculty-Initiated Withdrawals

Be advised that your instructors may be able to withdraw you from class, too, based on your attendance. At some colleges, instructors must withdraw students from their classes when the students miss a significant portion of the course instruction. Your instructors will tell you on the first day of class and will include in their syllabi exactly how many absences total a significant portion of course instruction. If you have missed several class meetings in a row, then your ability to make up the course content and pass the class is already jeopardized. Again, check the college website for the full policy and the most up-to-date information.

Excused Absences

According to most North Carolina community colleges' attendance and withdrawal policies, "An excused absence is defined as a planned absence." This is a significant change from high school attendance policies. Your college instructors are mostly very sympathetic people who are concerned about your well-being in addition to your education. However, under the current college policy, they are not able to excuse an absence after the fact. You must submit an Excused Absence Notification form at least 14 calendar days in advance to get your absence from class excused. See your college's website for more details about the excused absence policy and for the necessary paperwork. If you are in the US Armed Forces or National Guard, look for your college's policies regarding excused absences and your service.

Grades

Most colleges use the familiar grades of A, B, C, D, and F. At some North Carolina community colleges, students can also earn grades of AU (audit), CE (credit by exam), I (incomplete), P (pass), R (repeat), NS, (no show), W (withdrawal), and more. Your college's website always has the most up-to-date information about what grades you can earn at the college, and the class syllabus will identify what grades you can earn in a specific class. Many college instructors calculate grades in one of two ways: points or percentages.

Grade Calculations by Points

If your instructor uses **points** to determine your grade in the class, then each assignment will count a certain number of points toward a total number of available points. Your final grade will be calculated by dividing the number of points you earned by the total possible points.

Total Points You Earned/Total Points Possible for the Class = Your Grade for the Course

The table below shows an example of a class with 1,000 available points including points from three tests, a research paper, and a final exam.

Assignment	Points Possible
Test 1	200
Test 2	200
Test 3	200
Research Paper	300
Final Exam	100
TOTAL	**1000**

If your instructor calculates your grade using points, then you can simply add the points you earn on the individual graded assignments to determine your grade in the class. Then see your class syllabus to find out what letter grade your total point number is equal to. See the following expanded table for an example.

Assignment	Points Possible	Your Points Earned
Test 1	200	150
Test 2	200	165
Test 3	200	172
Research Paper	300	225
Final Exam	100	88
TOTAL	**1000**	**800**

The 800 total points earned convert into a letter grade of B according to the table that follows. For this easy example, you could also divide 800 into 1,000 to convert your points into a grade of 0.80 or 80%.

STUDENT NOTES

The number of points or the percentage of the total grade assigned to each individual assignment tells you not only how important it is to your overall grade in the course but also how important it is to the learning process in the class.

In the example to the left, the research paper is worth more points than the individual tests or even the final exam. This tells you that your grade on your research paper will have a big impact on your overall grade in the class and that the research paper will be a significant part of your learning process in the class.

STUDENT NOTES

Points Earned	Letter Grade
900–1000	A
800–899	B
700–799	C
600–699	D
599 or less	F

If you want to calculate your class grade before the end of the semester, you can divide the total number of points you've earned so far by the total number of points possible so far. For example, if you want to know your grade after the first three tests (but before the research paper and final exam), you can add 150, 165, and 172 to get a total of 487 points. Then divide 487 by the 600 points possible so far, and you'll get 0.8116 or 81.16%, which is a grade of B in classes that use a 10-point scale. See the table below for a visual representation of this example.

Assignment	Points Possible	Your Points Earned
Test 1	200	150
Test 2	200	165
Test 3	200	172
TOTAL	**600**	**487**

Grade Calculations by Percentages

Many college instructors use weighted percentages instead of points to calculate students' grades. If your instructor uses **percentages** to determine your grade in the class, then each assignment will count a certain percentage of your total grade. See the next table for an example of a class that has specific percentages assigned to tests, a research paper, and a final exam.

Assignment	Percentage of Total Grade
Tests	50%
Research Paper	30%
Final Exam	20%
TOTAL	**100%**

(Grade × %) + (Grade × %) + (Grade × %) =
Your Final Grade for the Course

STUDENT NOTES

If your instructor calculates your grade using percentages, then you must multiply your individual grades by the percentages that they count toward the total. Then add these numbers to find your total grade in the class. Look at the expanded table below to see an example. Notice that the table includes three test grades that you must first average to get the overall "tests" grade.

Assignment	Percentage of Total Grade	Your Grades Earned	Percent × Grade
Tests	50%	78, 83, 90 (average = 84)	42
Research Paper	30%	91	27.3
Final Exam	20%	93	18.6
		TOTAL	**87.9%**

Again, your class syllabus will tell you how to convert the percent grade into a letter grade. Most instructors will round the grade of 87.9% to 88%, which is a B according to the table of 10-point scale common letter grades below.

Percentages	Letter Grade
90%–100%	A
80%–89%	B
70%–79%	C
60%–69%	D
59% or less	F

To calculate your grade in a class that uses grade percentages, multiply your assignment grades by the percentage of the total.

In the example to the left, multiply 50% (or 0.50) by 84 (average of the three Test grades) to get 42. Repeat the multiplication process for the Research Paper grade (0.30 × 91) and the Final Exam grade (0.20 × 93). Then add 42 + 27.3 + 18.6 to calculate your class grade.

If you want to calculate your class grade before the end of the semester, follow the steps described above but then divide your grade percentage by the total percentage possible. For example, if you want to know your grade after the first three tests and the research paper (but before the final exam), follow the steps above to multiply your individual grades by the percentages assigned to get 69.3%. This is not your grade.

Assignment	Percentage of Total Grade	Your Grades Earned	Percent × Grade
Tests	50%	78, 83, 90 (average = 84)	42
Research Paper	30%	91	27.3
TOTAL	**80%**		**69.3**

STUDENT NOTES

Since Tests (50%) and Research Paper (30%) are 80% of your grade, you must then divide 69.3 by 0.80 because this grade includes only 80% of the total grade for the class. When you divide 69.3 by 0.80, you find that your class grade before the final exam is 86.6% or 87%.

If these examples of two methods of grade calculation are difficult to understand, keep in mind that many instructors will help you figure out how to calculate your grade in their class. If you have a question about how grades are figured in a specific class, then you can always visit your instructor during office hours for clarification. Or you might check the class learning management system website (for example, Canvas, Blackboard, or Moodle) for more information; many instructors post individual assignment grades and running averages on their class websites.

Your Grade Point Average

A **Grade Point Average (GPA)** is a calculated average of the grades you earn in your classes and is a common indicator of success in college. A high GPA will give you eligibility for certain scholarships and honor societies. It will look good on your résumé and will indicate to future employers your strong work ethic. It may also determine whether or not you can transfer to the university of your choice or into a specific major.

ESB Basic/Shutterstock.com

Most colleges calculate multiple GPAs that serve different purposes for students. At the end of each semester, the college will most likely calculate your cumulative GPA for you, so you can see how your grades in your most recent classes impact your overall GPA. When you graduate, the college will most likely calculate your program GPA as well. Both your cumulative and program GPAs will appear on your official college transcripts, which future employers and admissions counselors from other colleges and universities will see.

Cumulative GPA

The **cumulative GPA** frequently includes everything the student has ever taken at the college, regardless of whether the courses are on a student's Plan of Study or not. At some community colleges, the cumulative GPA includes developmental education, other pre-requisite courses, and courses outside of your program of study. However, at other colleges, developmental education courses are not included in GPA calculations. Likewise, some colleges include every attempt at a class in the cumulative GPA while other colleges don't include a first attempt when a student repeats a class. Check with your instructors, advisors, or college website to find out how developmental education classes and course repeats are considered in GPA calculations.

STUDENT NOTES

Consider the following example. A student takes several courses in the Architectural Technology Associate in Applied Science (AAS) program and then changes her program of study to University Transfer Associate in Arts (AA). She will receive a cumulative GPA that includes her Architectural Technology courses as well as her AA program courses. Your grades in every course you take, therefore, are important to your cumulative GPA even if they aren't on your current Plan of Study. And if you are returning to college after a previous unsuccessful attempt, then those previously earned grades—even if they were from 10 years ago—are still calculated into your cumulative GPA.

The cumulative GPA also usually includes every attempt at a class. For example, let's say a student takes MAT 171 (Precalculus Algebra) twice; he earns a D in the class the first time and a C the second time. Both the D and the C are calculated into his cumulative GPA. Again, check with your college website or college catalog to find out how your college's GPA calculation treats repeat attempts at a course. Likewise, both grades will likely appear on the student's college transcript.

Program GPA

Unlike the cumulative GPA, the **program GPA** includes only the courses on a student's Plan of Study. So the student who transfers out of Architectural Technology Associate in Applied Science (AAS) and into Associate in Arts (AA) will get a program GPA that excludes her Architectural Technology (AAS) classes. Her program GPA will only include the classes on the AA Plan of Study.

If you're transferring, your college or university may calculate your GPA differently than your community college. Check the transfer school's admissions department for clarification.

If a student has taken a class more than once, then the program GPA typically includes only the highest grade earned in the class. From the example above, the C in MAT 171 will most likely be calculated into the student's program GPA; his D in MAT 171 will probably not be calculated into his program GPA.

Although many college students think that you can replace a bad grade with a good grade in your GPA and on your transcript, this is a myth at most colleges. You must take every class seriously and earn the highest grades possible because all of your grades may count toward your cumulative GPA. Likewise, all of your grades appear on your transcript. If you suspect that you cannot pass a particular course, consider withdrawing from it and receiving a grade of W, which isn't calculated into your GPA. Be strategic about withdrawing from classes, though. If you receive financial aid, then you must demonstrate satisfactory academic progress through your program of study. In general, grades of W do not indicate satisfactory academic progress and may negatively impact your financial aid status. See pages 46–49 for more information about financial aid.

STUDENT NOTES

Many community college students can also earn grades like AU, NS, P, R, and W, which do not have any quality points associated with them.

Always check your class syllabus to see what grades are possible in each of your classes. And see your college website or college catalog for a full listing of the grades available to you.

Calculating Your GPA

Even though the college will probably calculate your GPAs for you, it is important to be able to calculate your own GPA, so you can track your progress during the semester and so you can anticipate the impact a single grade will have on your GPA. It is also beneficial to track your program GPA yourself since it may not be officially calculated by the college until you apply for graduation.

To calculate your GPA, you must know the number of credit hours assigned to each class you take, and you must convert the letter grade you earn into **quality points**. Use the table below to translate letter grades to quality points.

Letter Grade	Quality Points
A	4
B	3
C	2
D	1
F	0
AU, CE, I, P, R, NS, & W	Not factored into your GPA

Then multiply the credit hours by the quality points to find the total **grade points.**

Credit Hours × Quality Points = Grade Points

For example, if you make an A in HIS 111 (World Civilizations I, three credit hours), then you can expect to receive 12 grade points for the class because the A is worth four quality points, and three (credit hours) times four (quality points) is 12 (grade points). Add the total grade points for all of the classes you take in a semester and divide the total grade points by the total credit hours in the semester to calculate your GPA.

Total Grade Points ÷ Total Credit Hours = GPA

See the following table for an example. Notice that there are six grade points for ENG 111 because the three credit hours multiplied by the two quality points for the grade of C total six grade points. Similarly, there are nine grade points for PSY 150 because the three credit hours are multiplied by the three quality points for the grade of B. In each row, the credit hours are multiplied by the quality points to determine the total grade points for an individual course. In other words, multiply across but add down to calculate the totals.

STUDENT NOTES

Then the total grade points (39) are divided by the total credit hours (12) to calculate a GPA of 3.25.

Course	Credit Hours	Grade	Quality Points	Grade Points
ENG 111	3	C	2	6
PSY 150	3	B	3	9
ACA 122	1	A	4	4
PED 121	1	A	4	4
BIO 111	4	A	4	16
TOTAL	**12**		**TOTAL**	**39**
Total Grade Points ÷ Total Credit Hours = GPA				
39 ÷ 12 = **3.25**				

Knowing how to calculate your GPA can also help you understand the impact a single grade in a single class can have on your cumulative GPA. In the following revised example, the student earns a C in ACA 122 instead of an A. This lower grade brings the student's GPA down, but because ACA 122 is only one credit hour, the overall impact is small. Instead of an overall GPA of 3.25, the student's GPA is 3.08.

Course	Credit Hours	Grade	Quality Points	Grade Points
ENG 111	3	C	2	6
PSY 150	3	B	3	9
ACA 122	1	C	2	2
PED 121	1	A	4	4
BIO 111	4	A	4	16
TOTAL	**12**		**TOTAL**	**37**
Total Grade Points ÷ Total Credit Hours = GPA				
37 ÷ 12 = **3.08**				

However, a C instead of an A in BIO 111 has a much more substantial impact on the student's GPA because BIO 111 is a four-credit hour class. Compare the following table with the previous table. Earning a C in ACA 122 instead of an A changes the GPA from 3.25 to 3.08. But earning a C in BIO 111 instead of an A changes the GPA from a 3.25 to a 2.58, which is a significant difference. A GPA less than a 3.0 often indicates that a student is struggling in college.

STUDENT NOTES

Course	Credit Hours	Grade	Quality Points	Grade Points
ENG 111	3	C	2	6
PSY 150	3	B	3	9
ACA 122	1	A	4	4
PED 121	1	A	4	4
BIO 111	4	C	2	8
TOTAL	**12**		**TOTAL**	**31**
Total Grade Points ÷ Total Credit Hours = GPA				
31 ÷ 12 = **2.58**				

You can apply your understanding of how individual grades impact your GPA in two ways. First, when you have to make difficult decisions about which class to prioritize, you should almost always choose the class that has more credit hours associated with it. Inevitably, college students have multiple tests and/or assignments due in the same week. If you haven't managed your time appropriately, then you may have to choose to study for one test more than another test or to complete only one assignment on time. As you make this difficult decision, consider which class will have the bigger impact on your GPA.

Secondly, when you register for classes each semester, consider the impact of three four-credit hour classes if you are trying to build a full-time 12-credit schedule. There are certain advantages to balancing the four-credit hour classes with one- or two-credit hour classes; specifically, you can have a schedule of classes that vary in their demands and you can better prioritize the higher credit hours. Of course, there are advantages to taking fewer classes, too. Select your schedule strategically to benefit from these advantages.

Alexander Raths/Shutterstock.com

Academic and Personal Support

Your community college recognizes that your success requires additional support beyond the classroom. Numerous academic and personal supports are available to help students strengthen their likelihood for success. As you read through the following information, think about not only what resources would be of help to you now but also note additional assistance you may seek in the future. When a problem arises, students often find it difficult to manage the concern and also research possible resources. Learning these options now will allow you to act more quickly when difficulties do arise.

Advising

Academic advising is an interactive process that connects each admitted student with a college employee who can guide the student's academic decision making. Often, you are assigned an **academic advisor** after you have been admitted to a program. Advisors may be faculty within your program (for example, if you are in the Health Information Technology program, then your advisor is likely to be an instructor of Health Information Technology courses). Sometimes, advisors are faculty and staff from outside your department who have been trained to advise students in your program. Your relationship with your advisor can be one of the most important relationships you have with a member of the college personnel, but the quality of the relationship depends in large part on you.

At most colleges, you may contact your advisor for assistance at any point in the semester, but new students are almost always required to meet with their advisors in preparation for registration. Before registering for classes each semester, students must meet with an advisor to discuss their academic goals and to receive registration approval for the courses they select each semester. As you successfully progress through pre-requisite courses and into your program, your advisor may allow for this "meeting" each semester to take place over the phone or via email. In many programs, advisors have departmental guidelines that they must follow to determine which students to require face-to-face meetings of and which students to allow some flexibility. Even if your advisor doesn't require a face-to-face meeting for registration approval, you can still request an appointment to discuss your academic and career options. Keep in mind that advisors serve dozens of advisees each semester; make an advising appointment early to be able to get a convenient appointment with your advisor.

Prepare for a successful advising experience by reviewing what is expected of you as the advisee and what you can expect of your advisor.

STUDENT NOTES

Advisee Expectations	Advisor Expectations
To take the initiative to contact the advisor about questions or in preparation for an upcoming registration period	To be available to meet with advisees, including on multiple days of the week and at multiple times of the day
To maintain accurate records (see list that follows this table)	To be knowledgeable about the specific program and the college in general
To arrive on time for all scheduled appointments with advisors	To meet all scheduled appointments with advisees
To register for only the classes that the advisor approves based on pre-requisites and co-requisites	To provide sound advice about appropriate course sequences and appropriate course loads
To be forthcoming about progress made in classes and concerns about upcoming classes	To consider the advisee's academic performance in making recommendations regarding registration

See Chapter 5 for more explanations of these documents.

Advisees should keep an electronic or hardcopy advising folder with the following important documents and any other correspondences from the college:

- Any notices of acceptance from the college and/or your specific program of study, which may have been sent as either an email message or a hard copy of a letter sent to your home address
- The Plan of Study you were admitted under
- A Course Selection Guide (if applicable)
- Your placement test scores (if applicable)
- Unofficial transcripts from any other colleges you have attended (if applicable)
- Copies of any registration forms you complete with your advisor
- Your Academic Timeline (see page 181)

In addition to this personal advising relationship, students can take advantage of the expertise of personnel in your college's advising center or transfer center. In these offices, you will find valuable documents, including copies of Plans of Study, Transfer Guides, Course Selection Guides, and Articulation Agreements as well as information about placement testing, careers that your program is preparing you for, and university catalogs.

STUDENT NOTES

University transfer and other students interested in learning about their educational options at senior institutions are especially encouraged to use the college's transfer center and any online transfer information on the college's website. Here you will find information on Transfer Guides, Course Selection Guides, Articulation Agreements, admissions criteria for area universities, upcoming campus visits by college and university admissions officers, and financial aid.

Tutoring

Many colleges offer tutorial services for students who need additional help with particularly difficult classes. Tutoring varies from campus to campus. Some colleges have peer tutoring through which students tutor other students while other colleges employ professional educators with degrees in the subject they tutor (some are even instructors). Some colleges charge students a fee for tutoring; others offer free tutoring to enrolled college students. Some colleges maintain one central center with tables at which you can collaborate with an individual tutor. Others also maintain labs for online tutoring of subjects like math, while others offer an online tutoring platform that you can access via the internet. Check with your college's tutoring center to learn more about how to use this valuable resource at your school, including hours of operation and subjects tutored.

Although tutoring centers vary across North Carolina's community colleges, there are some basic similarities in their operations. For example, there are specific actions that the tutors can and cannot do to help you. Specifically, tutors can explain concepts to you and can help you understand directions or assignments. Tutors can also help you interpret instructors' suggestions and corrections on your work. Finally, tutors can help you build confidence in your own abilities and can help you develop study skills.

Keep in mind that the tutor's goal is to help you learn, not to get you a better grade on an assignment. You should not expect the tutors to do your work for you. Their job is to help you better understand the course content, so you can do the work for yourself. Therefore, tutors most likely will not correct or provide answers on assignments that will be graded. Also, tutors cannot predict your grade or tell you what an instructor expects. Finally, tutors cannot complete your assignments for you or help you with take-home exams.

To make the tutoring experience a successful one, bring your textbook, class notes, assignment sheets, and any other class materials that will be helpful. Also, prepare a list of specific questions that you have about the class content or assignment to share with the tutor.

FIVE SIGNS YOU MAY NEED A TUTOR:

1. **You don't understand how to do your homework.**
2. **You don't know how to begin an assignment.**
3. **You earned a low grade on a test or quiz.**
4. **You suffer from test anxiety.**
5. **You are easily distracted in class and when you study.**

STUDENT NOTES

Library

The college library is another useful campus resource, particularly for new college students. If your school has multiple campuses, a library may be available at more than one location. Check your college's website for locations and hours of operation each semester.

Most often, your student ID card serves as your library card, which will allow you to check out circulation materials, use materials on reserve, and access library computers. Circulation materials (including books, CDs, and audiotapes) can usually be checked out for two to four weeks, depending on your library's policies. Renewals are often available and often can be made online, in person, or by phone. Reserve materials (including some textbooks, sample tests and assignments, and DVDs) may be used in the library or checked out for a designated time period depending on the instructor's preferences.

In addition to circulation and reserve materials, your library will also have numerous periodicals that will only be available in the library. If you plan to read any of the dozens of current newspapers, magazines, or journals in your library, look for the periodicals section and expect to either read the item in the library or make photocopies of the material.

Your library is also a resource for copying and printing. Photocopying and printing costs vary from campus to campus, so make sure you check posted signs or check with a librarian before you print or make copies. Your library will also likely have a computer lab or access to computers to conduct research and possibly word processing and other software to complete assignments. Your library may also have wireless internet so that you can bring a laptop to work at one of the study desks located throughout your library.

Interlibrary loan services may be requested to access materials at another library. If you need a specific book or a journal article not available in your campus's library, then your librarian can request the book or article from other community college libraries or from university libraries. Any fees charged to your library for interlibrary loan materials may be passed on to you.

michaeljung/Shutterstock.com

STUDENT NOTES

Your library also features access to thousands of research resources through online databases, including NCLIVE, CQ Researcher, ProQuest, PsycARTICLES, and Literature Resource Center. These online databases can be accessed from computers on and off campus. Off-campus access is often restricted by password, but you can ask a librarian for the passwords you need. Computers on campus allow you to access the online databases without a password. Countless e-books are also available online through NCLIVE. Like the online databases described above, you may need a password to access the e-books from off campus.

Your library will also provide helpful information on citation guides, such as MLA, APA, and ASA. This information may be available on your college's library website as well. Your college librarians are familiar with multiple citation guides and can help you avoid plagiarism by citing your sources accurately. See page 15 for more information about avoiding plagiarism.

Remember, librarians are always willing to help students. If you need any assistance, don't hesitate to ask.

Computer Labs

Your college instructors will require that most of your assignments, including all papers, be typed. If you are not already familiar with a word-processing program like Microsoft Word, then you may struggle to meet the formatting guidelines for some of your college assignments. Take advantage of online tutorials, the help function in Word, and short courses through Continuing Education programs to improve your word-processing skills. Your campus's tutoring center may also offer a computer-use or digital literacy tutor who can help you improve your basic computer skills.

Campus computer labs are intended for educational purposes and offer services to support students' academic goals. In addition to printing abilities, campus labs will also offer internet access and word-processing software. Additionally, commonly used programs, such as Microsoft Excel or PowerPoint, will be available in most labs. If you don't have a working computer or printer or reliable internet access, then the computer labs will be a great resource for you. Learn the labs' hours and keep in mind that lab monitors are on duty in several labs to assist with basic computer questions.

Some labs may be designated for use by students in certain programs or classes and will provide hardware and software that are typically utilized in that field or in the course of duties associated with certain jobs. These labs may only be opened to students in specific courses and will likely have shorter hours, so make sure you are aware of the lab schedule and any criteria for use before you make plans to rely on that particular lab to complete an assignment.

FIVE TIPS FOR USING COMPUTER LABS ON CAMPUS:

1. **Save your work on a flash drive or jump drive.**
2. **Log out of any online programs such as Canvas, Blackboard, Moodle, or email after use. A student who uses the computer after you may be able to access your personal information if you don't sign out.**
3. **Ask the lab monitor when the computer lab is typically not busy, and then plan your visits accordingly.**
4. **Find a computer lab before you need it. The worst time to look for a lab is when you are desperate to print a paper right before class.**
5. **Print only what you need. If you need only 3 pages of a 20-page article, then print only the pages that you want.**

STUDENT NOTES

Most college computer labs open the first day of classes each semester and are closed on college holidays. Check the specific schedule on your campus. Don't assume the computer lab is always open.

Common Computer Lab Policies and Rules:

- Students must present a student ID card to use computer labs.
- While in the lab, students must abide by the college's appropriate use policy and posted lab rules.
- No food or drinks are allowed in the lab.
- Loud talking is prohibited and cell phones must be turned off or on vibrate.

Be mindful of the limits on free printing. Some labs charge for all printing; some limit the number of free pages per day or per semester; and some always provide free printing. The policy can vary from lab to lab on your campus. Know the costs before you print.

Wireless internet access may also be available on your campus, allowing you to access the internet on your laptop at various locations on campus. Check your college website for locations of wireless hotspots where you can access the internet remotely.

michaeljung/Shutterstock.com

Disability or Accessibility Services

North Carolina community colleges are dedicated to the success of all students. Students with physical, psychological, or learning disabilities may need additional academic supports, which are available through your campus's Disability Services office. Disability Services staff accommodate students with a variety of disabilities through services like individualized educational planning; support staff, including note-takers and interpreters; assistive technology; alternative testing arrangements; and priority assistance during registration. Plan ahead as much as possible to utilize these services since creating the individual plans and providing any required documentation may take several weeks.

Financial Aid

Even though community college tuition is considerably less expensive than tuition at senior institutions, several semesters of tuition can add up quickly. Therefore, the Financial Aid office is one of the first places new students look for when they begin their academic careers. Financial Aid options usually include grants, scholarships, work study, family federal loans, and the North Carolina Community College grant and loan program. However,

STUDENT NOTES

when most people discuss Financial Aid, they usually are speaking of need-based aid, such as Pell grants.

Eligibility for need-based financial aid is based on three factors:

1. financial need,
2. the number of credit hours you are taking, and
3. (sometimes) your program of study.

To find out if you are eligible for financial aid, you must complete and submit the **FAFSA** (Free Application for Federal Student Aid) online, which is available at studentaid.gov. Financial Aid staff can provide some help in completing this application if you need it. You must apply early and yearly for financial aid. Keep in mind that the process takes longer than most students anticipate.

Ways to Pay for College

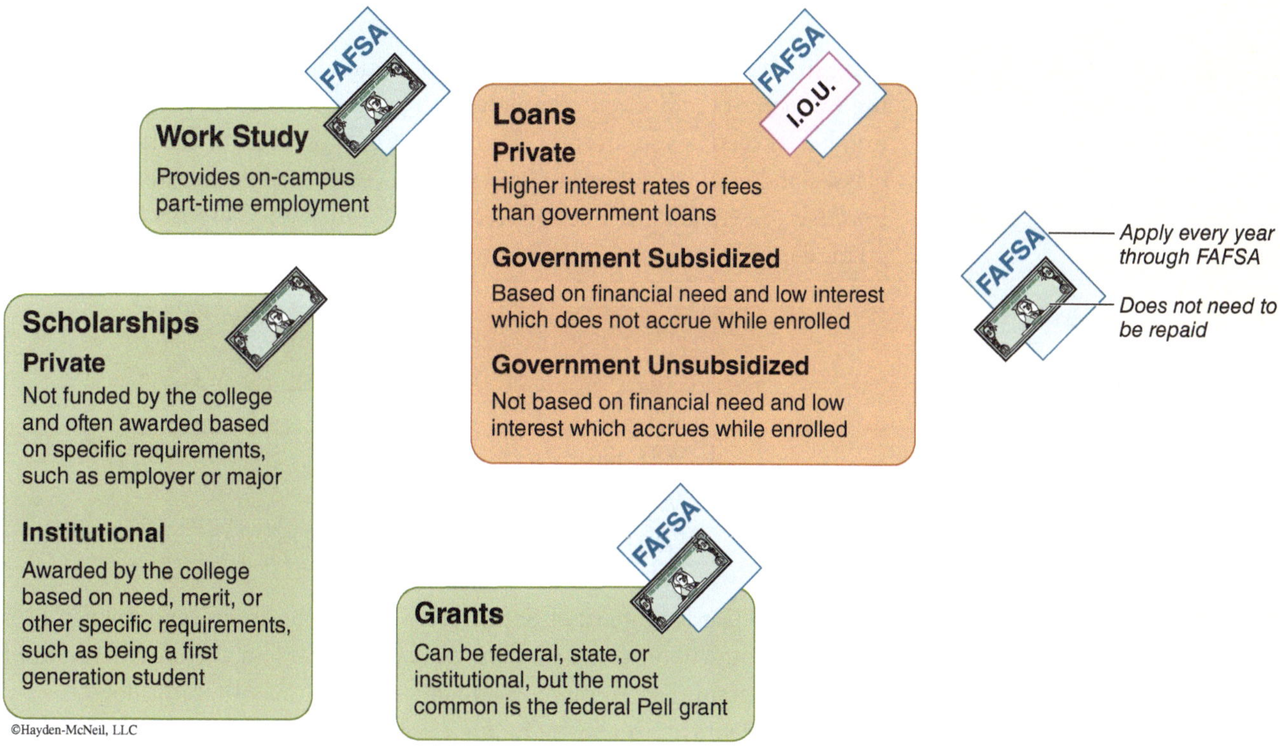

Again, keep in mind that acquiring financial aid is a process that takes time and good planning. See a financial aid advisor sooner rather than later.

STUDENT NOTES

FIVE STRATEGIES FOR MAINTAINING SATISFACTORY ACADEMIC PROGRESS (SAP):

1. Earn a C or better in all of your classes.
2. Before you withdraw from a class, speak to a financial aid officer about how the W grade will impact your completion rate.
3. Register only for courses that are listed on your Plan of Study.
4. Take advantage of campus resources, such as counseling and tutoring.
5. Track your cumulative GPA each semester.

If you receive a financial aid award, then you'll need to demonstrate satisfactory academic progress in order to maintain your financial aid eligibility. **Satisfactory academic progress (SAP)** is defined by the United States Department of Education as meeting the following standards:

1. Maintain a cumulative grade point average of 2.0 or higher (see page 36 for more information about cumulative GPAs);
2. Maintain a cumulative credit hour completion rate of 67 percent or higher; and
3. Attempt no more than 150 percent of the course hours required for graduation.

Your cumulative GPA is easy to track each semester. Many NC community colleges post students' GPAs on their Self-Service accounts. Log in to see if you meet the minimum standard of 2.0. If you attend a college that doesn't count your developmental education courses or first attempts at classes in your academic cumulative GPA, then your college probably does count your developmental education courses in your cumulative GPA for consideration for satisfactory academic progress.

You can also track your cumulative credit hour completion rate by dividing the number of credits you complete with grades of A, B, C, D, and P by the number of credits you attempt. For example, if you register for the following classes and earn the following grades, then your completion rate is 71.4% because you successfully completed 10 of 14 attempted credits (the W grade does not count as completion credit).

Course	Credit Hours	Grade
ENG 111	3	A
PSY 150	3	C
MAT 171	4	B
SPA 111/181	4	W

To meet the third standard of Satisfactory Academic Progress, just keep in mind that you will only receive financial aid for 150% of the credits required for your program. For example, if you are enrolled in a 60-credit degree program and you are receiving financial aid, then you will receive enough financial aid to pay for 90 credits (60 credits on the Plan of Study × 150% = 90 credits covered by financial aid). Or if you are enrolled in a 36-credit diploma program and you are receiving financial aid, then you will receive enough financial aid to pay for 54 credits (36 credits × 150% = 54 credits). This should be enough to cover the cost of the courses listed on your Plan of Study as well as any pre-requisite courses you may have to take.

STUDENT NOTES

For answers to frequently asked questions, descriptions of the different financial aid sources available, and the most up-to-date financial aid information, see your college's Financial Aid webpage or on-campus office.

Another great resource for college students who have questions about financial aid is the College for North Carolina (CFNC) website. CFNC has lots of information about the different sources of financial aid (for example, grants, scholarships, and loans) as well as information about the North Carolina 529 Savings Plan for college and some online financial literacy courses.

Common Financial Aid Myths

I must be a full-time student in order to receive aid.

- The amount of your award is determined by a federal formula and depends on the number of credit hours in which you are enrolled. For Pell grants, full-time is considered 12 credit hours. But Pell grants can be prorated. For example, if you are only taking 6 hours, then you will receive half the award.

I will receive a refund every semester.

- Students only receive a refund if their total aid package is more than their tuition. At most community colleges, you receive a refund because the tuition is very low. If you transfer to a university, you will likely not receive a refund.

Financial aid will pay for all my classes.

- Federal financial aid will only pay for classes listed on your Plan of Study or required as a pre-requisite or co-requisite, up to the amount of your award.

The only financial aid grants available are Pell grants.

- Financial aid packages often also include state and local grants, such as the NC Community College Grant, NC State Education Lottery Grant, or the State Student Incentive Grant. Even if you don't qualify for a Pell grant, you may qualify for other types of aid.

Everyone receives the same amount.

- Financial aid is based on the Student Aid Index (SAI), formerly known as the EFC (Expected Family Contribution), you receive from your FAFSA and varies by individual. It can also vary year to year for you if your income changes from one year to the next.

STUDENT NOTES

Academic, Career, and Personal Counseling

No matter how confident you are now in your ability to navigate the college culture and to prepare for your chosen career, read the following descriptions to learn of the many services available to you, most often through your campus's Student Development office. You may be surprised by the diversity and quality of services available.

Academic counseling usually provides educational planning and support for a student's current or future college goals. Academic counseling may be available through several departments on your campus: Admissions, Counseling, Advising, Registration, Enrollment Support, Transfer, Placement Testing, Student Development, or your academic program. No matter where your college houses these resources, you should have available to you someone who can provide guidance about choosing a program of study, selecting your courses, developing study skills, discussing transfer options, and/or addressing learning differences.

Career counseling can help students select a fitting professional path that matches their skills, interests, and values. Career counselors can also work with students to determine the steps to reach post-collegiate goals while still a student. Career counseling will most likely be available through a counseling office, student development office, or a career center. Common career counseling topics include finding career fields to match your personality and interest inventories (such as those described in Unit 2), accessing online career resources, learning of available paths to a career, discussing the variety of jobs within a field, advising about current internships and work opportunities, and discussing opportunities to network within the field.

Personal counseling is often limited to your college's counseling center. Because students' academic performance is often affected by their lives outside of the classroom, counseling staff are available to help students manage the aspects of their lives that might interfere with their academic performance. Counselors meet individually with students to provide encouragement and support, intervene in times of crisis, make referrals to community resources when necessary, facilitate relationship and communication skills, and help students identify and resolve personal issues. Counseling offices also frequently provide emergency financial assistance grants for students with a one-time, unexpected financial crisis that is preventing them from making successful academic progress.

Campus Police and Public Safety

Your college's safety office provides protection for college buildings, grounds, and parking lots. The office's safety officers respond to crime reports, fires, medical emergencies, traffic accidents, and other incidents requiring police or security assistance. The office may also provide other valuable services to students, such as creation and distribution of student identification cards and parking decals, first aid for minor injuries, lost and found, and police escorts for students on campus at night.

Know the location of your college safety office and its contact information. Your campus may have special phones to contact the safety office in case of emergency. It's a good idea to make mental note of their locations now in case a need arises.

STUDENT NOTES

Veterans' Services

To help veterans understand the policies and procedures pertaining to their education benefits, your college has staff in charge of coordinating and counseling students who are receiving veterans' benefits. Contact this coordinator on your campus to learn more about education benefits, including standards of academic progress for veterans and veterans' work study programs. You may also find much of this information on your college's website or on CFNC.org.

Health Services

Your college may offer student health services on campus, which you may contact for minor first-aid treatment or for referrals to community health providers for more significant illnesses or injuries. Your college may also offer health and/or accident insurance. Check to see what your campus in particular offers its student body.

Basic Needs Supports and Financial Resources

Recognizing that students need assistance with more than tuition and books to stay enrolled and focused on their coursework, NC community colleges are offering more resources for students' basic needs, such as supports for housing, utilities, childcare, food, health services, transportation, internet and computer access, and more. Often the college will connect students to area community agencies, but the college may also provide some of these services through the college, such as free bus passes, clothing closets, or food pantries on campus. Look for your college's resource center, counseling office, or emergency financial assistance program to connect with available supports or utilize NC211.org to find community resources that offer reduced-cost or free services and resources.

Community Service

The classroom isn't the only place that students can learn and contribute. Many community colleges have volunteer or community engagement offices that offer various community service opportunities through which

FIVE REASONS TO VOLUNTEER:

1. You want to learn more about a field before you commit to a program or job.
2. You are new to the area and you want to feel more connected, meet new people, or learn more about where you live.
3. You feel a responsibility to help others and would like to find a way to make a difference in someone's life.
4. You are highly skilled in a specific area, but you want to develop a more well-rounded skill set to appeal to future employers.
5. You are eager to apply what you're learning in the classroom to real life.

STUDENT NOTES

you can apply your skills and academic knowledge while volunteering at a non-profit or government agency. Volunteer work obviously benefits the community served, but it also provides students with important experiences, such as learning new skills, networking with potential employers, developing leadership abilities, and learning to be a part of a team or community. Civic responsibility, community engagement, and volunteering are becoming standard in academic and co-curricular programs at most senior institutions, and students hoping to transfer can improve their candidacy by illustrating a proven record of service to the community. Long-term volunteer commitments are especially impressive to senior institutions and employers.

Student Activities

Student organizations, campus events, and college-sponsored programs provide opportunities to develop friendships, leadership skills, and even job-related experience. Check with your student development or student activities office to learn more about your college's offerings, and take advantage of those that interest you.

Student Clubs and Organizations

Student groups provide excellent opportunities to get involved on campus, make new friends, network with students in your academic program, and build your leadership skills. Your membership in service organizations and honor societies, in particular, demonstrates your dedication to your academics and future career field. Participation in some of the organizations is by invitation only based on your academic standing or program enrollment.

See your college's website for information on how to get involved in student clubs and organizations. While you are there, look for links to the individual clubs for meeting times and locations. You may also find this information on bulletin boards around campus, especially in the student services building on your campus.

Minority Male Success Initiatives

One student organization that is common at North Carolina community colleges is a minority male success initiative or a minority male mentoring program. The goal of these programs is to provide additional supports for male students of color to support their academic success. Your college may provide a success coach or advisor or other college employee to serve as a point of contact for all of your academic, social, and basic needs. Participants may benefit from specific tutoring programs and small group discussions on the unique experiences of male students of color in higher education. Check your college's website to see if a program like this is available to students at your college.

STUDENT NOTES

Student Government

Your college will have a student government (often called the Student Government Association) that will coordinate and regulate activities and issues of concern to all students at your college. The organization represents students' voice as the official student government association on campus. Likely, the student leadership group meets monthly to discuss campus concerns, regulate campus activities, review or create procedures involving student organizations and activities, and respond to campus regulations that affect the student body as a whole. If you are interested in developing your leadership skills and participating fully in the college's student life, consider joining your campus's student government group.

dotshock/Shutterstock.com

Sports

Additionally, your campus may have intercollegiate sports teams that you can join. Many NC community colleges compete against other colleges within the National Junior College Athletic Association's Region X in such sports as basketball, baseball, softball, golf, volleyball, cross country, and esports. Check with your school to learn about upcoming games you can attend or to learn of opportunities to play collegiate sports, including information about trying out for the teams.

Campus Events

Your Student Development or Student Activities office (often in partnership with student clubs, organizations, or student government groups) will sponsor college-wide student events on campus. These events provide great opportunities to learn about the college's clubs and organizations, enjoy food

STUDENT NOTES

Record your goals for your cumulative GPA and program GPA on the tracking sheet on page 3 for easy reference in the future.

and drinks with your classmates, and build a sense of community on campus. Look for information about these events, especially around the beginning of the academic year.

Conclusion

Unlike in high school, college students are responsible for their own learning and their progression through individual courses and a program of study. When students can effectively read a class syllabus, attend and participate in class regularly, and meet other expectations of adult learners, then they are more likely to be successful in college. Similarly, college students should monitor their academic progression by anticipating and calculating grades and GPAs. Finally, your college campus contains a wealth of resources, including libraries, a tutoring center, financial aid offices, and student clubs and organizations. These co-curricular and extra-curricular resources can improve your college experience. As you reflect on how you might apply the information and strategies in this chapter, think specifically about how these concepts will make you a better prepared student and an advocate for your own learning.

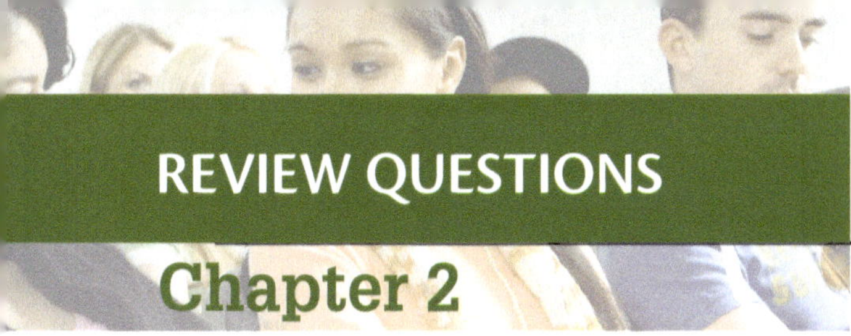

REVIEW QUESTIONS

Chapter 2

The College Experience

These questions will help you monitor and evaluate your learning, two important parts of metacognition.

1. Kourtnie and Kayla are sisters who are taking the same classes this semester: ENG 111 (Writing and Inquiry), CHM 151 (General Chemistry I), and ACA 122 (College Transfer Success). If Kourtnie earns a B in ENG, an A in CHM, and an A in ACA 122, then what will her GPA be?

To calculate the GPAs in questions 1–3, you need to know that the classes have the following credit hours associated with them:

ENG 111 = 3 SHC

CHM 151 = 4 SHC

ACA 122 = 1 SHC

ART 114 = 3 SHC

MAT 152 = 4 SHC

SHC stands for Semester Hours Credit, which is how credit hours are listed on many college documents.

2. Kourtnie and Kayla are sisters who are taking the same classes this semester: ENG 111 (Writing and Inquiry), CHM 151 (General Chemistry I), and ACA 122 (College Transfer Success). If Kayla earns a W in ENG, a W in CHM, and a B in ACA 122, then what will her GPA be?

3. Thomas is a first-semester student taking ACA 122 (College Transfer Success), ENG 111 (Writing and Inquiry), ART 114 (Art History Survey), and MAT 152 (Statistical Methods). The withdrawal date is approaching, and he is considering withdrawing from his MAT 152 class. Calculate his GPA with his grades as they are (B in ACA 122, A in ENG 111, B in ART 114, and D in MAT 152) and then calculate his GPA if he were to withdraw from MAT 152. When you compare the results, what advice would you give Thomas? Why?

REVIEW QUESTIONS

4. It is the third week of the semester. Dolly has registered for five courses because she is in a hurry to finish the Criminal Justice AAS program. Dolly is in ACA 122 (College Transfer Success), CJC 111 (Introduction to Criminal Justice), CJC 112 (Criminology), ENG 111 (Writing and Inquiry), and MAT 110 (Math Measurement and Literacy). She has realized that she cannot be successful in all of the classes at the same time because she also works 30 hours per week and has two small children. She wants to withdraw from one or more of her classes, but she doesn't know from which ones to withdraw. What college policies and procedures does Dolly need to understand to help her make this decision? What advice would you give her?

5. Ramon is taking the same English course for the third time. The first time, he earned a W because he hadn't turned in any assignments and was failing. The second time, he stopped attending class midway through the semester because he didn't like the instructor. Now he feels pressure to pass the class, so he can take other classes for his program. However, he did very poorly on the first test, and he's thinking of withdrawing from the class. What college policies and procedures does Ramon need to understand to help him make this decision? What advice would you give him?

6. Identify one financial aid myth and the reality that proves the myth wrong.

7. Match the person(s) on campus who could help in each situation. More than one response may be correct.

1. ___Instructor	**a.** You were absent from class and want to get the class notes.
2. ___Advisor	**b.** You need help preparing for an upcoming test.
3. ___Tutor	**c.** You are having doubts about your career goals and are considering changing your program.
4. ___Counselor	**d.** You have a question about one of the concepts in your textbook.
5. ___Classmate	**e.** You have gotten over a week behind in all of your classes and are experiencing extreme stress.

8. Imagine the ideal college campus. What offices, services, and other resources does your definition of an ideal college campus have?

9. Locate your college's mission on your college's website or in your student handbook. How do the college's campus resources serve the college's mission? Are there any additional resources that the college should offer in order to better fulfill its mission?

10. Find a list of student clubs and organizations on your campus. What are two that you're interested in joining now or in the future?

11. Samuel has worked as a lab technician in a research facility for over five years and is very self-directed and intelligent. However, he is experiencing some difficulties in his first semester in college. First of all, he is struggling in his math class because it has been so many years since he has studied algebra. Also, he wants to get more involved in campus life, but he hasn't had much success making friends in his classes. Finally, he isn't sure which degree program he should be in because he is considering transferring to a university. What resources in his college community should he explore to address each of his challenges? Why?

Discussion Questions

In Chapter 2, you located your college's mission statement. If you were to craft a personal mission statement for yourself as a college student, what would it be? What behaviors and practices will you need to habituate in order to fulfill your mission?

My Campus Contact List

Whom Do I Contact for…	Department	Location	Contact Information
Academic Advising			
Academic Records			
Applying for Graduation			
Career Counseling			
Changing Academic Programs			
Disability or Accessibility Services			
English as a Second Language Services			
Emergency Financial Assistance			
Financial Aid Counseling			
Food Pantry			
Instructional Concerns			
Insurance Information			
International Student Services			
Lost and Found			
Parking Permits			
Parking Ticket Payment			
Registration			
Scholarships			
Security			
Student Events/Activities			
Testing			
Textbooks			
Transcripts			
Transfer Information			
Tutoring			
Veterans' Education Benefits			
Withdrawing from a Class			
Work Study Programs			
As you identify additional resources you may need to contact on your campus, add that information below.			

antoniodiaz/Shutterstock.com

UNIT 1

Chapter 3

Wellness in College

Before you read this chapter, reflect on the following:

1. *Do you believe that the hard work you are willing to put into your classes and assignments will result in your success in college?*
2. *What healthy habits do you already have? What made you adopt these habits?*
3. *What worries you or causes you stress about being a college student?*

These questions will help you plan your learning, an important part of metacognition.

In addition to understanding higher education and adapting to your role as a community college student, college success will also require making adjustments in your personal life. Attending college is a great undertaking, and some students ignore or underestimate the changes they'll need to make to their personal behaviors and expectations outside of the classroom in order to succeed. Many students define college success narrowly, only in terms of GPA and graduation. This chapter expands the idea of college success by recognizing that you must take care of yourself in order to thrive in college. This chapter highlights the strategies you can use to maintain your wellness while enrolled in college, including several positive steps you can take to maximize your sleep, nutrition, and exercise habits that will keep you healthy and promote learning. Similarly, there are common traps that busy college students struggle to avoid that will inhibit your academic success.

STUDENT NOTES

Growth Mindset

This chapter (and every chapter of *Success by Design* as well as your entire ACA curriculum) is based in the idea that with dedication and hard work, people can learn and succeed, which is consistent with the theory of the growth mindset. Psychologist Carol Dweck researched and described a simple but ground-breaking construct called mindsets and identified two basic mindsets—or beliefs—that shape how we approach learning, working, and success. Individuals with a **growth mindset** believe that they can improve their intelligence and talent with practice, hard work, and resilience. People with a **fixed mindset**, on the other hand, believe that intelligence and talent do not change (that is, you are either born with a talent for a particular subject or you aren't) and that talent is all you need to be successful (that is, you don't have to practice or work at your talent). In her research, Dweck found that the most successful people in the world from a variety of professions, including sports, politics, music, and science, have a growth mindset. And the good news is that if you don't already have a growth mindset, you can cultivate one for yourself.

As a college student, you must already believe in some of the principles of the growth mindset. You are spending your valuable time and money to learn new concepts and skills, and you wouldn't waste these resources unless you believed you were capable of learning. However, some college students apply a fixed mindset to some aspects of college life. For example, when a student says "I am not good at math" (or writing papers or foreign languages, etc.), the student is communicating a fixed mindset that some people are good at math and other people are not good at math. The student is focusing on the performance of doing math rather than the practice of learning math. And perhaps more subtly, the student is giving himself permission to not do well in a math class because he isn't "good at math." Of course, some people have natural talents for certain subjects, and for some students math comes more easily than for others. However, under the right learning conditions and with varying degrees of effort, students can learn math. They have done so for centuries. And you are more likely to succeed in a math class if you minimize this kind of thinking (see the section later in this chapter on negative self-talk) and maximize your attention to learning.

Konstantin Chagin/Shutterstock.com

Read the table that follows for kinds of beliefs that individuals with growth mindsets and fixed mindsets regularly think, communicate, and demonstrate. Have you ever thought or said any of the statements?

Growth Mindset	Fixed Mindset
I can learn to do most anything.	I'm either good at it, or I'm not.
I like to try new things.	I stick to what I know.
My effort and my attitude impact my abilities.	When I'm frustrated, I give up.
Feedback is constructive and helpful.	Feedback is personal and critical.
When I fail, I learn.	When I fail, I'm no good.
I like when people recognize that I tried hard.	I like when people recognize that I'm smart.

STUDENT NOTES

If the fixed mindset statements sound familiar, note their growth mindset counterparts, and start building the habit of changing a fixed mindset into a growth mindset. In fact, as part of her research and publications on mindset, Carol Dweck identifies a four-step process to help change your mindset from fixed to growth:

1. *Learn to hear your fixed mindset "voice."*

   Notice when you say to yourself (or out loud) statements that reveal a fixed mindset. For example, when you are faced with an especially difficult assignment, do you ever think, "I can't do something so complicated" or "What if I fail and everyone sees that I don't belong in college?" Notice yourself thinking or saying comments that reveal a fixed mindset.

2. *Recognize that you have a choice.*

   How you react to challenges and criticism is your choice. Your instinct might lead you to a snap reaction to a challenge or criticism, but you can change your thinking.

3. *Talk back to it with a growth mindset voice.*

   Literally say out loud or make yourself think the entire sentence that counteracts a fixed mindset with a growth mindset. For example, if you think "I can't do something so complicated," stop yourself and think "This is going to be hard, but I can do it." Use the sentences in the growth mindset table above as a starting point.

4. *Take the growth mindset action.*

   After you voice the growth mindset, make the growth mindset choice. Act on the growth mindset by accepting challenges, asking for help when you need it, focusing on the learning process, and accepting criticism as an opportunity to improve next time.

STUDENT NOTES

As you read the rest of this chapter, look for opportunities to practice your growth mindset voice. For example, if you read a strategy that seems especially difficult and you catch yourself thinking "Oh, that would never work for me," try to change your thinking to "That would be hard, but I could try it" (or perhaps the more honest "I'm not willing to do the work that the strategy requires" if you just don't want to try it). Practice the four-step process as you read.

Identity Development

In addition to personal experiences, your sense of self is shaped by political, historical, and cultural contexts. Your new context—college—offers unique opportunities to deepen your understanding of your identity and to connect with others with similar identities. Having your identity affirmed and drawing strength and support from others who share similar identities can be incredibly helpful to your success and sense of belonging. For example, numerous research studies indicate significant benefits for college students who develop strong racial or ethnic identities, including improved mental health, greater academic performance, and increased self-esteem.

Racial Identity and Ethnic Identity

Colleges often offer ethnic studies courses and language courses, both of which researchers have found to be helpful to increase ethnic pride and a sense of affiliation. Outside the classroom, clubs and organizations such as the Black Student Union, Muslim Student Association, or Asian American Student Association can be found on many college campuses and can help students build supportive relationships. Additionally, colleges often offer minority mentoring programs, dance teams, multicultural fairs, or events like Black History Month and National Hispanic Heritage Month celebrations that provide opportunities to share traditions, showcase achievements, or build relationships. Participating in these events may help students feel more integrated into college culture, which is important for persistence and success.

Gender Identity and Sexual Identity

Similarly, many opportunities exist to explore and support the development of gender identity and sexual identity. Involvement in LGBTQ+ clubs or Pride Month celebrations or enrollment in gender studies courses can help students explore and affirm their gender or sexual identities. More colleges are utilizing allyship training, with Safe Zone being the most common in North Carolina higher education settings. After an LGBTQ+ Safe Zone training, faculty and staff display a "Safe Zone Trained" sticker outside their

STUDENT NOTES

offices to indicate a willingness to affirm, encourage, and support LGBTQ+ students.

Many identities and personal characteristics exist beyond those mentioned here. The intersection of multiple identities and the unique assets and challenges of students with intersectional identities are becoming more and more recognized. If you don't find a student group on campus that would be helpful in supporting your identity, you can meet informally or start your own official club by contacting your student government. Identity formation in college is important not only for your sense of self but also for how you see yourself within your new college community. Given the potential effects on your learning and development, investing the time to seek opportunities for affirmation and exploration could significantly improve your college experience.

Ideological Development

It makes sense that with a diverse student body, community college students should also expect to encounter diversity of thought as well. Students enter college with a wide range of beliefs and perspectives, and through coursework and interactions outside the classroom, students may find those points of view challenged. This can result in various feelings, some of which have positive associations: the joy of learning something new or the calm clarity that comes from understanding other perspectives. However, encountering viewpoints or expectations that differ from your own may also result in some less positive emotions, such as confusion, anxiety, or feelings of vulnerability due to incompatible or competing ideas.

The good news is that diversity is good for you. In fact, researchers at the University of Michigan found that students' experiences with diversity meaningfully and positively affected students' learning. Here are a few things to keep in mind when challenged by diverse perspectives:

1. **Embrace the opportunity to explore differences.** College is a unique space to discuss ideas openly. Utilize this time to explore complexities and discover opinions that differ from your own. Much of our thinking is automatic, but the active thinking and intellectual engagement in college are essential to academic, social, and cognitive growth.

2. **Keep in mind that the goal is understanding, not necessarily agreement.** Two seemingly opposing views can simultaneously exist. Rather than arguing which is right and which is wrong, it may be more helpful to try to understand the events or experiences that lead people to their different points of view. Such mutual understanding and respectful dialogue can result in better learning, help you make sense of your role within a multicultural society, and result in civil discourse of complex topics.

STUDENT NOTES

Healthy Habits—Sleep, Exercise, Nutrition

Most adults have heard the benefits of sleep, exercise, and nutrition on their physical and even emotional health. But did you know that these healthy habits also promote long-term memory and efficient learning?

Sleep

College students have a well-earned reputation for pulling all-nighters and not getting adequate sleep. Many college students don't realize that getting enough sleep is vital to not only their overall health but also their ability to learn and remember new concepts over the long term. Learning in college is cumulative, and sleep is critical to long-term memory. Even when we know that sleep is important, we sacrifice it to finish research projects and study for exams. However, research suggests that both the amount and quality of sleep are associated with your learning abilities and academic performance.

Antonio Guillem/Shutterstock.com

According to the National Sleep Foundation, adults between the ages of 18 and 64 need between seven and nine hours of sleep every night. Many sleep experts recommend that you experiment to find the right amount of sleep you need to perform your daily tasks to the best of your abilities. This includes concentrating during class, taking good notes, remaining alert while reading your textbooks, and performing well on tests and quizzes. The National Sleep Foundation recommends keeping a sleep diary to record when you go to sleep and wake up, how easily you fell asleep and stayed asleep, and how many times you woke up (to give you an accurate picture of your sleep habits). A sleep diary also helps you track your mood; your intake of caffeine, alcohol, and medications; and your exercise habits. Consider using the simplified sleep log at the end of this chapter or finding a sleep diary template online or creating your own to keep a record of your sleep habits for one week. This will help you create a baseline for improving on your sleep health.

Sleep is so important to learning and memory that many sleep experts recommend incorporating short naps (20–30 minutes) into your study practices. According to the American Psychological Association, our brains move new skills and concepts into long-term memory during sleep. So a study session followed by a short nap can help solidify new learning. And getting enough sleep can help improve focus and concentration, so after your good night's rest and nap, you are better prepared to read and remember new information. Just be careful to not let naps interfere with your overnight sleep. Your priority for physical health should always be getting a continuous 7–9 hours of sleep every night regardless of naps.

STUDENT NOTES

Consider too your circadian rhythm (or your body's internal clock that regulates when you feel sleepy and when you feel awake) and its impact on your academic performance. The National Sleep Foundation has published research indicating that most adults feel sleepiest between 1:00 and 3:00 p.m. and between 2:00 and 4:00 a.m. But "morning people" and "night owls" might experience some deviation in this pattern. You probably know when you are most alert and most sluggish during a typical day. Incorporate that understanding of yourself into the decisions you make about when to take classes and when to study. You should always do your most difficult work when you are most alert and your easiest work when you are tired. Think about whether taking morning classes and studying in the afternoon or evenings would work for your personal circadian rhythm. Or maybe studying first thing in the morning and then taking afternoon and early evening classes would be your preference. And consider the connection between your circadian rhythm and naps. In several sleep studies organized by the American Psychological Association, "night owls" benefited most from naps whereas "morning people" sometimes felt groggy or moody after naps.

Sleep deprivation is when you don't get enough sleep. Almost everyone has experienced brief periods of sleep deprivation and knows full well how it impacts their mood, decision-making, appetite, and energy levels. It is possible to recover from short-term sleep deprivation simply by getting enough sleep. For example, if you stay up late one night finishing a project, then you can catch up on sleep in the next few nights. Long-term sleep deprivation over the course of several weeks or months, however, might indicate a serious health problem and can lead to more serious consequences, such as weight gain, diabetes, stroke, and heart disease. If you have been experiencing sleep deprivation for weeks or months or years, talk to a health professional about strategies to help you improve your sleep. If you experience sleep deprivation the night or the week before final exams, then prioritize your sleep as soon as you are finished with your exams. Calculate how many hours of sleep you missed, and incorporate those hours into your sleep patterns for as many days as it takes. For example, if you usually sleep seven hours per night, and you stay up all night one night missing those seven hours (despite the advice provided here!), then you might add an hour of sleep every day for seven days or two hours of sleep for three nights and then an extra hour on the fourth night. Once you have gotten back on track, stay on track with 7–9 hours of sleep every night balanced with good nutrition and daily exercise.

STUDENT NOTES

Work schedules can sometimes interfere with sleep schedules. If you work a second or third shift, be sure to plan for sleep in your day, preferably 7–9 continuous hours. You might need to invest in room-darkening shades, an eye pillow, or a white noise machine to help your body adjust to sleeping during daytime hours.

Sleep Tips

Several national organizations, including the American Psychological Association and the National Sleep Foundation, recommend the following research-based strategies to maintain optimal sleep health:

- Go to sleep at the same time every night. Wake up at the same time in the mornings.
- Create a soothing bedtime routine. Consider reading for fun, writing in a journal, drinking hot tea, listening to calming music, or doing yoga or stretching.
- Avoid electronics at bedtime. Specifically, turn off the television and phones 30 minutes before sleep.
- Avoid "all-nighters" before tests. Your brain needs time to rest, so you can perform at a high rate during the test.
- Don't eat a big meal, drink alcohol or caffeine, or take drugs before going to sleep. All of these behaviors will interfere with optimal sleep.
- Exercise regularly (but not too close to bedtime).
- Limit naps to maximize sleep overnight.

Exercise

You are likely already familiar with the many benefits of regular exercise. It can reduce your risk of stroke, heart disease, obesity, and diabetes. It can also help improve your mood and lower anxiety. But did you know that exercise—especially aerobic exercise that gets your heart pumping—can also improve your brain function, which supports your learning? According to studies recently cited by Harvard Medical School and the American Psychological Association, exercise produces chemicals in the brain that improve concentration and learning. And it increases the size of the hippocampus, the part of the brain associated with learning and memory. Some studies even recommend exercising specifically four hours after a serious study session or learning new concepts, but other studies found positive results when test subjects exercised before a study session. Although we don't have clear guidelines on how best to schedule exercise, the research is positive that exercise can help us remember new concepts and remember them over the long term.

In addition to supporting physical fitness and mental fitness, exercise is a great way to overcome stress and anxiety, two common experiences for college students. According to the Mayo Clinic, any kind of exercise, including everything from walking and dancing to yoga and weight lifting, positively benefits all people, including everyone from the physically fit to the less than physically fit. Specifically, exercise helps the body release stress and tension, and it provides a mindful distraction from stressors like upcoming deadlines and incomplete assignments. As the semester gets busier and busier, prioritize exercise to increase the efficacy of your study sessions and to minimize your stress. See pages 76–77 for more information about dealing with stress as a college student.

Exercise Tips

Consider the following recommendations from the Mayo Clinic, the American Psychological Association, and the American Heart Association:

- Exercise at the same time of day to build and sustain the habit.
- Make it fun. Invite friends and family to join you. Try different activities to avoid monotony. Listen to music, audiobooks, or podcasts to entertain you while you exercise.
- Aim to exercise for 150 minutes per week. Most experts recommend 30 minutes per day for at least five days per week.
- If you don't already exercise, start slow with 10–15 minute exercise sessions.
- Experiment with exercising before class or a study session (and on a different day after class or a study session) to gauge how the memory and stress reduction benefits help you be a better college student.

STUDENT NOTES

Any and all movement improves learning. Try these additional strategies when you are on campus: park far from your classes to get a longer walk, take the stairs instead of the elevator, and walk around campus during breaks.

STUDENT NOTES

Nutrition

Healthy eating is also challenging as a college student, but its extensive and significant positive implications for your personal and academic success elevate the need to focus on diet even though it requires some effort. Studies show that nutrition affects every part of your body—maintaining your immune system, sustaining your energy levels, and supporting your well-being, mood, and mental health. Can you imagine being a successful college student without these? Conversely, a poor diet impairs cognitive function and memory, according to Harvard Medical School. If you aren't maintaining your nutrition by eating healthy foods and avoiding unhealthy ones, you are likely making things more difficult by thwarting your efforts to learn.

What you eat not only affects you now but can also have very serious repercussions on your future health. According to the *Journal of the American Medical Association*, poor diet is the biggest contributory factor leading to early death due to the preventable diseases associated with unhealthy eating, such as heart disease, diabetes, and cancer. In fact, diet was found to be a greater risk factor for premature death than tobacco, drug, and alcohol use combined. You're attending college to reach your future academic and career goals, and your personal health is essential to fulfilling these long-term aspirations. Changing unhealthy eating habits now can have long-term effects.

What exactly is unhealthy eating? Diets low in fruits, vegetables, whole grains, nuts, and omega 3 oils but high in red meat or processed meat, sodium, saturated and trans fats, and sweetened beverages have been found detrimental. Research indicates that regularly eating nutrient-rich foods (micronutrients such as omega 3, folate, and iron) and limiting nutrient-poor foods (such as junk foods and processed foods) provide the energy required for optimal cognitive function.

The United States Department of Agriculture (USDA) has created a visual guide to remind you of the portion sizes and variety of food to eat at every meal. As you can see, meals should consist of mostly vegetables and whole grains, with smaller servings of low-fat or lean proteins, fruits, and dairy.

STUDENT NOTES

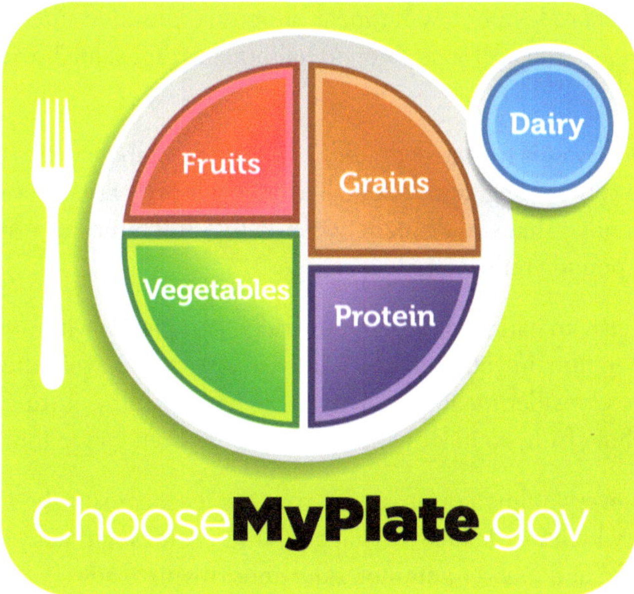

USDA Center for Nutrition Policy and Promotion

Additionally, when you eat can have an effect on your academic performance. According to the Centers for Disease Control and Prevention (CDC), extensive studies have shown a correlation between skipping breakfast and reduced focus, concentration, memory, and problem solving for students. Studies also indicate that regular breakfast eaters consume more micronutrients. For students, it seems the saying is true: Breakfast is the most important meal of the day.

Nutrition Tips

- Start small with just one or two changes, such as drinking more water or changing to whole grains. Other simple first steps might be to vary your foods (especially vegetables and protein), select the appropriate portion size, or select items for their nutritional quality.
- Eat breakfast and regular meals. If you're skipping meals due to lack of funds, see if your college is one of the many that has a food pantry on campus or offers other immediate food assistance for students.
- Read nutrition labels. Products often contain hidden sugars, sodium, and saturated fat.
- Limit sugar and caffeine. Avoid beverages with added sugar, such as sodas, sports or energy drinks, lemonade, fruit punch, and sweetened coffee drinks. Switch out sodas for sparkling water and add 100% fruit juice for flavor.

STUDENT NOTES

- Avoid processed meat such as lunch/deli meat, sausage, ham, and hot dogs. Eat more lean or low-fat meat or poultry, unsalted nuts and seeds, and omega-3 rich seafoods, such as salmon, sardines, anchovies, and trout.
- Drink more water to stay hydrated, keep your metabolism up, ensure digestive functioning, and reduce likelihood of overeating. It's generally recommended that you drink between ½ to 1 full ounce of water daily for each pound you weigh.
- Make it easy to eat right. Stock your fridge and pantry with nutritious food. Keep nuts in your bag as a handy snack, so you avoid the vending machine. Consider meal prepping on the weekends by cutting veggies and washing fruit, so healthy meals are ready when you're hungry.
- If you're overwhelmed or unsure of your choices, consult the USDA's website, which provides practical, simplified guides and videos to get you started and answer common questions: myplate.gov

How many of these nutrition habits do you incorporate into your everyday life? Pick a new one to try this week.

Traps to Avoid—Multitasking, Impulsivity, Procrastination, Negative Self-Talk, Imposter Syndrome, and Stress

In addition to developing or strengthening healthy habits around sleep, exercise, and nutrition, savvy college students also know which common traps to avoid. Specifically, multitasking, impulsivity, procrastination, negative self-talk, imposter syndrome, and stress are common experiences for college students, but they can and should be avoided whenever possible.

Multitasking

When does task shifting prove most ineffective or detrimental to you? Which of these tips would help the most?

Numerous news outlets have reported in recent years that there's really no such thing as multitasking, and neuroscience supports the headlines. When we think we are multitasking, we are almost always **task shifting**; we really can't complete two tasks that require the same mental energy and the processing part of the brain—especially learning new information —at the same time. In the rare instances in which we truly and successfully multitask (for example, listening to the radio while driving or quizzing a child on spelling words while cooking dinner), we are not learning new information; we are doing at least one activity that doesn't require the same kind of attention required for learning. According to the American Psychological Association, we lose time when we switch from one task to another. You may have experienced this feeling when you stop reading your textbook or other assigned reading to check a text message or look at social media. You lose time and concentration when you turn your attention back to the reading

STUDENT NOTES

assignment and try to remember where you left off. And you may have even had to start over from the beginning after the interruption.

In addition to lost time, your performance diminishes when you attempt two tasks simultaneously. For example, suppose it takes one hour to read a chapter in a textbook. Add TikTok, Snapchat, and texting to the reading, and now it takes 90 minutes to read the same chapter, and you won't remember what you've read as well as if you read it without task shifting. And you are more likely to make mistakes in your work if you complete an assignment while task shifting. The American Psychological Association has found that when we switch from task to task, we lose 40% in productivity. This is a huge loss for busy college students who don't have an extra 40% in their day.

Avoiding Multitasking Tips

- Eliminate distractions. Turn off the phone, TV, and other devices when you want to increase your productivity. Look for apps that will temporarily block access to social media sites or put your phone in airplane mode when you study. Try it at least once; you might be surprised by the impact it has on your concentration and memory.
- Schedule technology breaks. Set a timer for 15 minutes (or longer) and study without distraction for those 15+ minutes. At the end of the 15 minutes, check your phone or other device for missed messages, social media updates, or whatever other content you would have previously looked at while studying.
- Plan to do work in "batches." Spend a specific amount of time working on one class and then another specific amount of time on another class. Or focus your attention on checking email for messages from instructors and classmates and then shift your attention to completing your math homework.
- Practice deep concentration. Spend a significant amount of your day doing one thing deeply. This could be a 45–60 minute exercise session where you play basketball or practice yoga or go for a run without doing anything else at the same time. This will start to build the habit of "unitasking" instead of multitasking.

Muellek Josef/Shutterstock.com

STUDENT NOTES

Impulsivity and Procrastination

Impulsivity and procrastination are related problems that can originate in the same part of the brain, according to the magazine *Science*. They are similar in that they both reveal a lack of self-control and get in the way of accomplishing your goals. However, neither is a failure of ambition or spirit—and you can change your habits around both. Specifically, **impulsivity** is doing something now that can wait until later and **procrastination** is waiting do to something that you should do now. Neither supports your academic or professional goals. Procrastination is frequently a time management challenge (see Chapter 8 for more information about time management), but many people also avoid studying or completing assignments because they cannot control their impulses.

While the American Psychological Association draws a clear connection between impulsivity and gambling, violence, substance abuse, anxiety, and social disorders, impulsivity on a smaller scale is prevalent in many people's lives. Many of us experience impulsivity when we check one Facebook notification and then scroll through the newsfeed for several minutes and click on links to videos or articles that seem funny. In fact, impulsivity frequently manifests itself around smartphones and technology when we are continuously checking social media, scrolling endlessly, receiving constant notifications, and participating in group texts. The National Institute of Health has published research that draws a connection between procrastination and a lack of self-regulation, or the ability to resist social temptations when we should be working on academic or self-improvement activities. For many of us, smartphones or other technologies present social temptations.

Ways to Overcome Impulsivity and Procrastination

Note that many of the traps to avoid involve technology. While the internet and apps can support and enhance learning, our devices can be a major distraction to our long-term goals.

- Practice meditation or yoga to build the habit of getting deeply involved in one activity at a time and to quiet any racing thoughts.
- Use the things that distract you as rewards for sustained periods of concentration (for example, after studying for 30 minutes straight, check social media for 10 minutes). Start with short sustained periods if this is especially challenging for you. After 10 minutes, give yourself a 3-minute reward, and set a timer and then avoid looking at the clock.
- Identify what tempts you and plan around it. For example, put the phone on silent or in another room for at least 30 minutes.
- Create artificial deadlines (like the distributed practice strategy described in Chapters 8 and 11) to focus your attention.

STUDENT NOTES

- Set specific goals to give yourself a task to accomplish and some accountability around the task. Instead of "I will study for 30 minutes," say "I will create a practice test with questions from Chapters 6–8 in the next 30 minutes."
- Connect the activity that you should be doing to your short-term and long-term goals.

Negative Self-Talk

Everyone talks to themselves. Sometimes we maintain an internal communication or monologue; other times we speak the words out loud. In a rush to leave home at the start of the day, we might ask ourselves, "Where are my keys?" or "Do I need to take an umbrella with me?" Self-talk is common, but negative self-talk can be dangerous. If we change these benign questions to more critical thoughts like "What is wrong with me? Why can't I ever find my keys?" and "I don't want to be the idiot out in the rain with no umbrella again," we engage in negative self-talk and set ourselves up for failure. What we say to ourselves shapes our thinking and how we approach challenges. Likewise, negative self-talk can negatively impact motivation, stress, and time management. The more frequently you tell yourself that you aren't good at Spanish, the less likely you are to put forth the effort required to master the concepts in Spanish class. And the more frequently you earn less than ideal grades in Spanish, the more stress you feel around the subject.

Flamingo Images/Shutterstock.com

A recent study published by the American Psychological Association found that today's college students (especially those in the millennial generation) experience higher rates of perfectionism than previous generations of college students. The researchers point to a variety of potential causes, including wider expectations that more adults have college degrees and the ways in which we compare ourselves with other people via social media platforms and sometimes feel a sense of isolation as a result of those same social media platforms. Negative self-talk is a frequent feature of perfectionism. Perfectionists push themselves to be the best while at the same time criticizing themselves for the smallest missteps. This critical self-talk can feel paralyzing sometimes and can lead to procrastination. If you start an assignment late and you don't do well, then you can blame the low grade on the late start. Or you might delay starting an assignment because it seems difficult, and you don't want to ask for help or reveal that you don't know what to do.

STUDENT NOTES

Ways to Overcome Negative Self-Talk

- It isn't productive to worry about studying; just study. Try writing down the worries to get them out of your head and allow you to focus on studying more productively.
- Review the four-step method for developing a growth mindset at the beginning of this chapter for more strategies on changing the way you think about yourself and your abilities.
- Replace the negative self-talk with mantras like "This is hard, but I can do it" and "I am well prepared for class (or this test)." Try using the following examples of positive self-talk to counterbalance the negative self-talk:

What tasks, subjects, or events cause you to engage in negative self-talk? How can you counteract the negative self-talk?

Negative Self-Talk	Positive Self-Talk
High school was so easy for me. What's wrong with me?	College is very different from high school. I can succeed here, too.
Maybe I don't belong in college.	This is hard, but I have a plan.
This class is too hard.	There are lots of support systems here. I need to find the ones that will help me.
I studied last time and didn't do well. It doesn't matter how hard I try.	I need to use different learning strategies.
I don't know how to begin (a big assignment, a difficult course).	I can do this one step at a time.
I'm not good at math.	Other people have learned this, and so can I.

Imposter Syndrome

Similar to negative self-talk, imposter syndrome—the feeling that you don't belong or don't deserve to be in college—is often an unhelpful internal communication that may negatively affect college engagement and performance. Experts in imposter phenomenon, as it's also known, indicate that 7 in 10 adults experience imposter feelings at some point. However, some individuals may experience these feelings more routinely. For example, research in higher education, social psychology, and other fields have found that first-generation college students—the first in their families to attend college—may be more likely to experience feelings of imposter syndrome. Feelings commonly associated with imposter phenomenon include the following:

- worry that people will find out you're not as capable as they think you are,

STUDENT NOTES

- doubt that your achievements were deserved or earned, often attributing them to good luck and even going so far as to diminish your own successes,
- perfectionism or feelings that you must work even harder—often to impossibly high standards—to hide that you're a fraud or not as skilled as people think, or
- anxiety that people will find out that you don't have what it takes to be successful.

While not officially a diagnosis, imposter phenomenon is recognized by the American Psychological Association (APA), which also notes that imposter feelings can negatively affect self-esteem and may be accompanied by symptoms of anxiety or depression. The APA and the Cleveland Clinic recommend several actions to combat imposter syndrome:

- **Talk to others.** Beyond finding a sympathetic ear, talking to a friend and taking your internal communication external can help you hear how it may be irrational or illogical. It may also help you realize you're not the only one feeling this way. Speaking with a therapist can also help you change your negative thinking. Most colleges have counselors available for assistance with academic and personal challenges like imposter phenomenon.
- **Observe imposter feelings.** Notice when you experience feelings of inadequacy or fraud. Be ready with a response in these situations, such as recognizing the difference between feeling and fact by saying "I may think these things about myself, but it doesn't mean that they are accurate."
- **Note your accomplishments.** Remember what you do well to try to more realistically assess your abilities. Think through your common activities such as tutoring, running, or playing music to help you remember your strengths. Even tangible reminders such as a card from a friend or an instructor's email praising your work can help you more accurately take stock of your abilities. When you do reach an accomplishment or goal, celebrate those successes.
- **Embrace "good enough."** Everyone has room for improvement, but those who experience imposter phenomenon will overwork themselves to the point of burnout in order to overcompensate for perceived inadequacies. Instead of seeking perfection, try to get to a place where things are "good enough." For example, set limits to your time spent on a task; think about what a reasonable amount of time would be to spend on an assignment, and then cut yourself off when you reach that limit.

STUDENT NOTES

- **Stop comparing.** No one is perfect, no matter what their social media may show. Instead of holding your achievements up against others' accomplishments, focus on measuring your own successes with your personal values and more accurately and realistically setting your expectations.

Keep in mind that feelings of not belonging in college can also come from sources other than self-perceptions. The same feelings associated with imposter syndrome—feelings of inadequacy, intellectual self-doubt, or not belonging—can also stem from systemic oppression, which is when policies, practices, or procedures are rooted in bias, resulting in different experiences for students benefiting from systems of privilege than for students from marginalized groups. In other words, it may not be you but the institution that needs to take steps to change in order to address ways it may be unintentionally producing feelings of inferiority or not belonging in its students. The good news is that many colleges and universities are beginning to engage more deeply with the work necessary to become more equitable, inclusive, and anti-racist. If you'd like to be part of the student voice in this work, reach out to your college's student government association; Title IX or diversity, equity, and inclusion officer; or counseling office.

Stress

Stress is the way the body responds to some stimulus. A little stress can help you sharpen your focus during an exam or stay motivated to submit your best work in your college assignments. But a lot of negative stress can get in the way of effective learning. Stress is difficult to avoid in college. It is natural to feel stress from taking multiple classes, balancing competing demands and deadlines, and experiencing a lack of familiarity with higher education processes and expectations. In fact, there are countless causes of stress for college students, including the following:

- loss of financial aid
- balancing school with family and work responsibilities
- poor grades
- feeling behind or like you are the only student who doesn't understand
- start of a new semester
- mid-semester crunch of assignment deadlines and test days

STUDENT NOTES

- end-of-semester crunch of research paper deadlines, final exams, final projects and presentations
- forgetting to complete a homework or reading assignment
- bringing the wrong materials to class
- arriving late
- unclear long-term academic and professional goals

Just reading this list might have caused you some stress! It is critical that you learn to combat the negative effects of stress because of the potential short-term consequences (for example, difficulty sleeping, breathing deeply, or concentrating) and long-term consequences (for example, weight gain or elevated blood pressure). Stress can also diminish your productivity and ability to learn new concepts, which is critical to success in college.

Tips for Overcoming Stress

- Exercise to relieve stress. Experiment with aerobic exercise like playing tennis that elevates your heart rate and non-aerobic exercise like stretching.
- Practice yoga, meditation, and visualization strategies. There are free phone apps and YouTube videos that provide a good introduction to these techniques.
- Study regularly to learn course material and increase your confidence in the classroom and on tests. See Chapter 11 for a description of the benefits of maintenance studying.
- Talk to a counselor. Most college campuses have personal and academic counseling services; take advantage of these resources.
- Reward yourself for accomplishing small goals (for example, doing well on a test you studied for or turning in an assignment early). This will build your confidence and decrease your stress about the next test or assignment.
- Take control over what is causing you stress. Are you stressed because you arrive late to class every day? Leave earlier to arrive in time to get settled before class starts.

Which of these solutions would help the most with your current stressors?

STUDENT NOTES

Financial Literacy

A significant source of stress for most college students is managing their financial needs so that they can remain in school, realize long-term personal goals, and achieve independence. Financial responsibility begins with **financial literacy**—knowing how to create and meet your financial goals.

While talking about money may be stressful, the good news is you've already illustrated sound financial decision-making by choosing to attend a community college. Consider the following comparison of average annual tuition costs among your options for higher education within North Carolina.

Average Annual Tuition Costs in NC		
	In State	Out of State
Private universities	$26,751	
Public universities	$7,438	$20,438
Private 2-year colleges	$22,318	
Public community colleges	$2,542	$8,473

Your decision to attend a North Carolina community college—which have average annual tuitions of about $2,542 per year—has set you on a good financial path. Consider the following eight tips to continue making sound financial decisions while in college.

Set Financial Goals

In Chapter 7, you will learn about making SMART academic and career goals that are Specific, Measurable, Attainable, Realistic, and Time-bound. You should also make SMART financial goals. Consider making both a long-term and short-term SMART financial goal. Typical short-term SMART financial goals include paying off debt, saving for a particular item or event, or improving your credit. Long-term financial goals usually include planning for retirement, building wealth, or making large purchases.

Example of short-term SMART financial goal:

> I will eliminate my $3,245 credit card debt in 12 months by not using my credit cards for purchases, making all my payments on time, and getting a second job in the summer.

Example of long-term SMART financial goal:

> By 2032, I will save $15,000 for a down payment on my own house. I will have $20 from each paycheck directly deposited into my savings account; save 80% of every tax return in the same account; and go to school part-time to earn my degree so I can get a promotion and raise.

STUDENT NOTES

Create a Budget

Many people cringe when it's time to make a budget, but having a spending plan ensures that you're meeting your goals and establishing financial independence. The good news is that there are many helpful resources that make budgeting easy. CFNC.org offers a Financial Basics tool that allows students to explore key money management topics. Look for money management or budgeting apps, which make tracking expenses and saving for specific goals easy. There are also many free budgeting planners, such as the Monthly Budget Spreadsheet from collegeforadults.org.

No matter how you track your spending, there are a few basics for every budget. First, plan for a month at a time, making a list of incoming and outgoing money. If you have no idea how to set your monthly targets, consider keeping a spending diary, writing down every expense from rent to a pack of gum. Once you've seen where your money goes, set your limits for the next month. Keep in mind that your expenses should not exceed your income. If you spend more than you make, you should adjust your expenses and make cuts so that you're living within your means and avoiding debt.

Don't forget to think about hidden costs. For example, when budgeting for college expenses, don't just include tuition, but also books, fees, supplies, meal plans, transportation, parking, and technology, such as expensive calculators or computer equipment.

You may want to divide your budget into fixed expenses, such as rent or insurance payments, and variable expenses for things that might be more irregular, such as doctor's visits or eating out. Track your expenses several times throughout the month to monitor your spending and make sure you're on target. At the end of the month check to see where you met, exceeded, or failed your goals by comparing your actual spending against your projected expenses. Adjust your spending as needed to reach your goal.

Cut Costs

If your budget shows that you're spending more money than you're earning, you'll need to cut costs. The hardest but most important way to cut expenses is to examine your spending and to determine which items are needs and which are wants. We often believe many items are needs, when they really are not required. For example, it's nice to have a newer car, get frequent manicures, and eat out at restaurants, but these aren't actually necessities for most of our lives. If you're living beyond your means or are trying to achieve specific financial goals, you may need to sacrifice these discretionary expenses for a while in order to fulfill your financial plan. Eliminate wants from your budget; be cutthroat and don't rationalize things you would like to have or do over your bigger goals and dreams.

STUDENT NOTES

If you have trouble distinguishing wants from needs, consider tracking your purchases for an entire week. Write down your purchases every time you spend any amount of money. At the end of the week, consider which of these items were absolutely necessary and which were impulse purchases or wants. An easy way to do this is to pretend all of these items have been lost, stolen, or broken. Which ones would you replace immediately? These are needs. If you wouldn't have to replace the item right away, it was probably a want and that money could have been saved.

But cutting costs doesn't mean you have to go without having fun or looking good. Here are some very easy ways to save money while in school:

- Get reduced spa services on campus through the esthetician program or at a local beauty school.
- Check out movies for free through your campus library, which often has many new releases or blockbusters.
- Buy groceries and prepare your meals instead of eating out. The cost of seemingly cheap fast food meals add up quickly—and they're often less healthy than home-cooked meals.
- Look for free events in your community, such as concerts, outdoor movies, film screenings, or festivals.
- Plan ahead so you can get to the bookstore early to purchase used textbooks instead of new copies, which can be twice the cost.
- Check for student discounts for entertainment, shopping, or necessities. Many movie theatres, clothing stores, and insurance companies provide student discounts.
- Use campus computers and printers instead of purchasing your own desktop, laptop, printer, ink, and paper.

Understand Financial Aid

STUDENT NOTES

Make sure you've exhausted all your options for tuition assistance before you pay out of pocket. The paragraphs below will help you do some big-picture thinking about how you might use financial aid to support your academic goals. You'll find specific details about financial aid in Chapter 2, which includes information on your college's Financial Aid office, financial aid eligibility requirements, and satisfactory academic progress.

Your first step in obtaining financial assistance is completing the FAFSA every year. In addition to screening you for the Pell grant, Federal Supplemental Educational Opportunity (FSEO) grant, NextNC Scholarship, federal loans, and work-study eligibility, many scholarships or other forms of aid require you to submit your Student Aid Index (SAI) (formerly referred to as Expected Family Contribution or EFC) from your Student Aid Report, which you receive after submitting the FAFSA. The SAI indicates your Pell grant eligibility and is used by your college's Financial Aid office to determine your other aid options. Complete the FAFSA early and be in contact with your Financial Aid office well before the beginning of the semester to ensure you completely understand your specific aid package and the amount you will owe out of pocket. If you plan to transfer to a senior institution, using the Net Price Calculator tool at collegecost.ed.gov can help you prepare for tuition and fees beyond community college.

Most students know that senior institutions provide some scholarships for transfer students, but scholarships are also available at most community colleges. See your Financial Aid office for more information about when and how to apply for these opportunities. Since the applicant pool is smaller than for many state or national scholarships, your chances of receiving one of these scholarships could be greater, provided you meet the outlined requirements.

Consider checking with your employer to see if they provide scholarships or if there are any specific state-wide resources for your program arca. For example, Early Childhood Education program students can receive T.E.A.C.H. scholarships to complete community college coursework.

Unfortunately, there are several scholarship scams that trick many students every year. Be wary of scholarship sites that require you to pay fees up front, promise the scholarship information is only available through their site, claim that they are dispersing unclaimed aid, or guarantee scholarship money. Reliable scholarship sites include collegeboard.com and fastweb.com, but your scholarship search should start with your current college, intended transfer school, or employer.

STUDENT NOTES

Michaelpuche/Shutterstock.com

Use Available Resources

If you have cut expenses, are sticking to your financial plan, and have utilized financial aid but are still not meeting your budget, you might need to seek assistance. If you do need additional help, know that you aren't alone. In a recent survey by Temple University's Hope Center for Student Basic Needs, researchers found that 3 in 5 college students experience food and housing insecurities. To help students concentrate on their studies rather than their basic needs, community colleges have several supports and resources available to students, such as emergency funds to assist students with unexpected hardship, food pantries, child care assistance, and more. See Basic Needs Supports and Financial Resources on page 51 for more options. Finally, you can also check with your college's career office or job board to find additional employment opportunities. Don't be afraid to seek help.

Understand Credit

One of the reasons your financial decisions as a college student are so important is because of their potential effect on future financial goals. Your personal credit score follows you well beyond your college years, and some students must spend years working to improve the damage done to their credit scores in college. Your **credit score** is a number that banks and lenders use to determine how much risk they're taking in lending you money. A good credit score will help you qualify for larger loans and lower interest rates, which is important when seeking a home, car, or small business loan. Bad credit cannot only affect financial goals but also professional goals, too. Poor credit history can show up on a background check, limiting your employment offers or professional licensure eligibility.

STUDENT NOTES

Credit scores are most often adversely affected in college by accumulating excessive credit card debt or defaulting on student loans. Credit cards can be helpful tools in beginning to establish credit if used responsibly, meaning payments are made on time, limits are not exceeded, and balances are kept low. However, when you have limited income and large tuition bills, debt can accumulate quickly. Credit card interest rates are usually high, so debt can soon spiral out of control if your credit card becomes a main means of payment. To avoid high balances, charge only what you can pay off in full each month. If you already carry a balance, pay more than the minimum amount each month to get out of debt sooner, and make your payments before the bill is due in order to avoid last-minute problems and late fees. Failing to pay your bills on time hurts your credit score.

The other problem students encounter with credit comes from failing to make student loan payments. Unlike credit card debt, student loan debt remains with you for your entire life, even after bankruptcy. Like credit card late payments, delinquent, or late, payments for student loans hurt your credit score. Loans are considered to be in default if they are 270 days past due. Once in default, you will be ineligible for future loans until those past defaulted loans are reconciled. You can also be sent over to collection agencies, and you will be responsible for all collection fees as well. Additionally, your income tax return or paychecks could be garnished, and legal action can be brought against you until you've repaid your loan.

If you are already in default on a student loan or struggling to make credit payments, the most important thing to do is to take action. Ignoring the problem won't make it go away or get better. Consult reputable resources, seek help, and make a plan for reducing your debt.

Avoid Scams

Unfortunately, there are many businesses ready to take advantage of those strapped for money. Opportunistic lenders promise quick money but with extremely high interest rates or penalties for failing to meet very specific—and often impractical—terms. Predatory lending comes in a variety of formats: cash advances, payday loans, debt settlement, prepaid credit cards, rent to own stores, car title loans, or auto pawnbrokers. These services appeal to students because they offer a quick fix; however, they often deepen and perpetuate a cycle of debt since the convenience of quick money comes with excessively high interest rates, fees, and penalties. Avoid these services. Plan ahead and stick to your budget to avoid many of the draws of these predatory lenders.

STUDENT NOTES

Save

Saving may seem like the last thing you'll be able to do as a college student, but establishing a savings plan and good behaviors now can get you closer to financial goals. Start a habit of paying yourself first by opening a savings account and having money from your paycheck directly deposited into savings, even if it's just $5 a week. Put bonuses, financial aid reimbursements, or tax refunds in this interest-bearing account as well. Save your change and deposit it monthly into your savings account. You can even use apps to trick yourself into saving. For example, there are several apps that will round up purchases and place the "change" into your savings account. Although it may seem underwhelming to save your pocket change or only a few dollars a month, you will be glad to have that money when you need it.

Record a college wellness goal on page 3 for easy tracking.

Conclusion

The purpose of this chapter is to help new college students identify, evaluate, and strengthen their wellness strategies in a variety of aspects of college life. While community college students are very diverse in age, educational experiences, and goals, the benefits of positive identity development, sleep, exercise, and nutrition apply to everyone. Developing new healthy habits and avoiding traps like multitasking, impulsivity, negative self-talk, imposter syndrome, and stress will make you a stronger student and will prepare you for transfer to a university, entrance into a new career field, and success in many aspects of your life. One of the most powerful indicators of your long-term success is your mindset. When you approach your college classes with a growth mindset that allows you to embrace the challenges and learn from your mistakes, you are more likely to learn more deeply and succeed more generally.

REVIEW QUESTIONS

Chapter 3
Wellness in College

These questions will help you monitor and evaluate your learning, two important parts of metacognition.

1. In your own words, what is a fixed mindset? What is a growth mindset?

2. Use the wellness inventory below to self-assess your current habits and practices. If you mark **Never** or **Rarely** for any of the items, focus your attention on building up those healthy habits.

	Never	Rarely	Sometimes	Usually	Always
1. I get 7–9 hours of sleep each night.					
2. I go to sleep at the same time every night.					
3. I wake up at the same time every day.					
4. I eat a variety of fruits and vegetables.					
5. I avoid sugar and processed food.					
6. I limit caffeine.					
7. I eat breakfast.					
8. I drink plenty of water.					
9. I exercise 150 minutes per week (30 minutes per day over 5 days).					
10. I do a combination of aerobic and non-aerobic exercise.					

3. In your own words, how are impulsivity and procrastination similar? How are they different?

4. What are three new strategies you can use to overcome stress? Look for techniques you haven't previously tried.

REVIEW QUESTIONS

5. Which of the traps—multitasking, impulsivity, procrastination, negative self-talk, imposter syndrome, or stress—can you most relate to and why?

6. Alexandra is a first-semester community college student who plans to earn an AA degree and then transfer to Appalachian State University to major in Religious Studies. She is 26 years old and returning to college after an earlier attempt right after high school. She works full time, attends classes on multiple campuses part time, and has a spouse and two young children. After staying up all night to study for her first tests in two classes, she earned low Cs and started to doubt whether she's "college material." What advice would you give Alexandra to develop healthy habits and avoid common traps?

7. Use the simple sleep log that follows (or find a sleep log or sleep diary online) to track your sleep habits for one week. At the end of the week, look at your results, and answer the following questions:
    1. What surprised you about how much sleep you got?
    2. How could you change your habits before bed to increase the quality or quantity of sleep you get?
    3. How does sleep affect your mood, concentration, and ability to learn new information?
    4. What changes can you make to your sleep habits to improve your performance as a college student?

Simple Sleep Log

	Day 1	Day 2	Day 3	Day 4	Day 5	Day 6	Day 7
What time did you go to sleep?							
What time did you wake up?							
How many hours of sleep did you get?							
How many times did you wake up overnight?							
What woke you up?							
How would you describe the quality of your sleep?							
How did you feel the following day?							

Discussion Questions

What is a time when you approached a new activity or skill with a fixed mindset? How about with a growth mindset? Be specific. How were these approaches different for you? What were the outcomes?

REVIEW QUESTIONS

Unit 2

Shutterstock.com

GOAL DISCERNMENT

Goal discernment is the deliberate and systematic process of examining yourself and your options to make informed decisions about your future. You can apply the stages of goal discernment to make decisions about your academic and career goals. In fact, you may have already moved through the stages of goal discernment without realizing the benefits of the full process. If you are attending college after several years in the workforce, then you likely have already given some thought to what you like and dislike doing professionally. And if you are a recent high school graduate, then you may have done some research and academic writing on your potential careers. This unit of *Success by Design* will potentially strengthen or challenge your goals. The four chapters in this unit will prepare you for each of the three stages of goal discernment.

STUDENT NOTES

CHAPTER 4: Self-Assessment

First of all, you must assess yourself. What are your interests? What are your values? What are you good at? What is your ideal balance of your work and your personal life? How long are you willing to be a student? What are your strengths and learning style preferences? At this stage, you focus on your personality, your interests, and your values.

CHAPTER 5: Academic Goal Exploration

Second of all, you must do some research. What credentials are available to you at your community college? What are your options for transfer to a senior institution? What certification or training is required for your career interests? This stage of the process requires that you do some research about your academic choices.

CHAPTER 6: Career Goal Exploration

In addition to researching your academic options, you need to research to explore your career options. What is the job outlook? What is the starting salary? What opportunities for advancement exist? This chapter will complement the resources you discover in Chapter 5 but will focus on your professional choices.

CHAPTER 7: Goal Setting

Finally, you take action by setting goals based on your self-assessments and research. This chapter emphasizes the benefits of SMART goals. You'll also find resources to help you achieve your academic goals in a timely and thoughtful manner.

STUDENT NOTES

Important Learning Outcomes for Unit 2

- Identify your learning style preferences and develop strategies to support your learning style preferences.
- Research careers that match your personality traits, interests, and work values.
- Develop a strategic plan for completing community college academic goals, including certificates, diplomas, and/or associate degrees.
- Identify the rights and responsibilities of transfer students under the Comprehensive Articulation Agreement (CAA), including Universal General Education Transfer Component (UGETC) designated courses, the Transfer Assured Admissions Policy (TAAP), and the CAA appeals process.
- Evaluate additional options for transfer, including Bilateral Articulation Agreements and Uniform Articulation Agreements.
- Write academic goals that are specific, measurable, attainable, realistic, and time-bound.

STUDENT NOTES

Unit 2: Goal Discernment Tracking Sheet

As you read Unit 2, record the individual elements of your personal goal discernment in the table below. This will be a helpful record to track your personalized preferences and plans.

Holland Code/ Interest Finder Results	Top 3–5 Work Values
Program of Study or Major and Related Career Options	**Learning Style Preferences**
SMART Academic Goals	**SMART Professional Goals**

UNIT 2

Chapter 4

Self-Assessment

Phase4Studios/Shutterstock.com

Before you read this chapter, reflect on the following:

1. *What do you already know about your interests, values, and strengths?*
2. *Have you used the CFNC and NC Careers websites previously?*
3. *What do you want to learn about self-assessment and its role in the cycle of goal discernment?*

These questions will help you plan your learning, an important part of metacognition.

As you learned in the introduction to Unit 2, self-assessment is often the first stage in the cycle of goal discernment. **Self-assessment** is the systematic reflection on who you are as a person. Specifically, what are your interests, personality traits, and values? And how can these traits best inform your goals?

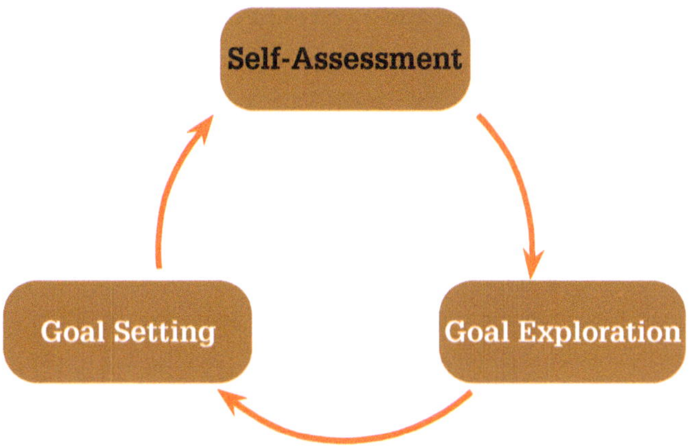

STUDENT NOTES

When you match your interests, personality, and values to your academic and professional goals, you can expect to be fulfilled both professionally and personally by your choices. You will feel satisfied with your choices and motivated to go to work even on days when you are tired or experiencing a disagreement with a co-worker. When you choose a career based on thorough self-assessment, these small distractions remain small distractions and your professional motivation remains high.

Many of us make decisions about our academic programs and future careers based on our superficial understanding of our own interests, personality, and values. But few of us take the time to be deliberate about identifying what exactly makes us unique and then search for academic programs and careers that suit us. The activities that follow will help you deliberately assess yourself, so you can make informed decisions (or confirm the decisions you have already made) about your goals.

Specifically, Chapter 4 includes the following useful self-assessment topics:

- personality and interests,
- work values,
- metacognition, and
- learning styles preferences.

Personality and Interests

The most common first step in self-assessment is to examine your personality and interests. Many college students choose their academic programs and future career paths based on their interests. For example, individuals who enjoy writing and following current events naturally become interested in journalism or media communications. Similarly, individuals who like a structured workday with few surprises may naturally become interested in careers like accounting or medical assisting. You can apply the information about Holland Codes on the next few pages and on the NC Careers website to explore your personality and interests as they relate to academic or career choices.

Holland Codes are a widely known and well-respected personality and interest assessment. Dr. John Holland, a psychologist, identified the six personality types in the Holland Codes that can be combined into 720 different patterns.

The Holland Codes hexagon shows the relationships of the personality types to one another. The codes closest together are more alike; the codes opposite from each other are least alike. For example, artistic individuals are not likely to also have many conventional characteristics (opposite) but will likely find they have several investigative and social preferences (closest).

STUDENT NOTES

Most people are a combination of types, and the combinations usually correspond with each other on the hexagon.

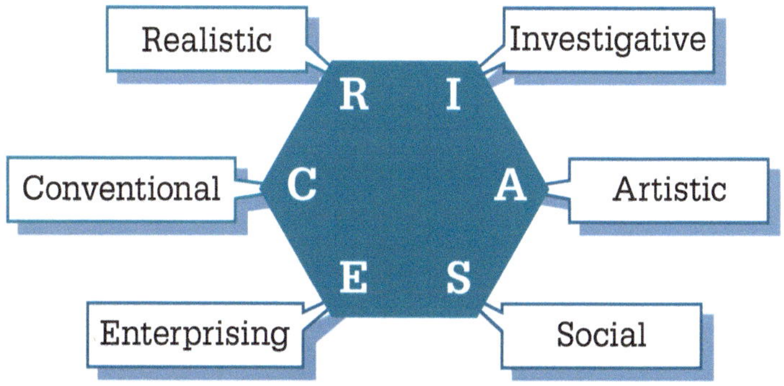

These types refer to both individual personalities and workplace environments. For example, a person's Holland Code might be CRI (**C**onventional, **R**ealistic, and **I**nvestigative) or SEA (**S**ocial, **E**nterprising, and **A**rtistic). Likewise, a specific career might be categorized as Conventional or Artistic.

Career counselors recommend identifying your personal Holland Code and then using your Holland Code to find similar work environments. People who work in environments that match their personality types are more likely to feel satisfied in their work lives. For example, if you have a very social personality, then not surprisingly you would prefer a workplace in which you have a lot of interaction with co-workers and/or the public. You might feel dissatisfied in a workplace where you must work independently with little opportunities to interact with other people.

Once you determine your Holland Code, use the table below to identify your compatible work environments. Notice that the compatibility is determined by the location on the hexagon. See "Step 2: Match Your Holland Code to Compatible Careers" on pages 96–97 for specific examples of careers.

Personality Type	Most Compatible Careers	Other Compatible Careers
Realistic	Realistic	Investigative and Conventional
Investigative	Investigative	Realistic and Artistic
Artistic	Artistic	Investigative and Social
Social	Social	Artistic and Enterprising
Enterprising	Enterprising	Social and Conventional
Conventional	Conventional	Enterprising and Realistic

STUDENT NOTES

You can also figure out your Holland Code by completing the Interest Finder activity on the NC Careers website.

See the instructions on how to log in to NC Careers and access the Interest Finder on pages 102–104.

Step 1: Identify Your Holland Code

Read the descriptions below and decide which personality type defines you the best. Next, choose which would be the second and third best descriptions of your personality. Write the three letters below. This is your Holland Code:

_____ _____ _____

R – Realistic People (Doers)

They like to work with machines, and they often like to work with their hands to build things. Their skills include having mechanical know-how, stamina to work outdoors, and the ability to operate machinery. They are often practical, love nature, and are good problem-solvers. They like working with things and tools.

I – Investigative People (Thinkers)

They like to explore ideas and analyze data. They have skills in math and science. Inquisitive, precise, and sometimes abstract thinking are characteristics of their personality. They like working with data and ideas.

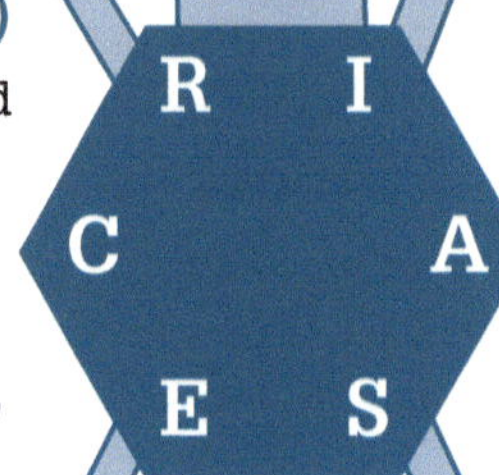

C – Conventional People (Organizers)

They like an organized and detail-oriented workplace. They are often skilled in finance, mathematics, and keyboarding. They see themselves as conforming, organized, and practical. They like working with data.

A – Artistic People (Creators)

They like to create, sing, dance, or write and prefer an unstructured work environment. They have skills in music, art, and/or communication. They value aesthetic qualities and are more likely to relate by indirect means through their medium. They like working with ideas.

E – Enterprising People (Persuaders)

They like to persuade and influence others in areas of business or politics. They perceive themselves as popular, self-confident, and social. They have skills in public speaking and leadership. Enterprising types like working with people and data.

S – Social People (Helpers)

They enjoy helping others and the community. They have skills in teaching, counseling, and getting along with others, and are sensitive to others' needs. They are cheerful, scholarly, and verbally oriented. They like working with people.

Step 2: Match Your Holland Code to Compatible Careers

Every profession requires more than just one talent. The chart on the following page organizes each career or workplace environment by its main characteristic only. Remember that according to the theory behind the

Holland Codes, you should look for a workplace environment that is compatible with your personal Holland Code.

R – Realistic People (Doers)

engineer, broadcast technician, landscape worker, barber, fire fighter, cook, auto mechanic, carpenter, surgical technologist, machinist, heavy truck driver, pest control worker, air traffic controller, roofer

I – Investigative People (Thinkers)

computer programmer, conservation scientist, financial analyst, microbiologist, physician, physician's assistant, pharmacist, chemist, biomedical engineer, food scientist, veterinarian, natural sciences manager, geologist, anthropologist, lab technician

C – Conventional People (Organizers)

bookkeeper, accountant, tax preparer, court reporter, cashiers, paralegal, bank teller, insurance underwriter, medical records technician, secretary/office worker, building inspector, computer operator

A – Artistic People (Creators)

commercial artist, singer, actor/actress, editor, author, music teacher, journalist, graphic designer, advertising manager, floral designer, animator, museum curator, photographer

E – Enterprising People (Persuaders)

salesperson, financial manager, construction manager, sports promoter, convention manager, lawyer, politician, real estate agent, marketing manager, business executive

S – Social People (Helpers)

nurse, physical therapist, occupational therapy assistant, teacher or teacher assistant, aerobics instructor, social worker, clergy, coach, dental hygienist, counselor, probation officer, paramedic, personnel director, home health aide

When you explore career options on well-recognized websites such as College for North Carolina (CFNC, previously College Foundation of North Carolina), NC Careers, and O*NET, you'll find careers organized by these Holland Code categories even if the websites don't refer to Holland Codes specifically. Knowing your Holland Code will help you efficiently search for compatible academic programs and careers.

Work Values

While it may be obvious to choose an academic program or career field based on your personality and interests, less obvious—but equally important—is the connection between your academic program or career field and your work values. Your **work values** are the elements of your personal belief system that are fulfilled from your career or workplace. If, for example, you

STUDENT NOTES

This list is obviously incomplete. Not every career is listed here. However, based on the careers that are listed, you can start to identify the characteristics of the individual careers that explain their categorization into a specific Holland Code category.

You can also log on to nccareers.org for additional career suggestions based on your Holland Code.

STUDENT NOTES

You can also identify your work values by completing the Work Values Sorter activity on the NC Careers website.

See the instructions on how to log on to NC Careers and access the Work Values Sorter on pages 102–104.

value variety or challenging work experiences, then you may become bored in a career that requires repetitive, simplistic work. Identifying your work values (like knowing your Holland Code) will help you make deliberate decisions about your future career. Not surprisingly, if you choose a career that matches your work values, then you are more likely to feel satisfied by your work.

Complete the following self-assessment to identify what types of satisfaction you expect from your work.

Step 1: Identify Your Work Values

Read the following list of satisfying results that individuals report getting from their careers. Rate the importance of each category using the following scale:

1 Unimportant or undesirable
2 Somewhat important
3 Very important to you in your career/job

___ **Advancement:** Have opportunities to work hard and move ahead in my organization

___ **Affiliation:** Be recognized as being associated with a particular organization

___ **Artistic:** Be involved in creative works of art, music, literature, drama, decorating, or other art forms

___ **Authority:** Have control over others' work activities and be able to partially affect their destinies

___ **Be Needed:** Feel that what I do is necessary for the survival or welfare of others

___ **Beauty:** Have a job which involves the aesthetic appreciation of the study of things, ideas, or people

___ **Community:** Work at a job in which I can get involved in community affairs

___ **Competition:** Pit my abilities against those of others in situations which test my competencies and in which there are win or lose outcomes

___ **Contact with People:** Have regular contact with the public

___ **Creative Expression:** Have opportunities to express my ideas, reactions, and observations about my work and how I might improve it verbally or in writing

STUDENT NOTES

___ **Creativity:** Create new programs and systems; develop original structures and procedures not dependent on someone else's format

___ **Decision-Making:** Have the power to decide policies, agendas, courses of action, etc.

___ **Exercise Competence:** Have opportunities to involve myself in those areas in which I feel I have talents above the average person

___ **Expertise:** Be respected and sought after for my knowledge and skills in a given area

___ **Fun:** Work in a situation in which I am free to be spontaneous, playful, humorous, and exuberant

___ **Help Society:** Make a contribution for the betterment of the world in which I live

___ **Helping Others:** Provide a service to and assist others as individuals or as groups

___ **High-Income Possibilities:** Work, which can lead to substantial earnings or profit, enables me to purchase essential items and the luxuries of life I desire

___ **Independence:** Be able to direct and control the course of my work, determining its nature without a great deal of direction from others

___ **Influence:** Be able to change and influence others' attitudes or opinions

___ **Integration:** Be able to integrate my working life with my personal life, involving my family or close friends

___ **Intellectual Status:** Be recognized as a person with high intellectual ability; one who is an authority in a given area of knowledge

___ **Job Tranquility:** Avoid pressure and the "rat race"

___ **Learning:** Be able to continually learn new skills and acquire new knowledge and understanding

___ **Location:** Live in a place which is conducive to my lifestyle and in which I can do the activities I enjoy

___ **Moral/Spiritual:** Have a sense that my work is important to and in accord with a set of standards in which I believe

___ **Orderliness of Environment:** Work in a consistently ordered environment where everything has its place and things are not changed often

___ **Personal Growth and Development:** Engage in work which offers me opportunity to grow as a person

STUDENT NOTES

___ **Physical Work Environment:** Work in a place which is pleasing to me aesthetically or beautiful to me

___ **Physical:** Do work which makes physical demands and in which I can use my coordination and physical abilities

___ **Predictability:** Have a stable and relatively unchanging work routine and job duties

___ **Pressure:** Have a job which involves working against time deadlines and/or where others critique the quality of my work

___ **Problem Solving:** Have a position that provides challenging problems to solve and avoids routine

___ **Productive:** Produce tangibles, things I can see and touch

___ **Recognition:** Be visibly and publicly appreciated and given credit for the quality of my work

___ **Relationships:** Develop close friendships with my co-workers and other people I meet in the course of my work activities

___ **Responsibility:** Be responsible for the planning and implementation of many tasks and projects as well as for the people involved

___ **Risk Taking:** Have work which requires me to take risks or accept challenges frequently

___ **Security:** Be able to depend on keeping my job and making enough money

___ **Status:** Have a position which carries respect with my friends, family, and community

___ **Supervision:** Be directly responsible for work which is done and produced by others under my supervision

___ **Time Freedom:** Be free to plan and manage my own time schedule in work; be able to set my own hours

___ **Undemanding:** Have work duties which demand very little energy or involvement

___ **Uniqueness:** Feel that the work I do is unique, novel, and different from others in some way

___ **Variety:** Do a number of different tasks; have the setting and content of my work responsibilities change frequently

___ **Work Alone:** Work by myself on projects and tasks

STUDENT NOTES

___ **Work on Frontiers of Knowledge:** Be involved in hard science or human research; work in a company that is considered one of the best in the business and strive for advances

___ **Work with Others:** Be a member of a working team; work with others in a group toward common goals

Step 2: Prioritize Your Work Values

Look back at the numbers you assigned to the individual work values on the previous pages. Note the values to which you assigned a "3." Now list below the three values that you would not be willing to compromise beginning with your most valued. These are your personal work values that should guide your academic and career goal exploration as well as your goal setting.

1. ______________________

2. ______________________

3. ______________________

This work values self-assessment was adapted from an activity developed by NC Careers. For more information, see nccareers.org.

As you explore potential majors and potential careers, keep your work values in mind and look for opportunities to match your values to your goals. In the same way that individuals who work in fields that are compatible with their personalities and interests can expect job satisfaction, people who seek out careers that fit their work values can expect to be personally and professional satisfied by their careers.

NC Careers

The NC Careers website features several useful self-assessment tools. Specifically, NC Careers allows students to complete interactive, self-scoring exercises that identify their personality and interests and their work values. Then the website identifies possible careers that match the self-assessment results. Additionally, NC Careers is a useful tool for goal exploration as you'll learn in Chapters 5 and 6.

Create a free nccareers.org account by following the directions on the following pages.

STUDENT NOTES

Step 1: Open an Internet Browser and Go to the NC Careers Website: nccareers.org

Notice all of the available links on the NC Careers homepage. You can investigate North Carolina careers, learn about college and university programs that prepare students for specific careers, identify strategies to overcome common barriers to employment like criminal records and disabilities, and explore apprenticeships and other on-the-job training opportunities.

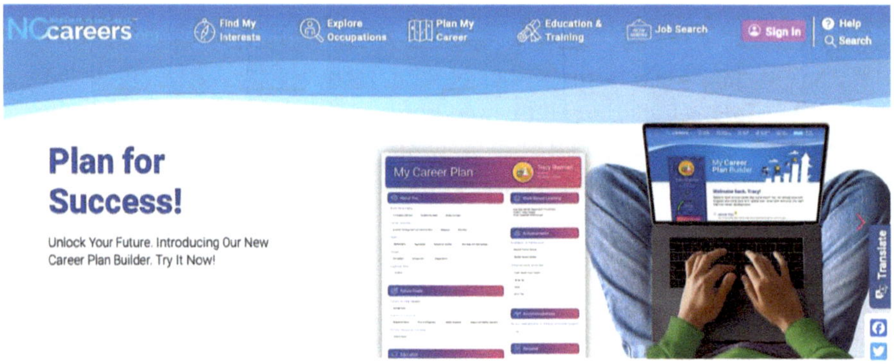

Step 2: Log on to NC Careers

NC Careers and College for North Carolina (CFNC) are in partnership and share log in credentials. If you used the CFNC website to apply for financial aid or apply for admission to your college, then enter your username and password on the NC Careers log on webpage.

If you are new to the NC Careers website, click on the SIGN IN link and then CREATE ACCOUNT to create a username and password for this website.

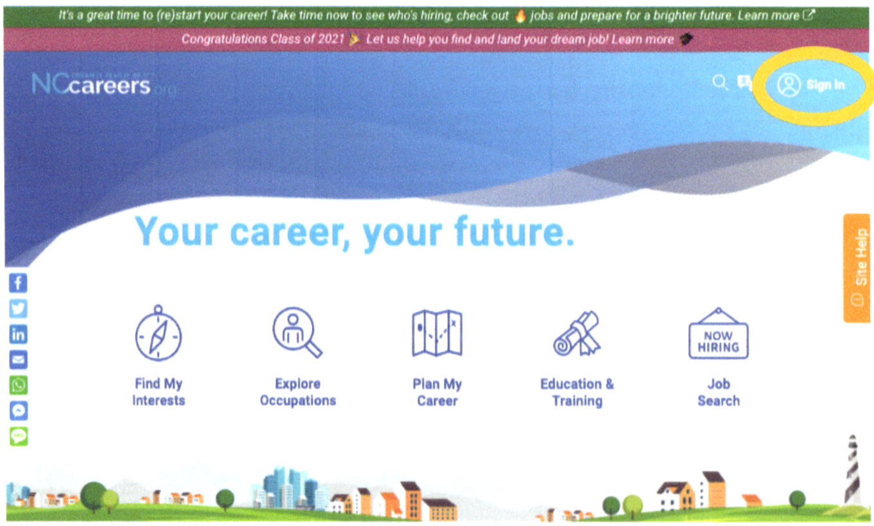

Step 3: Complete the "Create an Account" Page

Type in your personal information and create a CFNC and NC Careers account and password.

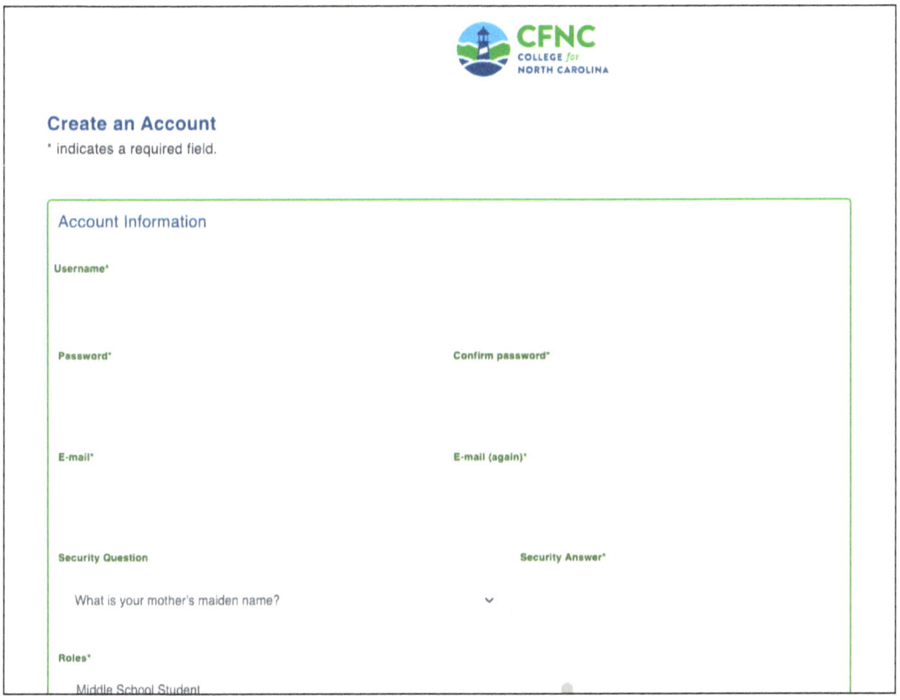

Step 4: Click on "Find My Interests"

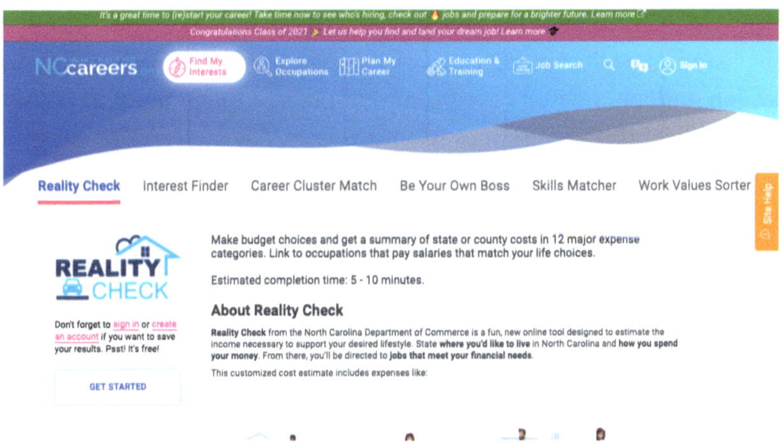

STUDENT NOTES

You will have to create a username and password on this page.

For your username, choose something that will be easy for you to remember, such as the first part of another college account like your school email address. Choose something you will easily remember for your password, too.

At the bottom of the page, you can type a question and answer that the website can use to send you your password if you ever forget it. Again, choose something easy to remember.

STUDENT NOTES

Step 5: Explore the Menu Options

You'll find several useful assessments on this webpage. Look for and complete the Interest Finder and Work Values Sorter. The Interest Finder will tell you your Holland Code (see the descriptions of the Holland Codes earlier in this chapter for more information). The Work Values Sorter will tell you your top two or three work values. Specifically, the Work Values Sorter will indicate your preferences for the following work values: Recognition, Relationships, Achievement, Support, Independence, and Working Conditions.

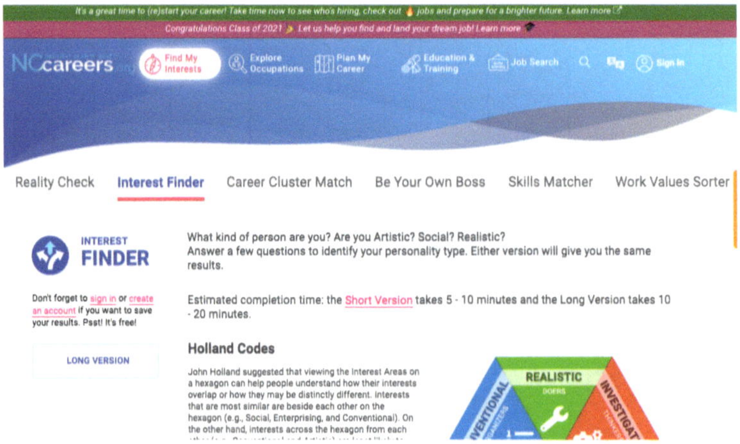

The NC Careers website will then report careers and clusters of careers that match your interests and your values. You can click on "Explore Matching Occupations" to find these matches.

You can then find information on the skills and requirements necessary for the jobs listed as well as average pay (for North Carolina and the United States), job outlook, related careers, and important links. You can refine the search based on your preferences in these areas (for example, only careers that have an expected increase in demand).

Step 6: Click on "Log Out"

When you finish working in NC Careers, click on "Log Out" before you close the internet browser. By logging out and logging in the next time you use the site, the site will save your information.

STUDENT NOTES

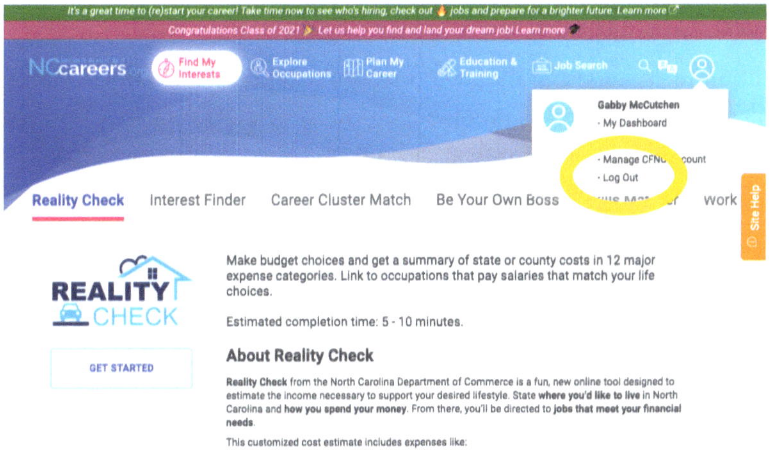

Sometimes students find that their results on the NC Careers inventories do not match the decisions that they have previously made about their academic and career goals. For example, a student might feel strongly that he wants to be a nurse, but not find the career of nursing matches his interests and work values. If this is your experience, then you might use the NC Careers website to explore careers that you hadn't previously considered that better match your self-assessment results. Or you might consider interpreting your self-assessment results a little more broadly.

This information provided on the NC Careers website will help you transition to the next steps in goal discernment: academic and career goal exploration.

Monkey Business Images/Shutterstock.com

CHAPTER 4: Self-Assessment

STUDENT NOTES

Metacognition

In addition to considering their professional interests and values, successful college students also use metacognition to help them learn strategically. **Metacognition** is, in its simplest definition, thinking about your thinking. This includes planning the best way to study for a specific class. For example, ask yourself questions to help you target your studying, such as, "What should I spend the most time studying? What did the instructor emphasize? How much time will I need to study in order to do well on the test?" With this planning step, you can realize that making flash cards can be a great technique for learning vocabulary for a biology or foreign language class, but flash cards are not usually a useful way to prepare for a philosophy essay exam that asks you to draw connections between philosophical concepts and the real world. Metacognition also helps you monitor yourself. As you're studying, check in with yourself by asking how well your chosen study strategies are working, what material you've mastered, or what material you are avoiding because it's confusing or hard. The final step in metacognition is to evaluate yourself, which is what self-assessment is all about. We use metacognition to evaluate our learning of new ideas when we create self-tests and quiz ourselves with our vocabulary flash cards. We also use evaluation to examine how well our study strategies worked and what might need to be altered for the next test.

These three phases of metacognition—planning, monitoring, and evaluating—are critical to developing as a learner. Throughout *Success by Design*, you'll use metacognition questions in the pre-reading and chapter review questions to help you become a more strategic student.

Learning Styles Preferences

There has been a lot of recent discussion about the value of learning styles among higher education instructors and researchers. Some researchers state that there is no scientific evidence supporting the value of learning styles or the attempts instructors make to teach to different learning styles. However, learning style preferences are still a useful way to categorize different kinds of teaching and learning inputs and activities. And when you know what kinds of learning inputs and activities you prefer, you can compensate for learning environments and instructors who don't provide those conditions in the classroom.

Your **learning style** is your preferred method for learning new information. Identifying your learning style is a critical step in metacognition. Your college instructors expect you to take responsibility for your own learning and to be able to learn in a laboratory or clinical setting, in study groups, in

STUDENT NOTES

online learning environments, and in individual study as well as in the classroom. Everyone has natural learning style preferences, and knowing your learning style provides you with the opportunity to take advantage of your natural strengths as a learner. Understanding your learning style preferences will help you improve your study habits and make sense of difficult subjects.

As you read about the learning style typologies below and complete a learning styles inventory, keep in mind that your learning style indicates your preference along a continuum. No one has exclusively only one learning style preference. It is important to take advantage of your natural preferences to make learning easy; however, it is also important to be able to adapt to learning environments that don't match your natural preferences. Savvy college students not only know their learning style preference, but they also try out less-preferred learning styles to accommodate certain types of class formats or instructors' teaching styles.

Shutterstock.com

Sensory Preferences

Learning styles are commonly organized into **sensory preferences**: visual, verbal, kinesthetic, and multi-modal. As you read the descriptions of each of the following sensory preferences, think about your personal sensory preferences.

Visual learners prefer visual representations of information (for example, charts, diagrams, pictures) to help them understand new ideas. They like instructors who show visual aids on the board or in PowerPoint slides. They also like textbooks that are printed in color and that have lots of pictures. Visual learners frequently highlight their textbooks and notes, and they use symbols in their notes to signify important concepts. When they take tests, visual learners can often remember information in a chart or graph more easily than information in sentences and paragraphs.

Verbal learners prefer lecture and discussion format classes. They may not take very good notes because they are so busy listening to the instructor and their classmates. When they study, they may read or quiz themselves out loud. Verbal learners frequently like to use audio recorders in class, so they can listen to the recording later to study the class content. They also like to participate in discussions either in class or with their instructors or classmates outside of class. When they see a chart or diagram, they have to translate the meaning into words, and then they often remember the explanations better than the chart or diagram.

Kinesthetic learners prefer to learn through using all of their senses (sight, touch, taste, smell, and hearing) and through hands-on, real-world applications. Kinesthetic learners often do not fully understand a concept until they can try it out for themselves in a laboratory or clinical setting. They like for their instructors to give them lots of examples of new ideas, and they often

STUDENT NOTES

remember the examples and their experiences better than they remember a list of vocabulary terms or other forms of concrete knowledge.

Multi-modal learners have some combination of visual, verbal, and kinesthetic learning style preferences. Multi-modal learners may have any two of the sensory preferences (for example, visual and kinesthetic or verbal and kinesthetic). Or they may have all three sensory preferences (visual, verbal, and kinesthetic). These combinations of learning style preferences give multi-modal learners great flexibility in learning in several different types of learning environments. While the student with the very strong visual preference may struggle in a lecture-only class, the multi-modal visual-verbal learner can more easily adapt to the lecture format.

Athanasia Nomikou/Shutterstock.com

Hemispheric Dominance

Another common learning style typology (that is just as debatable as the sensory preferences!) describes individuals' brain **hemispheric dominance**, or right-brain and left-brain preferences. The human brain is divided into two hemispheres with very different functions that work together for all types of thinking, learning, and activity. The two sides are described in very general terms below. As you read the descriptions of right-brained people and left-brained people, think about which characteristics best describe how you think and, therefore, hint at your personal hemispheric dominance.

The left side of the brain is responsible for use of language as well as logical and sequential thinking. **Left-brained** people typically pay attention to the steps in a process (for example, solving a math problem) or the details in a task (for example, spelling and grammar in writing an essay). Left-brained people also like using a checklist and completing tasks in a logical and sequential order. They have to understand the individual details of a new concept in order to understand the big picture.

The right side of the brain, on the other hand, processes visual input and is attentive to colors. **Right-brained** people are typically intuitive and global thinkers who rely on their instincts over methodical problem solving. Right-brained people resist making lists or schedules. They also prefer to work at their own pace and on what interests them in the moment, which can make them appear to be easily distracted. They can see a new concept's big picture readily and need to fully understand the big picture in order to be able to make meaning of its details.

Again, no one is exclusively left-brained or right-brained. But many of us do have a dominant hemisphere. You may find that you approach your college classes in a very left-brained logical, sequential way because college is so important to your personal goals and values. But in your personal life, you may prefer right-brained thinking.

Index of Learning Styles Questionnaire

STUDENT NOTES

You can probably identify your sensory and hemispheric preferences and patterns based on the simplistic definitions on the previous pages. However, you may have additional learning style preferences that you are unaware of. To more thoroughly identify the ways in which you learn best, complete the **Index of Learning Styles (ILS)** questionnaire, a learning styles preferences questionnaire developed by two professors at North Carolina State University. Your results on the ILS will give you a comprehensive picture of your learning style, including some sensory preferences (for example, visual-verbal) and some hemispheric dominance preferences (for example, sequencing-global and sensing-intuitive). It also measures your preferences in active and reflective learning.

Access the Index of Learning Styles questionnaire at learningstyles.webtools.ncsu.edu.

If after you complete the ILS, you are interested in knowing more about your personal learning style preferences, search online for the following well-known learning styles inventories and questionnaires:

- VARK Learning Styles Inventory,
- Howard Gardner's Multiple Intelligences, and
- Myers-Briggs Type Indicator.

When you complete the 44-question ILS, print your Learning Styles Results Form and examine your results carefully. You'll see your results reported along the same scales in the example below. Notice that your learning styles are reported along four continuums. Look for a red bar printed along each continuum. You may find that you have some strong preferences (for example, the score of 7 on the Visual end of the third continuum indicates a strong preference for visual learning). Or you may learn that you are well balanced on one or more continuums (for example, the score of 1 on the Sensing side of the second continuum).

NC STATE UNIVERSITY

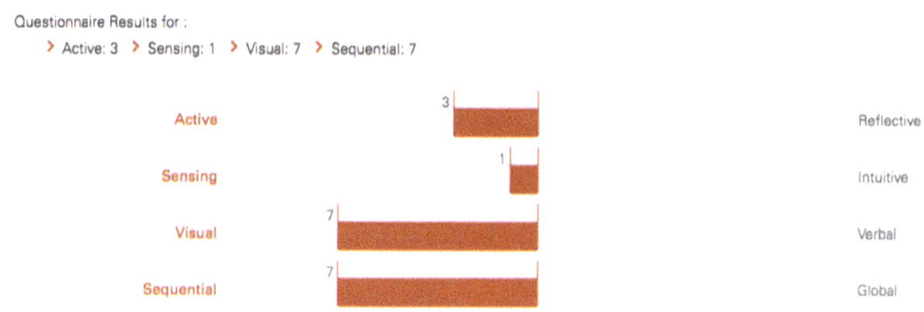

STUDENT NOTES

Keep your learning style preferences and these study recommendations in mind when you read Chapter 11: Study Strategies.

After you note your learning styles preferences as reported by the Index of Learning Styles, read the descriptions of each of the dimensions below and on the following pages to better understand your learning style preferences. You can read more thorough descriptions of each of the dimensions on the ILS website.

	Active Learners	Reflective Learners
Characteristics	• Understand information when they discuss, apply, or explain it to someone else. • Prefer group work to solve a problem. • Prefer to manipulate objects, do physical experiments, and learn by trying.	• Understand information when they can think about it quietly first. • Prefer to work alone to solve a problem. • Prefer to think things through, to evaluate options, and learn by analysis.
Recommendations	• Study in a group. • Find ways to apply new information, such as creating a practice test and quizzing other classmates.	• Don't just read and memorize material; think about how you could apply new information. • Summarize or restate your class notes in your own words.

	Sensing Learners	Intuitive Learners
Characteristics	• Like to learn facts. • Like solving problems using regular methods; dislike surprises. • Prefer concrete, practical, and procedural information.	• Like to discover relationships and possibilities. • Like innovation; dislike repetition. • Prefer conceptual, innovative, and theoretical information that provides overall meaning.
Recommendations	• Look for specific examples of ideas or concepts. • Find ways to apply new information to your own life. • Ask your instructor for applications to the real world.	• Look for connections between ideas. • Take the time to read and think about a question before you start answering it. • Take your time on tests; don't get impatient with details or checking your work.

STUDENT NOTES

	Visual Learners	Verbal Learners
Characteristics	• Remember what they see—pictures, graphs, diagrams, films, demonstrations. • Prefer visual representations of information.	• Remember words—what they hear and what they read. • Prefer to hear or read information. • Look for explanations with words.
Recommendations	• Find charts or other visual representation of new material. • Color-code your notes so all related topics are one color. • Create concept maps to organize new ideas.	• Write summaries or outlines of notes in your own words. • Work in groups to talk about lessons.

	Sequential Learners	Global Learners
Characteristics	• Understand ideas in linear steps. • Follow steps to find solutions. • Prefer to have information presented linearly and in an orderly manner. • Put together the details in order to see the big picture.	• Learn in large jumps without knowing how ideas relate. • Suddenly "get" it. • Can solve problems in new ways, but can't always explain how they did it. • Prefer a holistic and systematic approach to learning. • See the big picture first and then fill in the details.
Recommendations	• Outline lecture material in logical order. • Improve your global thinking skills by relating new ideas to things you already know. • Ask an instructor who skips from topic to topic to fill in any missed steps or missed material.	• Before you read a chapter, skim it to see the big picture. • Study the same subject for extended periods of time. • Be patient; it may be harder for you to understand the smaller pieces of a big concept.

STUDENT NOTES

Don't forget to record your Holland Code, work values, and learning style preferences on page 92 for easy reference.

Conclusion

After you have completed the multiple self-assessments described in this chapter, you should have a clearer understanding of who you are as a college student and a future professional. Whereas you may have had a vague idea of your personality, interests, and values previously, you can now describe these components of yourself using language that is common to career search and goal discernment. Similarly, you identified your learning style preferences by completing the Index of Learning Styles. These academic self-assessments can inform your goals, too, and can prepare you for long-term academic success.

REVIEW QUESTIONS

Chapter 4

Self-Assessment

These questions will help you monitor and evaluate your learning, two important parts of metacognition.

1. Look again at the descriptions in your Holland Code. What descriptions of your personality and interests are most accurate for you? What descriptions are not accurate? What one word best describes your codes?

2. In addition to your interests and values, what else should you take into consideration when choosing a career? List five questions that would contribute to the self-assessment stage of goal discernment.

3. Compare the results of your Holland Code self-analysis on page 96 and the results of the Interest Finder on the NC Careers website. How are they similar? If they are different, then which one is more accurate?

4. How well does your intended career match your interests and personality (as determined by the Holland Code and/or NC Careers website)? Identify the specific aspects of your interests that your career will help you fulfill.

5. Compare the results of your Work Values self-analysis on page 101 and the results of the Work Values Sorter on the NC Careers website. How are they similar? If they are different, then which one is more accurate?

6. How well does your intended career match your work values? Identify your work values that will be achieved in your chosen career.

7. Jasmine is a first-semester college student who is struggling in her math class. She always did well in math classes in high school, but she hasn't been in a math classroom in over 10 years, and she can't remember much from high school algebra. She knows that her strongest learning style preferences are visual, sensing, and active. Which of the three learning style preferences will help her most in math? Why? What is one strategy specific to that learning style that she should try?

8. Anthony is taking SPA 111 (Elementary Spanish I) and SPA 181 (Spanish Lab I) for the second time this semester. He dropped the classes last semester after he failed the first two tests. In one week, he will take his first test in Spanish this semester. He knows that his strongest learning style preferences are verbal and intuitive. Which of the two learning style preferences will help him most in preparing for the Spanish test? Why? What is one strategy specific to that learning style that he should try?

9. One common study technique that works for college students with different learning style preferences is flash cards. Fill in the table below with two strategies for visual learners to use flash cards and two strategies for verbal learners to use flash cards.

How Visual Learners Can Use Flash Cards Effectively	How Verbal Learners Can Use Flash Cards Effectively

10. Another common study technique that works for college students with different learning style preferences is writing practice test questions. Fill in the table below with two strategies for active learners to use practice tests and two strategies for reflective learners to use practice tests.

How Active Learners Can Use Practice Tests Effectively	How Reflective Learners Can Use Practice Tests Effectively

Discussion Questions

Reflect on your preferred learning style preferences. Share an example of when your learning style helped you understand or retain information effectively. How do you plan to apply your learning preferences to your coursework this semester? What is something you could do with your course materials that would align well with your individual learning style preferences?

REVIEW QUESTIONS

ESB Professional/Shutterstock.com

UNIT 2

Chapter 5

Academic Goal Exploration

Before you read this chapter, reflect on the following:

1. *What is the name of the credential you will earn from your community college?*
2. *How many of the ten community college credentials can you name?*
3. *What do you want to know about transferring to a senior institution?*

These questions will help you plan your learning, an important part of metacognition.

Now that you have clear definitions of your interests and values, it's time to explore your options. This means research. To ensure that you are on the right academic and career path, you need to research your goal options and look for connections to what you've learned about yourself in the self-assessment stage of goal discernment. This chapter of *Success by Design* will introduce you to several resources and concepts to help you move through the goal exploration stage of goal discernment. Specifically, it will focus on academic goal exploration.

As you consider your academic options, you should learn as much as you can about your chosen academic program and other related academic programs. Goals change, and the cycles of goal discernment are unending. Therefore, you may change your program or pursue additional programs based on what you learn from your research.

STUDENT NOTES

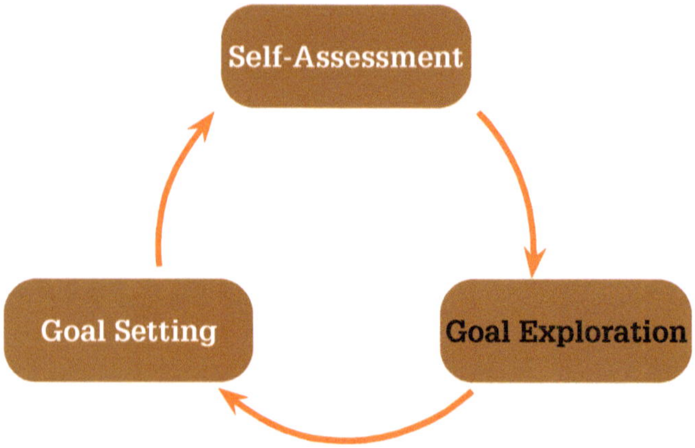

Chapter 5 will address the following very useful tools in academic goal exploration:

- Community college credentials;
- Programs of Study;
- Plans of Study, Transfer Guides, Course Selection Guides;
- Four options for transfer to senior institutions; and
- Demystifying transfer.

> Many colleges offer both AAS and AA/AS degrees in many of the same fields. For example, students who are interested in business careers may pursue an AAS degree or an AA degree. Business students who want to enter their new career fields immediately after graduation from the community college should pursue the AAS degree. Business students who want to transfer to a university and eventually earn a bachelor's degree should pursue the AA degree.
>
> If your desired career has both an AA/AS degree option and an AAS degree option, then consider how the different degrees will factor into your career focus and responsibilities.

Community College Credentials

Community colleges are unique institutions of higher education because they follow an **open door with guided placement policy** that allows them to admit any student who has earned a high school credential or its equivalent. Four-year universities and colleges, on the other hand, require minimum GPAs, standardized test scores, and completion of specific high school courses. They use competitive admissions processes to decide which students to admit and which students to reject. Because community colleges do not have competitive admissions, everyone who applies is admitted as a student. But North Carolina community colleges do consider students' high school GPAs and standardized test scores in placing students in college-level coursework. Students who do not have qualifying high school GPAs or standardized test scores may be required to complete some **placement testing** to make sure they are prepared for the college-level coursework in their programs. Placement tests commonly assess students' writing, reading, and math skills; students' scores indicate which classes they can begin taking. Later in this chapter, you will learn more about pre-requisite courses called developmental education courses that many students must take based on their placement test results.

Students attend community colleges for a variety of reasons. Some students want to complete a degree or other short credential to prepare for a new career, such as Clinical Trials Research Associate or Networking Technologies.

STUDENT NOTES

Other students choose to attend community colleges to earn a transferable associate degree before they move on to a senior four-year college or university, like North Carolina Central University or University of North Carolina–Greensboro. Still others take classes off and on for personal enrichment or because they haven't yet decided on a career or educational path.

Community colleges offer a variety of credentials that meet all of these goals. Most community college students are working toward an associate degree. North Carolina's community colleges offer the following associate degrees:

- Associate in Applied Science (AAS)
- Associate in Arts (AA)
- Associate in Engineering (AE)
- Associate in Fine Arts (AFA)
- Associate in Science (AS)
- Associate in General Education (AGE)
- Associate in Arts in Teacher Preparation (AATP)
- Associate in Science in Teacher Preparation (ASTP)

Check with your college to see which of these degrees are available to you.

Career and technical education students and health technologies students frequently enroll in **Associate in Applied Science (AAS)** programs. The Associate in Applied Science degree includes some general education courses, but it primarily focuses on major courses that prepare students for a new career. Common Associate in Applied Science programs include Nursing, Automotive Technology, Occupational Therapy Assistant, and Early Childhood Education.

University transfer students work toward the **Associate in Arts (AA)**, **Associate in Engineering (AE)**, **Associate in Science (AS)**, **Associate in Fine Arts (AFA)**, **Associate in Arts in Teacher Preparation (AATP)**, or **Associate in Science in Teacher Preparation (ASTP)** degree, depending on what they plan to major in at the senior institution. For example, students who plan to major in social work, education, psychology, or business should be Associate in Arts students. Students who plan to major in engineering should enter Associate in Engineering programs. Students who plan to major in biology, chemistry, or math are Associate in Science students. Students who plan to major in music and music education, art, or drama are Associate in Fine Arts students. Students who plan to major in education should enter Associate in Arts in Teacher Preparation or Associate in Science in Teacher Preparation depending on the requirements of the senior institution. In general, AATP students plan to teach subjects like English, history, social studies, and foreign languages while ASTP students plan to teach subjects like science, technology, engineering, and math.

STUDENT NOTES

Finally, students who want to take classes for their own personal growth earn the **Associate in General Education (AGE)** degree. The Associate in General Education degree does not prepare students for a new career, nor does it transfer to a senior institution.

In addition to degrees, all North Carolina community colleges offer **diploma** programs which require 36–48 credit hours. Diplomas often prepare students for specific careers, such as Licensed Practical Nursing and Carpentry.

Community colleges also offer **certificates** that are shorter credentials that typically demonstrate necessary requirements for professional certifications. Often students earn certificates as they work toward a diploma or associate degree. For example, a student may earn an Engine Performance Certificate as he completes the Automotive Technology AAS program. Certificates require 12–18 credit hours. Depending on the course offerings, students can complete several certificates to prepare them for a new career or for advancement in their careers as they work toward an associate degree.

Credential	Credit Hours
Associate in Applied Science (AAS)	64–76 credits
Associate in Arts (AA)	60–61 credits
Associate in Engineering (AE)	60–61 credits
Associate in Science (AS)	60–61 credits
Associate in Fine Arts (AFA)	60–61 credits
Associate in Arts in Teacher Preparation (AATP)	60–61 credits
Associate in Science in Teacher Preparation (ASTP)	60–61 credits
Associate in General Education (AGE)	64–65 credits
Diploma	36–48 credits
Certificate	12–18 credits

Programs of Study at North Carolina Community Colleges

On the next several pages, you will see most of the specific programs that are available at North Carolina community colleges as of Fall 2025. Check your college's website to see which programs are offered at your college.

Animals and Environment

- Agribusiness Technology
- Agricultural Systems Technology
- Animal Care and Management Technology
- Applied Animal Science Technology

- Aquaculture Technology
- Aquarium Science Technology
- Equine Business
- Equine Training
- Fish and Wildlife Management Technology
- Forestry Management Technology
- Golf Course Management Technology
- Greenhouse and Grounds Maintenance
- Horticulture Technology
- Hunting and Shooting Sports Management
- Landscape Gardening
- Outdoor Leadership
- Sustainable Agriculture
- Swine Management Technology
- Taxidermy
- Turfgrass Management Technology
- Veterinary Medical Technology
- Zoological Science Technology

Arts and Media

- Audio and Video Production Technology
- Digital Effects and Animation Technology
- Digital Media Technology
- Entertainment Technologies
- Film and Video Production Technology
- Graphic Arts and Imaging Technology
- Graphic Design
- Interior Design
- Metal Engraving
- Photographic Technology
- Professional Arts and Crafts: Sculpture
- Professional Crafts: Clay
- Professional Crafts: Fiber
- Professional Crafts: Jewelry
- Professional Crafts: Wood
- Sports Media Technology

Beauty and Personal Care

- Cosmetology
- Cosmetology Instructor
- Esthetics Instructor
- Esthetics Technology
- Manicuring Instructor
- Manicuring/Nail Technology
- Natural Hair Care Certificate

Business and Leadership

- Accounting and Finance
- Business Administration
- Business Analytics
- Entrepreneurship
- Leadership Studies
- Office Administration
- Project Management Technology
- Supply Chain Management

Education and Teaching

- Agriculture Education
- Early Child Care Workforce
- Early Childhood Administration
- Early Childhood Education
- Early Childhood Preschool
- Elementary Education Residency Licensure
- High School Adjunct Instructor
- Infant/Toddler Care
- Lateral Entry
- Library and Information Technology
- Occupational Education Associate
- School-Age Care
- School-Age Education

STUDENT NOTES

STUDENT NOTES

Engineering and Construction

- Aerospace Manufacturing Technology
- Applied Engineering Technology
- Architectural Technology
- Automation Engineering Technology
- Aviation Electronics (Avionics) Technology
- Aviation Management and Career Pilot Technology
- Aviation Systems Technology
- Civil Engineering Technology
- Computer-Aided Drafting Technology
- Electric Utility Substation and Relay Technology
- Electrical Engineering Technology
- Electrical Power Production Technology
- Electronics Engineering Technology
- Environmental Engineering Technology
- Geomatics Technology
- Industrial Engineering Technology
- Landscape Architecture Technology
- Laser and Photonics Technology
- Mechanical Drafting Technology
- Mechanical Engineering Technology
- Mechatronics Engineering Technology

Healthcare and Medicine

- Advanced Medical Coding
- Anesthesia Technology
- Associate Degree Nursing
- Associate in General Education—Nursing
- Biomedical Equipment Technology
- Breast Sonography (certificate)
- Cancer Information Management
- Cardiovascular Sonography
- Cardiovascular Technology (Invasive and Non-Invasive)
- Central Sterile Processing
- Clinical Trials Research Associate
- Computed Tomography and Magnetic Resonance Imaging Technology
- Cytotechnology
- Dental Assisting
- Dental Hygiene
- Dental Laboratory Technology
- Dialysis Technology (diploma)
- Emergency Medical Science
- Health and Fitness Science
- Health Information Technology
- Healthcare Business Informatics
- Healthcare Interpreting
- Healthcare Management Technology
- Healthcare Simulation Technology
- Histotechnology
- Human Services Technology/Addiction and Recovery Studies
- Human Services Technology/Social Service
- Interventional Cardiac and Vascular Technology
- Licensed Practical Nurse Refresher
- Magnetic Resonance Imaging
- Mammography
- Medical Assisting
- Medical Dosimetry
- Medical Laboratory Technology
- Medical Office Administration
- Medical Product Safety and Pharmacovigilance
- Medical Sonography
- Neurodiagnostic Technology
- Nuclear Medicine Technology
- Nurse Aide (certificate)
- Occupational Therapy Assistant

- Ophthalmic Medical Personnel
- Ophthalmic Surgical Assistant
- Optical Apprentice
- Opticianry
- Orthopaedic Technology
- Pharmacy Technology
- Phlebotomy
- Physical Therapist Assistant (1+1)
- Physical Therapist Assistant (2-year program)
- Polysomnography
- Positron Emission Tomography
- Practical Nursing
- Radiation Therapy Technology
- Radiography
- Recreational Therapy Assistant
- Respiratory Therapy
- Social and Human Services
- Speech-Language Pathology Assistant
- Surgical First Assistant
- Surgical Technology
- Therapeutic Massage

Hospitality and Food

- Baking and Pastry Arts
- Brewing
- Culinary Arts
- Foodservice Technology
- Hospitality Management
- Recreation and Leisure Studies
- Viticulture and Enology Technology

Languages

- Community Spanish Interpreter
- Interpreter Education

Law and Public Safety

- 911 Communication and Operations
- Basic Law Enforcement Training
- Criminal Justice Technology
- Cyber Crime Technology
- Emergency Management
- Fire Protection Technology
- Intelligence Studies
- Paralegal Technology
- Public Safety Administration

Real Estate

- BICUP Broker-in-Charge Update Course
- GENUP General Update Course

STUDENT NOTES

STUDENT NOTES

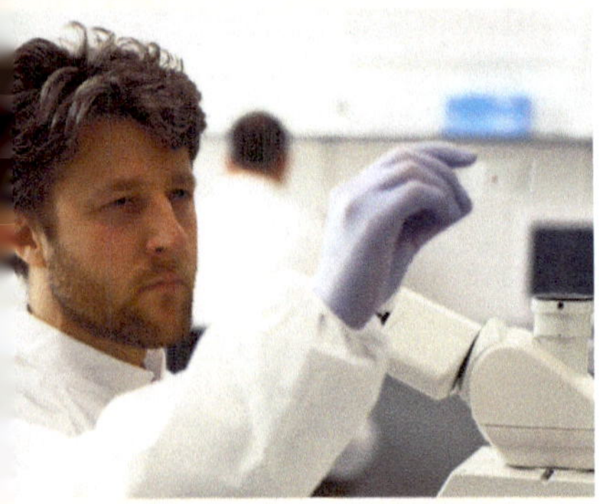

- Postlicensing 301 Broker Relationships and Responsibilities
- Postlicensing 302 Contracts and Closing
- Postlicensing 303 NC Laws, Rules, and Legal Concepts

Science and Research

- Agriculture Technology
- Biopharmaceutical Technology
- Bioprocess Technology
- Biotechnology
- Chemical Technology
- Environmental Management Technology
- Environmental Planning and Development
- Environmental Science Technology
- Marine Biotechnology
- Marine Science
- Marine Technology
- Nuclear Technology
- Sustainable Technologies

Tech and Computers

- Artificial Intelligence (AI)
- Computer Engineering Technology
- Geospatial Technology
- Information Technology
- Mission Critical Operations
- Simulation and Game Development
- Small UAS
- Small Unmanned Aircraft Systems
- Telecommunications and Networking Engineering Technology
- Telecommunications Installation and Maintenance
- UAS Operations Management
- UAS Operator Flight Training

Trades and Mechanics

- Air Conditioning, Heating, and Refrigeration Technology
- Alternative Transportation Technology
- Automotive Customizing Technology
- Automotive Light-Duty Diesel Technology
- Automotive Restoration Technology
- Automotive Systems Technology
- Boat Building (diploma)
- Boat Manufacture and Service
- Building Construction Technology
- Carpentry
- Collision Repair and Refinishing Technology
- Computer-Integrated Machining
- Construction Equipment Systems Technology
- Construction Management Technology
- Diesel and Heavy Equipment Technology
- Electric Line Construction Technology
- Electrical and Plumbing
- Electrical Systems Technology
- Electrical Vehicle Supply Equipment Technician Certification
- Facility Maintenance Technology
- Facility Maintenance Worker
- General Occupational Technology
- Gunsmithing
- Heavy Equipment Operation, Management, and Service
- Industrial Management Technology
- Industrial Systems Technology
- Lithium-Ion Battery Manufacturing
- Manufacturing Technology
- Marine Propulsion Systems
- Masonry
- Motorcycle Mechanics
- Motorsports

- Nondestructive Examination Technology
- Plumbing
- Race Care Technology
- Textiles Technology
- Welding Technology

Transport and Logistics

- Truck Driver Training (certificate)

University Transfer

- Associate in Arts
- Associate in Arts in Teacher Preparation (AATP)
- Associate in Engineering
- Associate in Fine Arts in Music
- Associate in Fine Arts in Theater
- Associate in Fine Arts in Visual Arts
- Associate in General Education
- Associate in Science
- Associate in Science in Teacher Preparation (ASTP)
- CCP to Associate in Arts in Teacher Preparation
- CCP to Associate in Science in Teacher Preparation

STUDENT NOTES

Plans of Study

When you are admitted to a specific degree, diploma, or certificate program, you will use that program's **Plan of Study** document to know what courses are required for a credential. Depending on what community college you are attending, your Plan of Study may be called Course Hour Requirements, Curriculum, Curriculum Standards, Checksheet, Degree Plan, Course Requirements, or Individual Graduation Plan.

The Plan of Study typically includes the required general education and major courses. Be sure to follow the Plan of Study for the year in which you were admitted to your program. For example, if you were admitted in 2025–2026, then you should use the 2025–2026 Plan of Study, not the 2024–2025 Plan of Study.

You may be required to take additional courses as pre-requisites or co-requisites to the courses required on your Plan of Study. These pre-requisite courses are typically listed at the bottom of the Plan of Study.

A **pre-requisite course** is one that you must successfully complete before enrolling in a higher-level course. For example, students must take and pass BIO 168 (Anatomy and Physiology I) before they can take BIO 169 (Anatomy and Physiology II). BIO 168 is a pre-requisite for BIO 169.

Some students also have to take **English as a Foreign Language (EFL)** courses as pre-requisites for their programs. If your first language is not English, then you may be required to take an additional placement test that may indicate that you need EFL courses to prepare you for the academic language skills you will need to be successful in college. EFL courses do not

STUDENT NOTES

count toward the required number of credits for your program of study, but your grades in EFL courses may count toward your cumulative GPA.

Another type of pre-requisites are **developmental education** courses. These are English and math classes that prepare students for success in college-level courses. Developmental education classes have course numbers under 100, like ENG 025 or MAT 035. If your high school GPA or placement test results indicate that you need any developmental education courses, then you are required to take and pass them, but the developmental education credit hours do not count toward the total number of credits required by your Plan of Study. For example, if you place into developmental education courses and you plan to earn the 60–61 credits required for the AS degree, then you may actually have to complete 66 or 68 or 70 credits depending on how many developmental education classes you need. The grades you earn in developmental education classes may count toward your cumulative GPA and will probably count toward your Satisfactory Academic Progress if you are receiving financial aid (see Chapter 2 for more information about GPAs and financial aid).

Some developmental education courses are co-requisites to first-level English and math courses. A **co-requisite course** is one that you must complete at the same time as a required course. For example, some students must take ENG 045 and ENG 111 in the same semester based on their placement. ENG 045 is a co-requisite for ENG 111. Not all co-requisites are developmental education courses, though. At some colleges, PHY 110 (Conceptual Physics) and PHY 110A (Conceptual Physics Lab) must be taken in the same semester. PHY 110 and PHY 110A are co-requisites at those colleges.

Plans of Study are frequently organized to list non-developmental education pre-requisites separate from the required courses for the credential and to list co-requisites that are required for all students regardless of college placement in the same semester. Also, your advisor can help you plan your schedule to take into consideration any pre-requisites or co-requisites.

Your semester-by-semester class schedule and eventually your transcript will probably not look exactly like your program's Plan of Study because of any combination of the following reasons:

- You may have to first complete pre-requisites, like some developmental education courses.
- You may have to complete additional co-requisites, like ENG 045 and MAT 045.
- You may take fewer (or more) courses than are listed in a single semester on the Plan of Study.
- You may enter your program in a different semester than the first one listed on the Plan of Study.

STUDENT NOTES

In addition to paying attention to pre-requisites and co-requisites as you read your Plan of Study, consider credit hours and contact hours.

Credit hours are the number of hours associated with a particular class. Each Plan of Study requires a certain number of credit hours. The credit hours are used to calculate your GPA and determine your tuition bill each semester.

Contact hours, on the other hand, are the number of hours you spend in class each week. For example, CIS 110 (Introduction to Computers) is three credit hours and four contact hours. If you take CIS 110, then you'll receive three credits on your transcript, and you'll be billed for three credits. But you'll actually spend four hours in class each week.

Look for credit hours and contact hours on most Plans of Study. You will often have to add the "class hours," "lab hours," and "clinical hours" on the Plan of Study to determine the total number of contact hours. If you can't find the credit hours and contact hours on your Plan of Study, then you can look up the hours associated with each of your classes on your college's website.

Now is a good time to look for your Plan of Study at your college. Most colleges post Plans of Study on their website. And most Plans of Study include the details described in this chapter. Look specifically for credit hours and contact hours. Look also for the organization. For example, is the Plan of Study in chronological order (first semester, second semester, etc.)? Or is the Plan of Study organized by discipline (required Natural Sciences courses, required Humanities/Fine Arts courses, etc.)? Typically, university transfer Plans of Study (Associate in Arts, Associate in Engineering, Associate in Fine Arts, Associate in Science, Associate in Arts in Teacher Preparation, and Associate in Science in Teacher Preparation) are not in chronological order, and they include some choices for students to make about exact courses. Therefore, the information about Transfer Guides and Course Selection Guides in the next section is very important for university transfer students.

STUDENT NOTES

Transfer Guides and Course Selection Guides

University transfer Plans of Study typically list disciplines or categories of courses that are required for the degree. Within these disciplines, there may be several courses listed that students can select from. University transfer students have a lot of choices to make. Therefore, in addition to choosing to pursue the AA, AE, AFA, AS, AATP, or ASTP degree, university transfer students should also select a Transfer Guide or Course Selection Guide. These documents list which specific classes are preferred for a specific major at a specific university.

Under the 2014 Comprehensive Articulation Agreement, a resource was developed for community college transfer students. **Transfer Guides** (previously called Baccalaureate Degree Plans) are lists of courses recommended by North Carolina public universities to prepare transfer students for success in specific majors at the universities. Universities develop the Transfer Guides to best prepare students for success upon transfer to the senior institutions. Transfer Guides list the courses students should take at the community college and the courses that students will take at the university. They provide a complete plan for the four years students spend earning a bachelor's degree.

For the most up-to-date list of Transfer Guides, check the UNC System website at northcarolina.edu, CFNC.org, or the website of the university you plan to transfer to.

In addition to the Transfer Guides, individual community colleges have developed resources to help their students transfer seamlessly to senior institutions. Your college might have **Course Selection Guides** or other documents that list the recommended courses for not only graduation from your institution with an associate degree but also transfer into a specific major at a specific university. For example, if your college serves a lot of students who are interested in majoring in Social Work, then there may be a Course Selection Guide or other useful document that lists the requirements for majoring at Social Work at several area universities. Check your college's website or college catalog for information about what resources are available to transfer students at your college. These documents typically list the recommended courses for the associate degree and do not include the required courses at the university.

Now is a good time to research the various Transfer Guides and Course Selection Guides that are available at your college. As you review these documents, notice that the recommended coursework is different, especially in Natural Sciences and Mathematics. Also notice that the credit hours may be listed as SHC ("Semester Hours Credit") but that the contact hours may not be listed. You can always look up the contact hours for specific courses on your college's website.

See your college's website or speak to an advisor about what document will be the most useful to you as you prepare for transfer to a senior institution.

STUDENT NOTES

Four Options for Transfer to Senior Institutions

As you explore your academic goals, you'll need clarification about your transfer options. There are several options, and you should weigh the advantages and disadvantages of each to determine which option is best for you. No matter what associate degree you pursue at your community college—AAS, AA, AE, AFA, AGE, AS, AATP, or ASTP—you have the opportunity to transfer your classes and your degree to a senior institution. The four paths to transfer also offer lots of choices in terms of how quickly students can transfer and how easily their community college classes will transfer.

TIPS FOR A SEAMLESS TRANSFER:

Earn a C or better in your classes. Articulation Agreements won't protect your transfer classes if you don't have a grade of C or better.

Do your homework. University websites have lots of information about transfer admissions. Many universities state exactly which classes they want transfer students to bring to the university.

Use your college's resources. Look for advising and transfer centers on your campus to help you better understand the CAA and find out which Bilateral Articulation Agreements and Uniform Articulation Agreements you are eligible for.

Option 1: No Degree or AGE Degree

Some students, often called **visiting students**, take just a few classes at the community college and then transfer to a senior institution. As long as you are taking classes that are transferable and that are college-level and you earn a C or better in your classes, then you can transfer whenever you are accepted to the senior institution, and the Comprehensive Articulation Agreement (CAA) will protect your classes. Other students choose to pursue the AGE degree, which is not designed for transfer. But the AGE degree may include several transferable courses. If you plan to transfer, the AGE may not be the best choice for the maximum number of transfer protections. But AGE students can benefit from the CAA similar to visiting students who do not earn a community college credential.

The **Comprehensive Articulation Agreement** is a North Carolina agreement that states that all community college courses that are designated as transferable will transfer to all public North Carolina universities and to private North Carolina colleges that have signed on to the agreement. The CAA protects transfer to all public North Carolina universities to help students have a seamless transfer experience. The public North Carolina universities include all of the following institutions in the UNC-system:

- Appalachian State University
- East Carolina University
- Elizabeth City State University
- Fayetteville State University

STUDENT NOTES

- North Carolina A&T State University
- North Carolina Central University
- North Carolina State University
- UNC Asheville
- UNC Chapel Hill
- UNC Charlotte
- UNC Greensboro
- UNC Pembroke
- UNC School of the Arts
- UNC Wilmington
- Western Carolina University
- Winston-Salem State University

Many private colleges have also chosen to follow the CAA, but not all of them. Private institutions that agree to follow the provisions of the CAA sign on with the ICAA, the Independent Comprehensive Articulation Agreement. If you plan to transfer to a private university, then you should make sure that the university will accept the classes you take at the community college. Similarly, if you plan to transfer to an out-of-state school, then you will need to do some additional research to make sure your community college classes will transfer since the CAA is a North Carolina program.

The CAA classifies transferable courses in three categories:

1. **Universal General Education Transfer Component (UGETC) courses**
2. **general education**
3. **pre-major/elective courses**

UGETC designated courses are guaranteed to transfer and to be applied toward the senior institution's lower-division general education course requirements. General education and pre-major/elective courses are also guaranteed to transfer, but the senior institution can decide whether the course will count as part of general education or elective credit if the transfer student does not graduate with an associate degree prior to transfer. UGETC courses that you take at the community college can count as general education courses and pre-major/electives, but pre-major/elective courses cannot count as general education courses.

STUDENT NOTES

Lisa F. Young/Shutterstock.com

Students who plan to transfer before they earn an associate degree are limited to transferring the following number of UGETC credits:

Discipline	Maximum Number of Credits Community College Students Can Transfer without the Associate Degree
English Composition	6 credit hours
Humanities/Fine Arts/ Communications	9 credit hours
Social/Behavioral Sciences	9 credit hours
Mathematics	8 credit hours
Natural Sciences	8 credit hours

If you earn this many transferable credits at a community college, then it is in your best interest to complete the associate degree before you transfer. See Option 2 for transfer for the benefits of earning the AA or AS degree.

You can always look at the community college course description to find out if a particular course is transferable. And if you do not plan to earn a degree before you transfer, then it is critical that you look for and accurately interpret the transfer statements on the course descriptions. For example, ENG 111 (Writing and Inquiry) is a transferable UGETC course. (The details in the following table are from the Combined Course Library resource on the North Carolina Community College System website.) You can tell that ENG 111 is a transferable UGETC course because the last sentences of the course description say so. This means that ENG 111 will transfer, and it will count toward the English composition requirement at the university.

STUDENT NOTES

ENG 111 Writing and Inquiry

Class 3 Lab 0 Clinical 0 Work 0
Credit 3

This course is designed to develop the ability to produce clear writing in a variety of genres and formats using a recursive process. Emphasis includes inquiry, analysis, effective use of rhetorical strategies, thesis development, audience awareness, and revision. Upon completion, students should be able to produce unified, coherent, well-developed essays using standard written English.

College Transfer
This course has been approved for transfer under the CAA as a general education course in English Composition.
This course has been approved for transfer under the ICAA as a general education course in English Composition.
This is a Universal General Education Transfer Component (UGETC) course.

Contrast the course description for ENG 111 with the course description for ENG 273 that follows. African-American Literature is also a transferable course, and it is protected by the Comprehensive Articulation Agreement to be guaranteed to transfer. But it will not count toward your English composition requirement. It will transfer as a pre-major/elective course only.

wavebreakmedia/Shutterstock.com

STUDENT NOTES

ENG 273 African-American Literature
Class 3 Lab 0 Clinical 0 Work 0 Credit 3 This course provides a survey of the development of African-American literature from its beginnings to the present. Emphasis is placed on historical and cultural context, themes, literary traditions, and backgrounds of the authors. Upon completion, students should be able to interpret, analyze, and respond to selected texts. **Minimum State Pre-requisites** Take One: ENG-112, ENG-113, or ENG-114 **Minimum State Co-requisites** None **College Transfer** This course has been approved for transfer under the CAA as a pre-major and/or elective course requirement. This course has been approved for transfer under the ICAA as a pre-major and/or elective course requirement.

Finally, some community college courses are not transferable at all. The course description for non-transferable courses doesn't say anything about the Comprehensive Articulation Agreement or the transferability of the course.

We can sometimes tell whether a course is non-transferable by the course number. We know that BIO 092, CHM 094, ENG 025, ENG 045, MAT 025, MAT 035, and MAT 045 are not transferable courses because the course numbers are less than 100. Any course that has a course number less than 100 will not transfer.

Students who transfer before they complete an associate degree will have their transcripts evaluated course by course by the senior institution admissions office. The university will decide how the transferable credits transfer, for example, as general education or pre-major/elective courses. If you do not complete an associate degree, then you will be required to take additional general education courses at the university in order to fulfill the university's general education requirements.

arek_malang/Shutterstock.com

Option 2: The AA and AS Degrees

The Comprehensive Articulation Agreement offers students who complete an Associate in Arts or Associate in Science degree at a community college considerably better protection than students who don't earn a degree before they transfer.

STUDENT NOTES

All North Carolina community colleges are approved to offer Associate in Arts (AA) and Associate in Science (AS) degrees. The AA and AS degrees require a minimum of 30 credit hours of UGETC designated courses and additional general education and pre-major/elective courses. The AA and AS degree programs require 60–61 credit hours total. The CAA requires that transfer students earn a grade of C or better in their transfer courses and an overall GPA of 2.0. See your Plan of Study and Transfer Guide or Course Selection Guide for a list of the courses required for these degrees at your community college.

There are five significant benefits to earning the AA or AS degree before you transfer.

The first benefit of earning an AA or AS degree before you transfer is that all 60–61 credit hours will transfer as a package when you are accepted to the university. That is, all of the courses within the degree program will transfer together. And you will have fewer classes to take at the university than if you transfer before completing the AA or AS degree because you will be given academic credit for more classes from the community college. Bachelor's degree programs typically require 120 credit hours; by completing the AA or AS degree, you are halfway finished with the requirements for the bachelor's degree. The CAA recommends that students identify their major and the senior institution that they plan to transfer to before completing 30 credit hours. That way, you have plenty of time to take the courses that are preferred by both the major and the senior institution you choose.

Secondly, the AA and AS degrees include the maximum UGETC designated courses that you can complete at the community college, so when you are accepted to the university, you will have fulfilled the university's lower-division general education core requirements. You will not have to take additional lower-division general education courses. However, do be advised that there may be additional university courses required of you beyond the lower-division general education core courses depending on the requirements of individual majors and senior institutions. The CAA prevents universities from requiring transfer students to take courses or fulfill university expectations that they do not require of their native students. However, there may be university requirements (for example, service-learning experiences) that native students fulfill in their freshman or sophomore years that you will have to fulfill later.

Rawpixel.com/Shutterstock.com

Thirdly, you will transfer as a junior. You will be able to move even more quickly into your major electives and toward graduation with a bachelor's degree. You'll also be eligible for the privileges that students with junior status receive, for example, early registration and preferred parking on campus.

Fourthly, completion of the AA or AS degree satisfies the University of North Carolina **Minimum Admission Requirements (MAR)** and **Minimum Course Requirements (MCR)**. The MAR include specific

STUDENT NOTES

standards for high school GPA and ACT or SAT test scores. When you earn the AA or AS degree, you do not have to submit your high school GPA or ACT/SAT test scores to the university. The MCR specify the number of high school units students must have completed to be considered for admission to the university. If your high school transcript does not include all of the courses required by the MCR, then you may not be considered for admission to the senior institution without the AA or AS degree.

Finally, you can take advantage of the **Transfer Assured Admissions Policy (TAAP)**, which states that students who earn the AA or AS degree are guaranteed admission to one university in the UNC-system, though not necessarily to the school of the student's choice. To qualify for TAAP, you must earn an AA or AS degree from a North Carolina community college, pass all of your transferable classes with a C or better, and have a cumulative GPA of 2.0 or higher. And you must be in good standing and eligible to return to the school you are transferring from. If you are not admitted to the university or universities that you apply to, then you should visit the College for North Carolina (CFNC) website to find out how to take advantage of the Transfer Assured Admissions Policy.

Again, the purpose of the CAA is to improve the transfer of credits from North Carolina community colleges to the University of North Carolina system schools. If upon transfer you think that the terms of the CAA were not honored, then you have the right to use the **Transfer Credit Appeal Procedure** to present your argument. Look for a link to the Transfer Credit Appeal Procedure on your college website or on the North Carolina Community College System website: nccommunitycolleges.edu.

Option 3: The AATP, ASTP, AE, AFA, and select AAS degrees

The third option for transfer is **Uniform Articulation Agreements** that protect students in select degree programs as they transfer to universities to pursue bachelor's degrees. There are Uniform Articulation Agreements available to Associate in Arts in Teacher Preparation, Associate in Science in Teacher Preparation, Associate in Engineering, Associate in Fine Arts, Associate in Applied Science in Nursing, and Associate in Applied Science in Early Childhood Education program students. The Uniform Articulation Agreements exist between multiple North Carolina community colleges and multiple—but specific—public UNC-system universities. And the number of Uniform Articulation Agreements is growing. Check the North Carolina Community College System website at nccommunitycolleges.edu for the most current information.

The first Uniform Articulation Agreement (UAA) helps students transfer their Associate in Arts in Teacher Preparation and Associate in Science in Teacher Preparation and went into effect in Fall 2021. The Uniform

STUDENT NOTES

Articulation Agreement includes a list of community college courses that meet the admissions requirements for the 15 UNC System Educator Preparation Programs (EPPs). Students who earn the AATP or ASTP degrees and want to transfer into one of the EPPs must earn a C or better in all transfer courses and a minimum 2.7 GPA on a 4.0 scale. The UAA does not guarantee admission, and additional admissions criteria at the senior institution may be required. The UAA document lists the courses that AATP and ASTP students should take at the community college to prepare for a seamless transfer to one of the EPPs.

All 58 of the North Carolina Community Colleges and 15 UNC senior institutions participate in the Uniform Articulation Agreement for education. Here are the 15 universities:

- Appalachian State University
- East Carolina University
- Elizabeth City State University
- Fayetteville State University
- North Carolina A&T State University
- North Carolina Central University
- North Carolina State University
- UNC Asheville
- UNC Chapel Hill
- UNC Charlotte
- UNC Greensboro
- UNC Pembroke
- UNC Wilmington
- Western Carolina University
- Winston-Salem State University

The Uniform Articulation Agreement that guides the transfer of Associate in Engineering students into Bachelor of Science in Engineering programs was approved in Fall 2015. The Uniform Articulation Agreement includes a recommended list of community college courses that meet the admissions requirements for all Bachelor of Science in Engineering programs in UNC-system universities. This list functions like a Plan of Study or curriculum standard for AE students.

However, the Uniform Articulation Agreement does not guarantee admission since engineering programs are typically very competitive. In order to be protected by the Uniform Articulation Agreement, Associate in Engineering students must graduate with the AE degree and must earn a C or better in each course and a minimum 2.5 GPA on a 4.0 scale.

STUDENT NOTES

While 33 North Carolina community colleges have been approved to offer the AE degree, only five UNC senior institutions participate in the Uniform Articulation Agreement for engineering. Here are the five universities:

- East Carolina University
- North Carolina A&T State University
- North Carolina State University
- UNC Charlotte
- Western Carolina University

The third Uniform Articulation Agreement helps Associate in Fine Arts (AFA) students. There are three AFA degrees: AFA in Visual Arts, AFA in Music, and AFA in Theater. The Uniform Articulation Agreement includes a recommended list of community college courses that meet the admissions requirements for the corresponding Bachelor of Arts programs in UNC-system universities. This list functions like a Plan of Study or curriculum standard for AFA students. Students must earn a C or better in each course and a minimum of 2.0 GPA on a 4.0 scale to qualify for the protections of the AFA Uniform Articulation Agreements. The UAAs for AFA degrees do not guarantee admission to the university or to competitive admissions programs.

AFA in Visual Arts students can transfer to senior institutions to earn Bachelor of Fine Arts (BFA) degrees. AFA graduates who meet the criteria will fulfill the entry requirements for the participating BFA programs and will have completed the general education course requirements for the BFA degrees.

There are 31 North Carolina community colleges that offer the AFA in Visual Arts, but only 7 participating universities in the AFA for Visual Arts Uniform Articulation Agreement (the name of the degree is in parentheses):

- Appalachian State University (BFA in Studio Art)
- East Carolina University (BFA in Art)
- UNC Asheville (BFA in Art)
- UNC Chapel Hill (BFA in Art)
- UNC Charlotte (BFA in Art)
- UNC Greensboro (BFA in Studio Art)
- Western Carolina University (BFA in Art)

STUDENT NOTES

AFA in Music students can use the UAA to transfer to participating UNC universities to earn a Bachelor of Music degree. There are 17 North Carolina community colleges that offer the AFA in Music, and 10 participating universities in the AFA for Music Uniform Articulation Agreement:

- Appalachian State University
- East Carolina University
- North Carolina Central University
- UNC Chapel Hill
- UNC Charlotte
- UNC Greensboro
- UNC Pembroke
- UNC School of the Arts
- UNC Wilmington
- Western Carolina University

Finally, AFA in Theater students can use the UAA to transfer to participating UNC universities to earn a Bachelor of Arts with a focus on theater. Eleven North Carolina community colleges offer the AFA in Theater, and 11 participating universities in the AFA for Theater Uniform Articulation Agreement:

- Appalachian State University (BA in Theater Generalist)
- East Carolina University (BA in Theater Arts)
- Fayetteville State University (BA in Theater)
- North Carolina Central University (BA in Theater)
- UNC Asheville (BA in Drama)
- UNC Chapel Hill (BA in Dramatic Art)
- UNC Charlotte (BA in Theater)
- UNC Greensboro (BA in Drama)
- UNC Pembroke (BA in Theater Arts)
- UNC Wilmington (BA in Theater)
- Western Carolina University (BA in Stage and Screen)

The fourth type of Uniform Articulation Agreement helps students who have earned an AAS in Nursing in order to become a Registered Nurse (RN) go on to a Bachelor of Science in Nursing (BSN) program. The AAS in Nursing Uniform Articulation Agreement guides AAS degree-seeking students in selecting courses that will help them meet the minimum requirements for BSN programs. Some North Carolina community colleges offer an AGE in Nursing degree to help students meet the course requirements of the

STUDENT NOTES

nursing UAA. Like the other Uniform Articulation Agreements, completion of the required courses does not guarantee admission; nursing is another competitive academic program. In order to be protected by the Uniform Articulation Agreement, AAS in Nursing students must graduate with the AAS degree and must earn a C or better in each course and a minimum 2.0 GPA on a 4.0 scale. University nursing programs are allowed to require community college students to take no more than a maximum of two courses or six credits beyond the Uniform Articulation Agreement for admission to a specific school of nursing. The Uniform Articulation Agreement for AAS in Nursing states that universities cannot require students to complete more than 128 credits in order to earn the BSN.

While 55 North Carolina community colleges offer AAS degrees in Nursing, only 11 universities have agreed to participate in the Uniform Articulation Agreement benefitting the community college graduates:

- Appalachian State University
- Fayetteville State University
- East Carolina University
- North Carolina A&T State University
- North Carolina Central University
- UNC Charlotte
- UNC Greensboro
- UNC Pembroke
- UNC Wilmington
- Western Carolina University
- Winston-Salem State University

The fifth Uniform Articulation Agreement guides the transfer of AAS in Early Childhood Education students into senior institutions that offer either the Bachclor in Birth–Kindergarten major with a teaching licensure option or the Bachelor in Early Childhood without a teaching licensure option. To benefit from the protections provided by this Uniform Articulation Agreement, students must have a 2.0 GPA upon graduation and earn a C or better in all of their courses. Like the previously described UAAs, this one does not guarantee admission to the university, and AAS degree students must meet the minimum admissions requirements for the receiving university, including minimum GPA and for some universities, minimum Praxis exam scores. Also like the previously described UAAs, this document lists the courses that students should take to prepare for a seamless transfer. If an AAS in Early Childhood Education student is eligible for the protections under the UAA, then 60 of the required 64–76 credits will transfer and count towards the 120-credit bachelor's degree. Eligible transfer students

STUDENT NOTES

will be granted junior status, but may also be required to complete additional courses at the university beyond the general education courses they completed at the community college.

All 58 North Carolina community colleges offer the AAS in Early Childhood Education. The following 12 universities offer a bachelor's degree in Birth–Kindergarten Teaching with a licensure option and have signed on to the UAA:

- Appalachian State University
- East Carolina University
- Elizabeth City State University
- Fayetteville State University
- North Carolina A&T State University
- North Carolina Central University
- UNC Charlotte
- UNC Greensboro
- UNC Pembroke
- UNC Wilmington
- Western Carolina University
- Winston-Salem State University

And the following eight universities offer a bachelor's degree in early childhood with a non-teaching licensure option (the name of the major is in parentheses) and have signed on to the Uniform Articulation Agreement:

- East Carolina University (Family and Community Services, Child Development Concentration)
- Elizabeth City State University (Child, Family, and Community)
- Fayetteville State University (Birth–Kindergarten Non-Teaching)
- North Carolina A&T State University (Child Development and Family Studies)
- North Carolina Central University (Family Consumer Sciences, Child Development and Family Relations Concentration)
- UNC Greensboro (Early Care and Education)
- Western Carolina University (Early Childhood)
- Winston-Salem State University (Early Intervention and Preschool Concentration or Business Optional Concentration)

If you are enrolled in an AATP, ASTP, AE, AFA, AAS in Nursing, or AAS in Early Childhood Education program, find the appropriate Uniform Articulation Agreement for your program and use it to be sure you are

STUDENT NOTES

registering for the right courses and meeting the expectations for admission into the corresponding bachelor's degree program.

Also be advised that additional UAAs continue to be developed for students at North Carolina community colleges. Specifically, new agreements for students who plan to transfer to private universities in North Carolina are among the most recent additions to the menu of Uniform Articulation Agreements. Private universities have signed on to UAAs as Independent Colleges and Universities to ease transfer for community college students who major in psychology, sociology, music, theater, visual arts, teacher preparation, and nursing. See the North Carolina Community College System website or your college's advising or transfer center for more information on these UAAs with private universities.

Option 4: The AAS Degree

The previous options for transfer focused on students who are currently enrolled in degrees that are designed for transfer to senior institutions. North Carolina community colleges also offer Associate in Applied Science (AAS) degrees, which prepare students to enter new careers immediately after graduation. AAS degrees are not designed for transfer. Individual community colleges can offer dozens of these degrees, including Paralegal Technology; Architecture Technology; Brewery, Distillation, and Fermentation; Respiratory Therapy; and Industrial Systems. However, many students who complete AAS degrees find that they want to continue their education with a bachelor's degree. It is critical that these students understand the protections granted to them as community college students.

The Comprehensive Articulation Agreement (CAA) does offers some protection, but it does not protect AAS degrees the same way it protects AA or AS degrees.

All Associate in Applied Science degrees require some Universal General Education Transfer Component (UGETC) designated courses, and these courses are transferable and protected by the CAA. For example, ENG 111 (Writing and Inquiry), PSY 150 (General Psychology), and COM 231 (Public Speaking) are listed on many AAS Plans of Study. These individual UGETC courses can transfer to the university and count towards the university's required lower-division general education requirements.

The AAS Plans of Study also include specific program or major courses. For example, the AAS in Occupational Therapy Assistant requires several courses with the OTA prefix (OTA 110, OTA 120, OTA 245, etc.). Most AAS programs or major courses are not designed for transfer to all universities and similarly are not protected by the Comprehensive Articulation Agreement. If you are unsure of whether your courses are designed for transfer, look for the course description.

STUDENT NOTES

Although the CAA doesn't apply to many AAS courses, students can frequently transfer their AAS degrees to senior institutions through Bilateral Articulation Agreements, which allow AAS students to transfer their entire degrees to a university. **Bilateral Articulation Agreements** are transfer agreements between a specific university and a specific community college. They are for specific degree programs. For example, Cape Fear Community College and UNC Wilmington have a Bilateral Articulation Agreement to help students who graduate from Cape Fear with an AAS degree in Radiography transfer to UNC Wilmington to earn a bachelor's degree in Radiography. Similarly, Stanly Community College and Winston-Salem State University have a Bilateral Articulation Agreement for students who earn an AAS degree in Accounting to then go on to earn a bachelor's degree in Accounting.

AAS degree students should look to their community college's website or college catalog for an up-to-date list of Bilateral Articulation Agreements that are available to them.

See the following table for a summary of the similarities and differences among the Comprehensive Articulation Agreement, Bilateral Articulation Agreements, and Uniform Articulation Agreements. As you review the table, note which associate degrees are protected by which articulation agreement(s). Also note which community colleges and which universities participate in the articulation agreement(s). Finally, you'll see at the bottom of the table the standards that you must meet in order to qualify for the protections afforded by the agreements.

STUDENT NOTES

	Comprehensive Articulation Agreement	Bilateral Articulation Agreements	Uniform Articulation Agreements
What does it protect?			
• Transfer of individual courses	✔		
• Transfer of AA and AS degrees	✔		
• Transfer of AAS degrees		✔	
• Transfer of AATP, ASTP, AE, AFA, and select AAS degrees (AAS in Nursing and AAS in Early Childhood Education)			✔
Which colleges participate?			
• All NC community colleges	✔		
• All public UNC universities	✔		
• Some private NC universities	✔	✔	✔
• Specific NC community colleges that have signed agreements with specific four-year colleges and universities (usually public UNC universities)		✔	
• All NC community colleges that offer the specific degrees	✔	✔	✔
• Public UNC universities that have chosen to participate		✔	✔
How can students benefit?			
• Transfer in-state from a NC community college to a NC university	✔	✔	✔
• Earn a C or better in all courses	✔	✔	✔
• Earn a minimum GPA of 2.0 (Note that some UAAs can require a higher GPA)	✔	✔	✔

Fortunately, there are many resources available to help you decide which senior institution is right for you. University websites often have webpages specific to transfer admissions. Also, college recruiters often visit community college campuses, and they can be a great resource for information about the university.

STUDENT NOTES

The College for North Carolina website is another useful resource in academic goal exploration. See the screenshot and information on page 145 to learn more about how to use CFNC for academic goal exploration.

Demystifying Transfer

Once you understand your transfer options as a community college student and select the best path for your academic and career goals, you'll need to think more about how the transfer process works. In particular, you'll need to understand how potential senior institutions view transfer students and the specific steps you should take to transfer.

Transfer enrollment has increased over the last 10 years. There are over 17,000 transfer students in the UNC 16-university system, and 10,000 of them come from NC community colleges (as opposed to transfer from private colleges, out-of-state, or from within the UNC-system).

You have many factors in your favor as a transfer student. First, you have a better chance of getting into a senior institution as a transfer student than as a high school student. Admission rates for transfer students are usually the same as admission rates for entering freshmen, but the applicant pool is much smaller. Sometimes the admission rate is even higher for transfer students. For example, UNC Chapel Hill admitted approximately 15% of its 66,535 applicants for Fall 2024, but about 36% of its 4,721 transfer applicants were admitted. Transferring from a community college greatly improves your chance of admission.

Another factor in your favor is that transfer students have proven themselves to be successful at the college level and are a safer bet for senior institutions, meaning transfer students are more likely to graduate than incoming first-year students. More and more senior institutions in North Carolina are increasing their recruitment of transfer students for this reason.

As a potential transfer student, you'll have many questions. Read below for answers and resources to put you on the best path to successful transfer to a senior institution.

How do I find potential transfer schools?

- Search CFNC for programs and majors that interest you. Click on "Plan Your Future" and then scroll down to find and click on "Plan for College." Scroll down to find the "Explore Programs and Majors" link. Click on "Explore Programs and Majors" and then enter your area of interest in the search box (for example, finance, education, or psychology). Look at results options and then select the ones that interest you the most. From there, click on "Schools Offering This Major" and select

"Bachelor's." Here you will find the senior institutions in North Carolina offering the program you're interested in. In addition to finding potential transfer programs, the results also help you learn about related careers, opportunities to specialize, and options for graduate school.

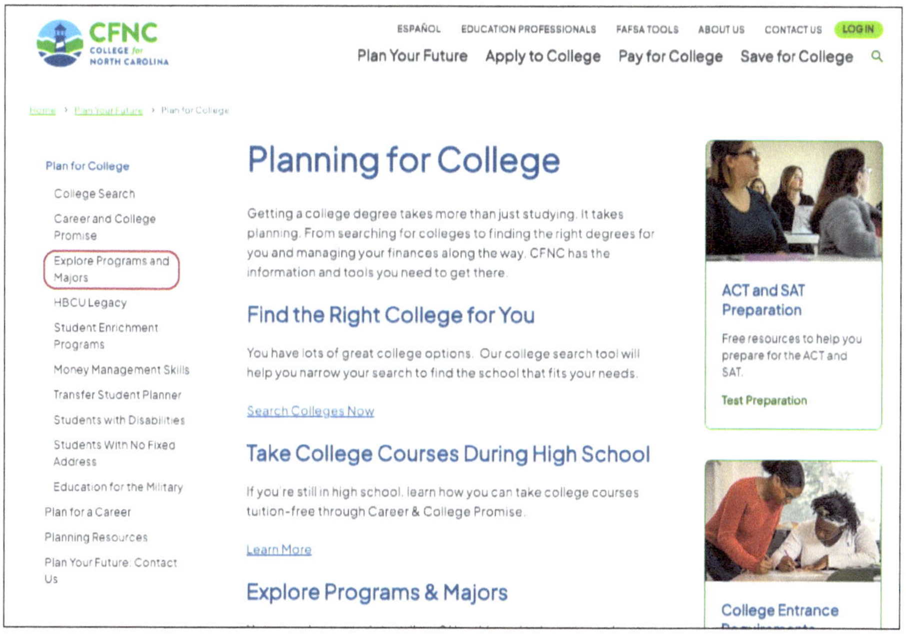

- Learn more about applying to a specific university as a transfer student. On the same Planning for College webpage pictured above, click on "College Search." Use the filter on the left side of the screen to focus your search. Click on the universities that interest you, and look for transfer acceptance rates and numbers, minimum transfer requirements, application deadlines, FAFSA numbers, cost, and statistics on the average amount and type of aid offered to students.

You can also search North Carolina public and private colleges and universities (including community colleges) by name, major, alphabetical listings, locations, and other search parameters. You can even incorporate the results of the Interest Finder and Work Values Sorter (see page 102 for more details) into your search for a major if you are undecided.

- Narrow your list to 3–4 schools. Once you find schools offering your program, compare and contrast the areas of specialization within those programs. For example, while multiple schools may offer a finance degree, one may offer a concentration in insurance and risk management while another specializes in accounting. Consider your professional goals and interests in order to determine which program and school is a better fit for you.

- Don't worry about cost. While you're narrowing your list, don't rule out schools based on tuition just yet. Many private schools offer scholarships for transfer students specifically and will also provide financial

STUDENT NOTES

See page 102 for a step-by-step guide to creating a CFNC and NC Careers account. If you already have an account, then click on the "Log on to My CFNC" to access your account and bypass the account creation process.

STUDENT NOTES

assistance for first-generation, minority, or low-income students. Graduating debt-free or with little debt doesn't always mean you have to go to the cheapest school.

Gino Santa Maria/Shutterstock.com

I know what schools and major I'm interested in. Now what?

- Check out transfer admissions requirements for each school. Make sure to look for transfer admissions specifically, not just admissions.
- Find and follow pathways to ensure you're taking the best classes. Explore the NC Community College Transfer webpages at northcarolina.edu/students/transfer/ncccs/ to learn more about course equivalencies and Transfer Guides and find contact information for transfer counselors at senior institutions.
- Make sure your classes transfer and consider the benefits of transferring with a degree or without a degree. See the Four Options for Transfer outlined earlier in this chapter for more information.
- Speak to a transfer counselor at the specific institution you're interested in. While you may know the requirements for admission to the university, you need to know if there are any additional requirements necessary to enter your specific program.
- Consider a campus tour or visit to narrow your choices. Colleges and specific majors might offer open houses or information sessions for potential students. Or you could attend a campus event to see if the campus environment matches your priorities. Seeing the campus firsthand and talking to current students can be valuable experiences.

What do I need to know about admission?

- Often, you will need to be admitted to two places: the senior institution (NC State, for example) and the individual college or program (College of Design or College of Engineering). The college or program may have additional requirements (minimum GPA, coursework, etc.) beyond the admissions requirements for the university.

- Note the advertised minimums to be admitted to a university and your program, but also inquire about what scores, GPAs, and coursework are usually required to be competitive. While schools may or may not provide minimum GPA requirements, you should know the numbers for the average admitted transfer student. For example, while UNC Chapel Hill says it looks at the student's application holistically and does not list GPA minimums, you should know that their admitted transfer students had an average of a 3.7 GPA.
- Keep application deadlines in mind and plan ahead. Find transfer application dates on individual school's websites or on the CFNC.org webpages mentioned earlier.

STUDENT NOTES

What should I ask a transfer admissions counselor?

- How many transfer applications do you receive for this program, and what percent is usually accepted?
- What are the minimum requirements for a transfer student to this program?
- What makes a student competitive for this program? What's a competitive GPA?
- How transfer-friendly is this school? Does it offer transfer scholarships, orientations, or mentoring? Specific transfer advisors?
- What are transfer student success rates in this program? How do they differ from native students' success rates?
- Do you have specific suggestions about course selection if I intend to apply to this program?

What other things should I keep in mind?

- Students need to decide their intended transfer university and major within the first 30 hours of their associate degree, if not sooner. Doing so will allow you to follow a specific Transfer Guide or Course Selection Guide for your intended program and senior institution, ensuring you're taking the right coursework. Doing so will also help you minimize the number of courses, length of time, and cost at the community college. And it will help you maximize the protections available to you under the appropriate articulation agreement.
- Your GPA from your community college does not transfer to the senior institution.

STUDENT NOTES

- Complete the FAFSA for your transfer school to learn the amount of aid you may receive. You can find the school's FAFSA number on the school's website or on CFNC.org.
- Once you transfer, plan to attend transfer student orientations and activities; the community of other transfer students can be invaluable in your first semesters of transition.
- There are scholarships specifically for transfer students. Nationally, look into Jack Kent Cooke, Coca-Cola, and Phi Theta Kappa scholarships. Also check specific organizations, such as the Hispanic Scholarship Fund, which has transfer-specific scholarships. At the local or institution level, check with the university for transfer-specific funding. For example, NCCU offers transfer student scholarships based on GPA. Community college students with a 2.75 or above from their community colleges are eligible.
- When applying to senior institutions, consider including three different types of schools: a school that you'll likely be accepted into easily, a more competitive program that's realistically a good fit, and a reach school that may seem too competitive or costly but is still a good match for your interests.
- Consider how your AP credit will transfer. If you received course credit for AP classes at your community college, remember that you may not receive the same credit at the senior institution if you transfer before you receive your degree. For example, an AP score of 3 may give you credit for ENG 111 at your community college, but NC State requires an AP score of 4 to receive credit for the first level of composition. If you transfer before you receive your degree, your AP credit for ENG 111 will not count at NCSU.
- Community colleges only provide credit for courses that they offer. If you have some credits from a senior institution that did NOT transfer to the community college, consider whether this credit can transfer to your 4-year institution in another way. Your community college may not have recognized your fish and wildlife management course, but your senior institution might.

What's it take to be competitive?

1. **Strong GPA (above 3.5)**
2. **Hard courseload, which means the right classes and added levels of engagement, such as honors or service-learning projects**
3. **Extracurricular involvement that demonstrates leadership skills and long-term commitments and interests**
4. **Recommendation letters**
5. **Well-written admissions essays**

STUDENT NOTES

wavebreakmedia/Shutterstock.com

Conclusion

Successful community college students understand not only the specific requirements for their chosen program of study, but also how their program fits within the larger community college structure. As you have likely noticed by now, community college students are very diverse in age, and you may return to the community college in the future to pursue a different credential. After studying the concepts in Chapter 5 and applying them to your own Plan of Study and Transfer Guide or Course Selection Guide, you are well prepared to make realistic decisions about your academic future. You are also ready to look toward your career options, as you'll see in Chapter 6.

If you haven't recorded your program of study on page 92, do so now for easy reference.

STUDENT NOTES

REVIEW QUESTIONS

Chapter 5
Academic Goal Exploration

These questions will help you monitor and evaluate your learning, two important parts of metacognition.

1. Match the community college credentials with their definitions.

___ Certificate

___ Diploma

___ Associate in Arts

___ Associate in Science

___ Associate in General Education

___ Associate in Applied Science

___ Associate in Science in Teacher Preparation

___ Associate in Fine Arts

___ Associate in Engineering

___ Associate in Arts in Teacher Preparation

a. a degree (60–61 credit hours) that prepares students to transfer to a university and major in education and prepare to teach subjects like English, history, social studies, and foreign languages

b. a degree (64–65 credit hours) designed for individuals wishing to broaden their education, with emphasis on personal interest, growth, and development

c. a degree (60–61 credit hours) that prepares students to transfer to a university and major in education and prepare to teach subjects like science, technology, engineering, and math

d. a degree (60–61 credit hours) that prepares students to transfer to a university and major in fields such as English, fine arts, foreign languages, history, philosophy, psychology, or sociology

e. a degree (60–61 credit hours) that prepares students to transfer to a university and major in engineering

f. a degree (64–76 credit hours) that prepares students for a particular career

g. a credential requiring a shorter time commitment from students, specifically 12–18 credit hours

h. a degree (60–61 credit hours) that prepares students to transfer to a university and major in fields such as biology, chemistry, geology, mathematics, or physics

i. a degree (60–61 credit hours) with an emphasis on courses such as art, drama, or music

j. a credential requiring a shorter time commitment from students, specifically 36–48 credit hours

2. Identify at least one advantage and one disadvantage of the four options for transfer to a university.

Option 1: No Degree or AGE Degree

Advantages	Disadvantages

Option 2: AA and AS Degrees

Advantages	Disadvantages

Option 3: AATP, ASTP, AE, AFA, and select AAS Degrees

Advantages	Disadvantages

Option 4: AAS Degrees

Advantages	Disadvantages

Discussion Questions

What did you learn in this chapter about your specific credential at the community college and how it best aligns for transfer and/or career? With this information, what is one specific question you want to take to your next advising appointment?

Stephen Coburn/Shutterstock.com

UNIT 2

Chapter 6

Career Goal Exploration

Before you read this chapter, reflect on the following:

1. *What do I already know about my future career? How did I learn this information?*
2. *Who could tell me more about my future career?*
3. *What are three characteristics of reliable websites for academic and professional research?*

These questions will help you plan your learning, an important part of metacognition.

In addition to researching what academic options you have at your community college and beyond, you should also consider your career options. You can use the career goal exploration resources in this chapter to find the careers that best suit the personality, interests, and values you identified through the various self-assessment tools in Chapter 4. As you learned in Chapter 4, individuals whose personality, interests, and values match their careers can expect to experience a high level of job satisfaction from their careers. Use the resources described in this chapter to identify careers that suit your personal characteristics.

As you move through the career goal exploration process, be mindful of what you learned about your academic goals, too. Different college credentials prepare you for different careers. When you research a specific career, pay careful attention to the education and training required to enter that career. You may find that you already have the necessary education, or you may discover that you will need several credentials beyond the associate degree in order to enter the career.

STUDENT NOTES

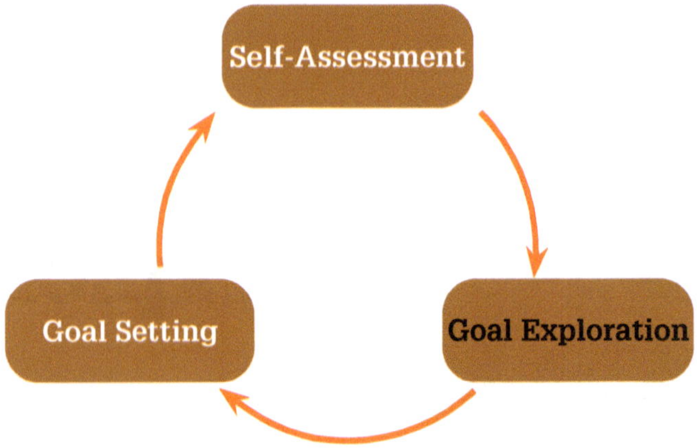

Chapter 6 will address the following very useful tools in career goal exploration:

- Occupational Outlook Handbook,
- NC Careers,
- Other online resources,
- Informational interviews,
- Job shadowing,
- Volunteering,
- Job fairs, and
- Résumés and Cover Letters.

Occupational Outlook Handbook

The **Occupational Outlook Handbook** is published every two years by the United States Department of Labor's Bureau of Labor Statistics. It is a reliable source of information about a wide variety of careers across the United States. Specifically, you can use the Occupational Outlook Handbook to research a career's daily job tasks, starting and average salaries, projections about the growth of the career, related fields, and links to professional organizations and other useful online resources.

You can find a hard copy of the Occupational Outlook Handbook in many libraries, including many community college campus libraries. You can also use the Occupational Outlook Handbook online at bls.gov/ooh/. See the following screenshots to learn how to use this very useful online tool for career exploration.

When you open the Occupational Outlook Handbook online, look for the search field "Search Handbook" in the right-hand corner of the page. Type the career that you want to explore in the search field.

STUDENT NOTES

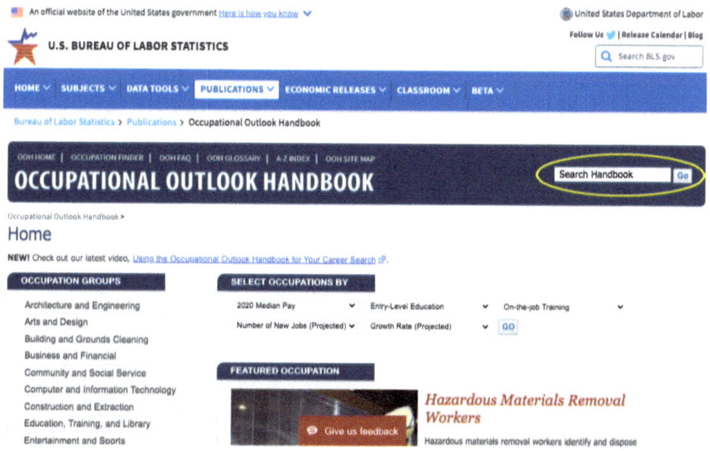

The screenshot below shows the result of a search for "respiratory therapist." On the results page, you can find useful information about respiratory therapists. Notice the tabs at the top of the page that identify the content available on this specific career. Specifically, look for "What They Do," "Work Environment," "How to Become One," "Pay," "Job Outlook," "State & Area Data," "Similar Occupations," and "More Info."

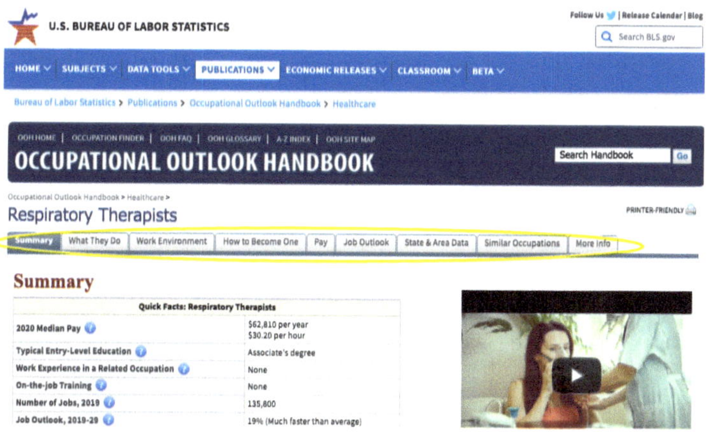

Depending on your search terms, you may have to find your career in a results list. For example, if you type "nurse" in the BLS search engine, then you'll get a results page with links to resources for "Registered Nurses," "Nurse Anesthetists, Nurse Midwives, and Nurse Practitioners," "Licensed Practical and Licensed Vocational Nurses," "Nursing Assistants and Orderlies," and so on. Click on the result that matches your personal career goal.

Note, too, the URL for the links on the search results page, and select links with "ooh" in the web address. The code "ooh" refers to the Occupational Outlook Handbook. If you choose a web address without "ooh" in it, then you may find yourself looking at Occupational Employment Statistics (which are helpful, but not the full picture) or resources for K–12 students

STUDENT NOTES

(which are also helpful, but not as thorough as the Occupational Outlook Handbook).

Likewise, you may need to use different search terms to find your career choice. For example, students in the AAS Early Childhood Education program should search for "Preschool Teachers" or "Child Care Workers." AA students who plan to major in psychology at a senior institution would use the search terms "Psychologist," "Psychiatrist," or "Guidance Counselor," depending on which career they specifically plan to enter (and depending on how many credentials they are planning to earn).

NC Careers: Explore Occupations

You learned about the NC Careers website in Chapter 4 as a resource for self-assessments and in Chapter 5 in the discussion of academic goal exploration. This site is also a very useful tool in career goal exploration.

Go to nccareers.org and click on "Explore Occupations" to research careers by job title, clusters (or fields such as "Education and Training"), or even based on your personal results on the Interest Finder. As you read your search results, keep in mind that the salary information, job outlook projections, and other facts in NC Careers are specific to North Carolina whereas the Occupational Outlook Handbook lists national averages. On the NC Careers website, you can even search by region of North Carolina to see how salaries and the number of jobs within a particular field vary in different parts of the state.

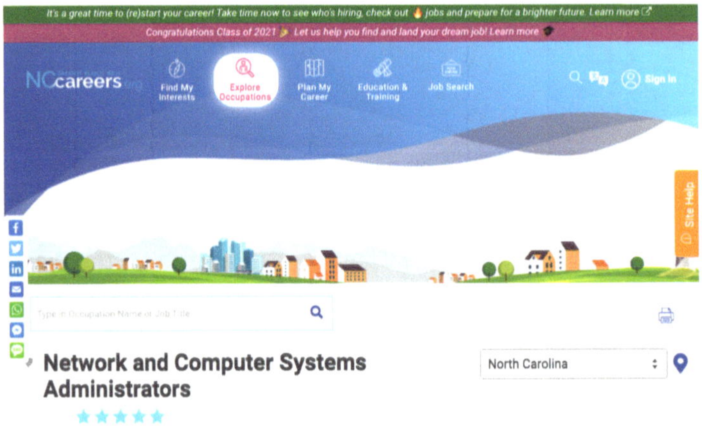

On the "Explore Occupations" webpage, look for annual salary data, job duties, common job titles, similar occupations, and education and training.

Finally, many of the career webpages on NC Careers include video clips of professionals in various careers. The videos can help you visualize how you might use the skills and knowledge you are learning in the classroom, lab, and/or clinical setting.

Plan to spend the time necessary getting familiar with the NC Careers website, so you can take advantage of this incredibly rich source of information on North Carolina education and career opportunities.

STUDENT NOTES

Other Online Resources

The Occupational Outlook Handbook and NC Careers are only two of hundreds of websites that can be useful in the career goal exploration stage of goal discernment. Look for websites that offer more than salary information; useful career goal exploration sites are comprehensive, like the Occupational Outlook Handbook and NC Careers. As you look for additional online resources, think critically about what makes a website good. Four general criteria for website analysis include:

Accuracy

A reliable website contains information that is correct. The website is updated regularly and verified by a trustworthy source. The website is also proofread carefully for spelling and grammar errors.

Authority

A reliable website is also sponsored by a knowledgeable author or agency. Look at the domain at the end of the URL for information about the website sponsor. For example, a .com website is a commercial site and often exists for the sole reason of selling a product. A .edu website, on the other hand, is published by an educational organization, and a .org website is published by a nonprofit organization. These are websites that exist to provide information, not to sell you a product.

Objectivity

A reliable website may or may not be designed to persuade viewers. If the site is trying to persuade viewers, consider the message carefully. Look specifically for the quantity and types of advertisements on the page for insights into its objectivity.

Currency

A reliable website is kept up to date. Look for information at the top or bottom of the page about when the website was published or last updated. Avoid websites that reference information that is several years out of date. As you know, many career fields are dynamic and the education required for a specific career as well as the average starting salary can change in a span of just a few years.

The following types of websites most often meet these criteria:

College and university websites

Links on college and university websites specific to majors and departments

Academic and professional organizations

Websites for companies you may want to work for

Links on your community college's website to your chosen department or Program of Study

Links from the Occupational Outlook Handbook or NC Careers websites

STUDENT NOTES

Monkey Business Images/Shutterstock.com

A career goal exploration website that consistently meets these criteria is O*NET OnLine (onetonline.org/). Like NC Careers, the O*NET website uses the language of the Holland Codes and work values to sort careers and match individuals with appropriate careers. Also, the websites provide trustworthy information about the following aspects of individual careers: job descriptions, typical job responsibilities, required skills and abilities, average salaries, and projected growth.

Consider exploring the O*NET website if the NC Careers and Occupational Outlook Handbook websites provide you with insufficient information about careers that interest you.

Informational Interviews

In addition to your online research, you can also gather valuable information about your future career from other people. In an **informational interview**, you interview someone who is working in the career, company, or industry that interests you, so you can learn more about the career, company, or industry. Conduct an informational interview after you've done some research on your own, so you can ask any questions that you've thought of as a result of your research. Use the following guidelines to get the most benefit from an informational interview.

Before the Interview

STUDENT NOTES

Figure out what you want to get out of the interview. Are you interested in learning about a specific job, trends in the industry, or your interview subject's personal experiences? Use the following categories and questions to guide your preparation for the interview.

Questions about the Job
• Describe what you do on a typical day at work. • What kind of schedule do you typically work? • What is the most difficult part of your job? • Where does your job fit in your company's staffing chart? What are the entry-level positions or more advanced positions?
Questions about the Company
• What opportunities for advancement exist at this company? • What is the average length of time that people stay with this company? • What is the culture of this company? (for example, collaborative, competitive, individualistic, supportive) • Is the company growing now? Is the number of employees growing or shrinking?
Questions about the Individual
• How long have you been working in this career? • What is your favorite part about your career? • What do you wish you had known about your career before you started working? • How well did your educational program prepare you for your career?
Questions about the Industry
• What opportunities for advancement exist in your career? • How is technology changing the career? • How frequently do people move in and out of this industry? • What work-related values are most important for this field? (for example, achievement, recognition, relationships, support)
Questions about You
• What advice do you have for someone who wants to begin working in your career field? • How well do you think I would fit in at your company? • What kind of position will my degree/diploma/certificate prepare me for? • In addition to earning my degree/diploma/certificate, what else should I do to prepare for this career? (for example, volunteering, internships, learning a second language)

STUDENT NOTES

Keep in mind that the informational interview gives you one person's opinion. If you catch someone on a bad day or if you interview someone who dislikes her job, then you may get a very negative opinion.

If this happens to you, consider interviewing a second person, so you'll have two perspectives to compare and contrast.

To set up the interview, email or call the person that you want to interview. To help you appear to be the serious college student that you are, use professional language. Avoid text-messaging lingo and inappropriate slang. Also, be polite. Say "please" and "thank you," to indicate your respect. Finally, provide flexibility. Don't expect your interview subject to meet with you immediately. You may have to offer a few dates or times to meet if your schedules are very different.

During the Interview

Arrive early to the appointed location of the interview. Start by introducing yourself if you don't already know your interview subject. Tell the person a little bit about yourself, including what you are hoping to learn from the informational interview.

Bring up to 12 questions for a 30–45 minute interview, but prioritize the questions in case the discussion runs long, and you don't have time to ask all of your questions. During the interview either record the conversation (with the interview subject's permission) or take lots of notes.

Finally, be mindful of your interview subject's time. For example, if you have arranged for a 30-minute conversation, then keep an eye on your watch and thank the person for her time at the end of 30 minutes. Ask for her email address or phone number in case you have follow-up questions.

After the Interview

Transcribe your recording of the informational interview or review your notes as soon as possible, so you can fill in any holes in the conversation based on your memory. If you find any gaps in your notes or understanding, ask follow-up questions in an email message.

Also, be sure to thank your interview subject for her time and expertise. This is just good manners, but it is a professionally wise action, too. Your interview subject may one day be a hiring supervisor who reviews your résumé or application for employment.

Finally, compare the results of the interview with other sources of knowledge, for example, other informational interviews, research, and personal experience. Informational interviews are most useful when they are part of a larger career goal exploration effort.

STUDENT NOTES

Shutterstock.com

Job Shadowing

Like the informational interview, job shadowing is a great way to learn about your potential career. **Job shadowing** is spending a half-day or whole day following someone at work, so you can see for yourself what the job requires. Like the informational interview, job shadowing requires planning before the experience and some follow-up after the experience.

Job shadowing is particularly useful for the following types of college students:

- Students who don't know what to expect from the day-to-day experience of working in their future career field,
- Students who don't already know anyone who works in their career field of interest,
- Students who are undecided or trying to decide between two or more possible careers, and/or
- Students who are unclear about the relationship between their chosen academic credential and their chosen career.

Use the following guidelines to get the most out of a job shadow experience.

Some challenges in job shadowing include the following:

- **It can be hard to find people to job shadow. Start networking now to find someone to job shadow.**
- **You must rely on the generosity and availability of someone working in your future field.**
- **Some careers may not accommodate job shadowing. For example, you can't easily sit in on a drug or alcohol counseling session due to privacy concerns.**

STUDENT NOTES

Before the Job Shadow

Come prepared with questions, and prioritize your questions in case you face time constraints. The informational interview questions on page 161 are also appropriate job shadow questions. Likewise, the tips for setting up an informational interview on page 162 apply also to scheduling a job shadowing experience.

During the Job Shadow

Dress appropriately (for example, business attire for an office setting, comfortable shoes for a healthcare setting). You are not going on an interview, so you don't have to wear interview attire. Focus instead on fitting in to whatever setting you will be in. Also, be unobtrusive and observant. Take notes and ask questions when the time is appropriate.

After the Job Shadow

Write the person that you shadowed a personal thank you note. In your note, include specific details that were useful to you, for example, information your job shadow mentor showed you or told you.

Like with the informational interview, compare the results of the experience with other sources of knowledge, for example, informational interviews, research, and personal experience. Keep in mind that the work environments and cultures vary from company to company.

Volunteering

Volunteering is another way to explore your career options. When **volunteering**, you assist a non-profit or government organization that works to address an unmet community need, such as food insecurity, and you are not compensated for your work.

Volunteering is useful for students at all stages of career goal discernment and has many benefits beyond refining your career path. Use the guidelines below to get the most out of a volunteer experience.

Before Volunteering

First, consider your goal for volunteering. If you are unsure of your intended career, try several episodic or one-time service events to learn about yourself, your preferred work environments, your skills, and your work values in action.

STUDENT NOTES

If you're more certain of your career path, look for long-term opportunities (usually at least a six-month commitment) that will provide the greatest opportunity for deep learning for you and a beneficial impact for the community organization. Look for volunteer positions that will provide specialized training, allow you to work closely with professionals in your intended career, or offer a potential "promotion" to increased volunteer responsibility.

Before contacting a service organization, assess how much time you could realistically devote each week to volunteering. For long-term opportunities, you will likely also need to factor in time for orientation or training.

Finally, make sure you're committed to the organization's cause and are passionate about helping others. You're volunteering to learn and connect with people in your field, but you're also there to provide a service and improve your community and others' lives.

During Volunteering

If the organization provides an orientation, pay attention to expectations, such as appropriate dress, client confidentiality, and other behavior guidelines for volunteers.

Treat your volunteer work like a trial period or interview. It could be! Show up on time, call if you'll miss a shift, and take pride in your work. Introduce yourself to others and network. Remember names, ask questions about the work or organization, and let others know your interests and goals. Conversely, don't sit around waiting for someone to ask you to help; take initiative and show enthusiasm for the work. Volunteering, like most career experiences, requires flexibility, so keep an open mind and practice your adaptability.

Where to Find a Volunteer Opportunity

- **Your college's student activities or community engagement office.**
- **Your local volunteer center.**
- **Websites such as volunteermatch.org or idealist.org.**

After Volunteering

Reflect on your experiences to further your career goal discernment. Based on your volunteer experiences, do you adapt well? Are you a better communicator than you thought? Do you like to lead? Do you prefer established procedures or the opportunity to be creative? Once you learn more about yourself, consider whether your intended career path matches your abilities, interests, and values.

Like with the informational interview and job shadow, compare the results of the experience with other sources of knowledge, such as research and personal experience. Remember that work environments and cultures vary. Consider additional volunteer work to further pursue your interests and important skills.

STUDENT NOTES

Job Fairs

As you have learned, career goal discernment requires more than picking a field. It also means establishing contacts and gaining critical skills. **Job fairs** are another good way to gain these since they provide opportunities to make contact with potential employers and to practice interview skills. On college campuses, job fairs are usually coordinated through your career services department and are usually held in a large auditorium with rows of tables. Area businesses and organizations send a recruiter or representative to staff a table or booth in order to fill specific positions or recruit talent for the company. Job fairs allow attendees the convenience of speaking with many potential employers all in one place. You'll likely attend multiple job fairs. Many students attend job fairs as a student in order to find employment while attending college. After graduation, students also attend career fairs in order to attain positions within their career fields.

Even though it may seem a little early to attend a job fair, there are many benefits to starting now. Most students feel some nervousness when talking about themselves and their qualifications. It can also be intimidating to approach a recruiter. Practice these skills now so you'll be more confident when seeking a professional position after graduation.

Before the Job Fair

Research and practice are critical for a positive job fair experience. First, find out which companies will attend and then spend at least 10 minutes looking into any of interest. Specifically, look at their websites to learn more about their mission, operations, locations, size, and open positions.

Prepare your résumé and have someone look over it. If you haven't, set up a professional email address to list at the top of your résumé and to provide on sign-up sheets at the booths. Print several copies of your résumé to bring with you, along with a pen and small notebook to take notes. Dress as if you were preparing for an interview, but make sure you're comfortable. Silence and put away your phone.

Prepare your elevator speech: a 20–30 second pitch that explains who you are, why you're interested in the company, and how your skills or qualifications are a good match. Practice this multiple times so you'll feel confident when you introduce yourself to recruiters.

Also create a list of two to three questions to ask. See the "Questions about the Company" on page 161 for some sample questions. You can write your questions in your notebook ahead of time so you won't forget if you get nervous. Do not ask about pay or time off; those can be discussed later if you receive an official job offer.

STUDENT NOTES

Finally, employers sometimes conduct interviews on the spot. When planning your day, budget extra time in case you have the opportunity to interview during the job fair. You can also look online for common interview questions so that you can feel prepared should the opportunity arise.

During the Job Fair

Once you arrive, strategize when you'll visit each of your top targets. You may want to begin with a company that isn't your top choice to work out any nerves.

Approach each booth confidently, making eye contact with the recruiter and shaking hands. Have your résumé easily available so that you can hand it to the recruiter and reference specific information when mentioning qualifications or skills. Also, remember to slow down. Most of us talk too fast when nervous, and you want to exude confidence and interest. Ask your questions. At the end of your conversation, make sure you get the recruiter's business card and let them know you look forward to continuing the conversation soon.

Finally, don't get distracted from your purpose: finding a job. Avoid attending with a group of friends or classmates if they'll be a distraction. Also, don't load up on freebies. Taking a free pen or two is fine, but you don't want to be juggling swag from another company when talking to a recruiter.

After the Job Fair

Reflect on the experience. What went well? What will you do differently at future job fairs or interviews? Save notes and business cards from important conversations.

Follow the recruiters' instructions for applying for any positions of interest. If the company doesn't have any current positions that are a good fit for you, email the recruiter to say you appreciated the opportunity to discuss the company and hope they will keep you in mind should an opening arise.

Résumés and Cover Letters

When you are ready to attend job fairs as a job seeker and apply for jobs in your new career, you will most likely need to create two professional documents: a résumé and a cover letter.

A **résumé** is a document that formally presents your experiences and skills. You will likely create a résumé when applying for a job, internship, or scholarship. In fact, you may already have a college application résumé if you are a recent high school graduate. A résumé allows you to highlight your

STUDENT NOTES

education and work experiences, along with any awards and honors. The formality of the document keeps it clear and concise while outlining your strengths as a candidate.

A **cover letter** accompanies a résumé and gives you the opportunity to introduce yourself as a candidate, explaining your specific interest in the position as well as tailoring your skills and experiences to the role. Cover letters are formal letters that typically include a professional greeting, specific details about your accomplishments, and a request for an interview. Strong cover letters showcase your personality and fit.

Use the following list of tips to create attention-getting résumés and cover letters:

- **Be specific.** Include the names of relevant degrees, courses, industry certifications, and other programs that prepare you for successful employment at the company. While you may be able to use the same résumé to apply for multiple jobs in the same industry, you will likely have to write different cover letters for different jobs or at least make significant changes to your cover letter for jobs at different companies. Be sure to include the exact job title you are applying for on the cover letter.
- **Be brief.** In general, your résumé and cover letter should each be one page in length. Most jobs require online applications in addition to résumés and cover letters, so you should be strategic about highlighting only the most relevant information in your résumé and cover letter. Many career advisors recommend including only the last 10 years of employment history on your résumé. Successful résumés often include multiple sections with bulleted lists that are easy to read and understand quickly.
- **Be grammatically correct.** Demonstrate your strong attention to detail with a résumé and cover letter that are free from spelling, punctuation, and grammar errors. Consider using templates in Microsoft Word, Google Docs, or NC Careers to help with formatting, so you can pay extra attention to the content and grammatical accuracy of the documents.

Most community colleges have a Career Services office that can provide support in creating résumés and cover letters. Additionally, Writing Center tutors are available to help you with wording and correctness. And the NC Careers website has additional useful strategies on the "Job Search" webpage. When you are ready to apply for that first job in your new career, you have lots of useful resources to support a successful job search.

Conclusion

The most thorough career goal exploration combines academic research and personal experience. In order to really know what to expect from a future career, you should compare the facts and figures you learn about from online resources with the personal experiences you hear about in informational interviews and with the personal observations you make during a job shadowing, volunteering, and or job fair experience. Only then can you realistically anticipate what to expect from your future career.

STUDENT NOTES

Now is a good time to reflect on what you have learned from your career goal exploration. Be sure to add any new career options to your record on page 92.

STUDENT NOTES

REVIEW QUESTIONS

Chapter 6

Career Goal Exploration

These questions will help you monitor and evaluate your learning, two important parts of metacognition.

What is the best source of information to answer the following career goal exploration questions? Consider the specific resources from Chapter 6: the Occupational Outlook Handbook, NC Careers, other online resources, the informational interview, job shadowing, volunteering, and job fairs.

1. What is the average starting salary?

2. How does a specific company evaluate its employees' performances?

3. What are the credentials required to begin a specific career?

4. What are the credentials required for a specific job at a specific company?

5. What are the daily tasks of a specific career?

REVIEW QUESTIONS

6. What opportunities for advancement exist in a specific career?

7. Where in North Carolina and in the United States are the most jobs in the industry located?

8. What are some related jobs?

Discussion Questions

What are two new pieces of information you learned about your career? Where did you learn the information? How do these two facts inform your decisions in the next semester? In the next two years?

UNIT 2

Chapter 7

Goal Setting

Armadillo Stock/Shutterstock.com

Before you read this chapter, reflect on the following:

1. *When have I previously set and achieved a goal? Why was I successful?*
2. *When have I previously set and not achieved a goal? Why was I not successful?*
3. *How many semesters will it take for me to earn my community college credential? How can I know for sure?*

These questions will help you plan your learning, an important part of metacognition.

This chapter will introduce you to several resources and concepts to help you begin to set goals based on the thoughtful reflection in the self-assessment stage and the thorough research in the goal exploration stage. Goal setting, like a lot of the concepts in this textbook, is an art and a science. You can learn to improve your goal-setting skills by following the advice on these pages. But until you put the concepts into practice and make the necessary adjustments to make them work for you, you'll just be going through the motions, and you won't see the real benefits of setting and then accomplishing your goals. As you read this chapter, think about your specific academic and professional goals.

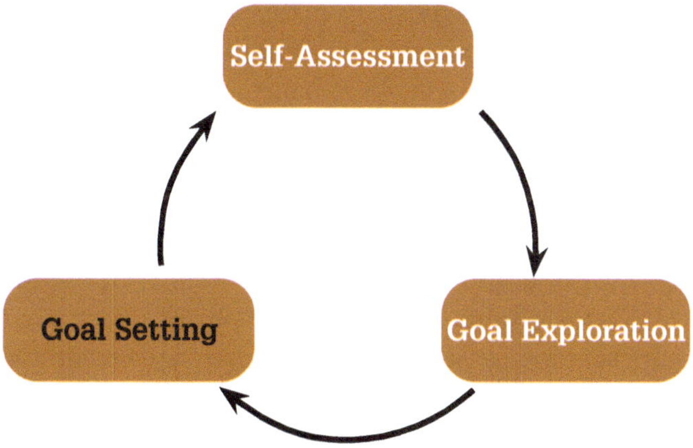

STUDENT NOTES

Specifically, Chapter 7 will address the following very useful tools in career goal exploration:

- Strategies for effective goal setting,
- SMART goals,
- Community College Goal Setting Action Plan, and
- Academic Timeline.

Strategies for Effective Goal Setting

Goal setting is a purposeful way to focus your mind and your energy on what you value most. Goals provide us with a meaningful structure to articulate what we really want for ourselves. Goals also keep us motivated and help us live proactive, not reactive, lives.

Goals can take you from where you are now to where you want to be. You can set goals to improve your study habits, to earn a specific credential, to transfer to a university, and/or to enter a new career field. Knowing your specific and personal goals can also help motivate you to stay focused in difficult or uninteresting classes. Leverage your long-term goals to help you achieve short-term success. Use the following strategies to set the most useful goals for yourself:

wavebreakmedia/Shutterstock.com

- **Reflect on the self-assessment stage of goal discernment.** Take into consideration what you learned about yourself from the self-assessments. Write goals that reflect your interests, personality, and values. These goals will be more meaningful to you than a goal that you think you should have for yourself or a goal that someone else sets for you. If you discover that the results of your self-assessments contradict the goals you have previously set for yourself, then think critically about whether you need to revise your goals based on your recent reflections.
- **Incorporate your knowledge from the goal exploration stage of goal discernment.** Use what you learned from your research to make your goals as specific as possible. For example, if you learned that you need a graduate degree like a master's degree to qualify for your chosen career, then write an academic goal that includes the specific required graduate degree. You might also include any preliminary credentials (associate or bachelor's degrees) you will earn along the way as objectives that will lead to the larger, long-term goal.
- **Write down your goals.** This is an important step in differentiating between goals and dreams. Consider posting them where you will see them and be reminded of where you are going. You might write your goals on Post-it Notes and put them by the bathroom mirror or car dashboard to remind yourself what you are working toward. Dr.

STUDENT NOTES

Gail Matthews, a psychology professor at Dominican University of California, conducted a research study in which 76% of the adult participants who wrote down their goals and checked in weekly with a friend to share their progress achieved their goals. This group outperformed the adult participants who just thought about their goals and achieved their goals within the same time frame at a rate of 43%.

- **Use "I will..." statements.** When you begin your goal statements with these very important words, you give your goals the power to motivate you. A goal that begins with "I will" is much stronger than "I kinda want to."
- **Prioritize your goals.** None of us multitasks as well as we tell ourselves we do. Nor can we concentrate on many goals simultaneously. Organize your goals into short-term goals and long-term goals. Your short-term goals might be related to your academic goals, for example, grades you'll earn this semester or the credential that you'll earn from your community college. Long-term goals, on the other hand, are more likely to be your professional goals, like the career you'll enter when you finish your credential or the path you'll take to advance in your career field. Just make sure that your short-term goals and long-term goals are related, so they'll be meaningful and motivational.
- **Write performance goals, not outcome goals.** As you think about your academic and professional goals, consider how much control you have. According to mindtools.com, when you set performance goals (instead of outcome goals), you have control over those goals. For example, in preparation for a test, a performance goal would be studying for a specific amount of time or using a specific study strategy. An outcome goal would be to make an A on the test. You might study for a test longer than you've ever studied before and still not make an A because of test anxiety or a distracting testing environment. If you had set an outcome goal of making an A, then this will be a defeat. However, if you set a performance goal of studying for a specific length of time, then you can feel the satisfaction and self-confidence from achieving this goal. And you will be motivated to continue your strong study habits.

Shutterstock.com

- **Anticipate obstacles.** The Center for Performance Psychology recommends visualizing successful completion of a goal, which can help you identify potential obstacles. Also, if you set a goal that you never accomplish, then you should use the experience as an opportunity to learn more about yourself. Did you not reach the goal because it was too big or difficult? Because you were not motivated to do the work that it required? Because you got distracted by a new goal? Whatever the reason, use it to write a better goal the next time. Consider the size and scope of the goal and how easily it fits into the other aspects of your life.

STUDENT NOTES

See page 270 for more information about acronyms.

SMART Goal Setting

As you decide what you want to accomplish academically and professionally, write out your goals and ask yourself if your goals are SMART. Many companies, academic coaches, success workshops, and college courses use the acronym SMART to help employees and students clarify and strengthen their goals. Each letter in the word SMART stands for a characteristic of a well-written goal. Consider the following very common academic goal as you read about **SMART goals.**

"I will make good grades."

Specific

You are more likely to do the work required to achieve a specific goal than a general goal. For example, "I will make good grades" is not specific because different students define good grades differently. Some students consider A's, B's, and C's to be good grades while others consider only A's and B's to be good grades. A more specific goal is "I will make all A's."

Measurable

Establish a way to determine whether or not you achieve your goals. When you can measure your goals, you can figure out how well you are progressing and adapt when necessary. For example, at the end of the semester, you can look at your unofficial transcripts and see if you made all A's or not.

Attainable

Make sure it is possible to achieve the goal. For example, if your goal is to earn all A's, but you are a full-time student and a full-time employee with no time to study for your classes, then your goal may not be attainable. Set yourself up for success rather than failure by writing goals that are possible.

Realistic

More specifically, make sure it is possible for you as an individual to achieve the goal. To reach your goals, you must be *willing* and *able* to do the work that your goals require. For example, if your goal is to earn all A's, and you are willing to put in the work that is required to earn A's, then your goal is realistic. But if you don't prioritize your time to study, then your goal is unrealistic.

Time-Bound

Establish a deadline, so you can know when to evaluate whether or not you have achieved your goal and to create a sense of urgency. Looking back at the poorly written goal, when is the student going to make good grades? This week? This semester? This year?

STUDENT NOTES

Look at the following examples to see how to change vague goals into SMART goals.

Vague Example 1: I will get more sleep.

SMART Revision: I will get a minimum of 8 hours of sleep this month by turning off the lights and putting away all devices by 11:00 p.m.

This SMART goal is specific and measurable (*get 8 hours of sleep each night*), attainable, and timebound (*this month*).

The only SMART criterion that is questionable is whether or not this goal is realistic. If this individual is willing to turn off the lights and put away devices at 11:00 p.m., then it is a realistic goal.

Vague Example 2: I will pass my classes.

SMART Revision: I will earn a B in BIO 111 and an A in ENG 111 this semester.

This SMART goal is specific and measurable (*naming the exact grades and the exact classes*), attainable (*students can earn these grades*), and time-bound (*at the end of the semester, you will see your final grades*).

The only criterion that is questionable is whether or not the goal is realistic. If this student is willing and able to do the work required to earn these grades, then it is realistic. If the student is unwilling or unable to do the work required, then it is not realistic.

Vague Example 3: I will be successful.

SMART Revision: I will be a self-employed accountant in five years.

This SMART goal is specific (*self-employed accountant*), attainable (*it is possible to earn an AAS degree in Accounting in less than five years*), and time-bound (*five years*).

Again, the only questionable criterion is whether or not the goal is realistic. If this student is willing and able to do the work required to earn the AAS degree and then do the work that is required to become self-employed, then it is realistic. If the student is unwilling or unable to do the work required, then it is not realistic.

Shutterstock.com

STUDENT NOTES

Below is a Durham Tech student's academic SMART goal. Notice that it includes a specific credential that she planned to earn and a timeline.

> "In Fall 2028, I will transfer to North Carolina State University and enter the College of Management to earn a Bachelor of Science in Business Management with a concentration in Entrepreneurship. By then I will have an Associate in Arts degree from Durham Tech. In order to be admitted to NC State, I will keep my GPA at 3.0 or higher. I will have to stay in school full time to keep my financial aid, so I'll need to go to Durham Tech for six semesters (counting summer terms) in order to get my AA degree. I will graduate from North Carolina State University in Spring 2030."

The same student developed an equally strong professional SMART goal. This particular student had developed a business plan in one of her business courses, so her professional goal includes details that many first-semester students are not ready to include just yet. However, most college students can identify for themselves the basic features of a professional goal (for example, the career, the timeline, and the connection between the academic goal and the professional goal).

> "I will open my own pet-sitting small business in 2030. I will continue to work as a part-time pet sitter while I am a Durham Tech and NCSU student to stay connected with the field. I will use the time between graduation and when I open my own business to find investors and execute my business plan. By 2035, I will employ 8 to 10 part-time workers to take care of the company's day-to-day operations."

bonvoyagecaptain/Shutterstock.com

As you write your own academic and professional SMART goals, use these examples as a guide, and your goals will be just as effective. And then put your SMART goals somewhere you will see them regularly to help you stay motivated and achieve them.

Community College Goal Setting Action Plan

Students in various academic programs can have similar goals. On the following pages are several lists of steps to complete each semester to help you achieve your goals. The chronology of the plan below is a recommendation. You may decide to do some of the activities earlier or later than what is recommended here. You may also find that it will take you longer than four semesters to complete your specific community college program. Add whatever individualized goals you've set for yourself in the margins.

STUDENT NOTES

First Semester

- Choose a program and credential that matches your career goals.
- Draft an Academic Timeline (see page 184), so you can anticipate how long it will take to finish your credential.
- Orient yourself to your community college and start to explore the resources available to you, including career counseling, academic advising, and transfer advising.
- Connect with your academic advisor (see pages 41–43 for tips on working effectively with an academic advisor).
- Create an electronic or hardcopy advising folder and keep all of your important documents in it, for example, your Plan of Study, your Transfer Guide or Course Selection Guide (university transfer students only), your Academic Timeline, your registration forms, and important messages from your advisor.
- Take your first-semester classes seriously. If your classes are easy for you, then use this semester as an opportunity to develop a strong GPA. If your classes are difficult, then get the help you need to pass them. It is difficult to bring up your GPA after just one bad semester (see pages 36–40 for more information about GPAs).

Second Semester

- Research what additional credentials you will need to succeed in your career.
- Revise your Academic Timeline (see page 184) based on any new understanding of course availability/scheduling or input from your advisor.
- Look for scholarship information on your community college's website. Many scholarships require that applicants be enrolled in a specific program.
- Meet with your advisor to select your classes for the next semester and to ask any questions you have about completing your credential.
- Research universities that offer your intended major if you plan to transfer. Watch for university recruiters to visit your community college, and visit university campuses during "open houses."
- Keep a list of classes you have completed or review your unofficial transcript.
- Look for extracurricular activities that support your goals.
- Monitor your GPA and notice the impact your grades in a single semester can make on your cumulative GPA.

Many universities have specific application deadlines. If you plan to transfer to a senior institution, then find out when the university accepts transfer applications. Don't forget to check for financial aid application deadlines, too.

Third Semester

- Review your Academic Timeline (see page 184) and make changes as needed. As you finish pre-requisites and enter your program of study, you may find that you have fewer course options each semester. It will become much more important that you plan a few semesters in advance the further into your Plan of Study you get.
- Update your list of classes you have completed or review your unofficial transcript.
- Meet with your advisor to select your classes for the next semester and to ask any questions you have about completing your credential.
- Find opportunities to get involved in your future career field. Look for volunteer opportunities, internships, or co-op experiences. You can put your newly developed skills to work while networking with future professional colleagues.

Fourth Semester

- Meet with your advisor to conduct an unofficial degree audit. Bring your unofficial transcripts and/or your Plan of Study with the classes you have successfully completed checked or highlighted. This will help you identify any classes you still need to take.
- Meet the graduation application deadline for your community college. Some colleges encourage students to apply for graduation a semester before they plan to complete their program of study. Even if you don't plan to participate in the commencement ceremony, you may need to apply for graduation. Your application will trigger an official degree audit process that will confirm for you that you have completed all of the required coursework for your credential.
- If you are an AA, AE, AFA, AS, AATP, or ASTP student, then schedule an appointment with a transfer admissions counselor or advisor at the university. Bring a list of questions that you have about transfer. Follow up with a thank you note.
- If you are an AAS or diploma student, then take advantage of networking opportunities such as job fairs or informational interviews. See a career counselor on campus for assistance with creating or updating your résumé and preparing for interviews.

When you finish the Academic Timeline (see the next section), revisit this timeline and add or move steps to the semester appropriate to your personal timeline.

STUDENT NOTES

Academic Timeline

The **Academic Timeline** is a chronological and individualized list of the courses you plan to take to earn your specific credential. You can write out an Academic Timeline on paper or on the following pages, and at many North Carolina community colleges, you can enter your Academic Timeline in Self-Service. As you learned in Chapter 5, your semester-by-semester class schedule will probably not look exactly like your program's Plan of Study because of any of the following reasons:

- You may have to first complete pre-requisites or additional co-requisites, like developmental education courses.
- You may take fewer courses than are listed in a single semester on the Plan of Study.
- You may enter your program in a different semester than the first one listed on the Plan of Study.
- You may transfer in credits from previous college experiences.

The Academic Timeline is a useful tool to help you synthesize all of the information you learned about yourself, your program, and your future career in the previous stages of goal discernment. Read the example Academic Timeline that follows and then use the tables on the next pages to plan the sequence of the classes you will take to earn your specific credential. Start with the Plan of Study or Transfer Guide/Course Selection Guide that will lead to the credential you will need to accomplish your professional goals.

Shutterstock.com

Hints for Completing the Academic Timeline

Use your Plan of Study and Transfer Guide or Course Selection Guide to complete the Academic Timeline.

- If you are in a career/technical program or health technologies program, then use the Plan of Study.
- If you are a university transfer student, then use your Transfer Guide or Course Selection Guide.

STEP 1: Include any transfer credit or previously completed college credits that will count toward your degree. List these credits in the Semester 1 table at the beginning of the Academic Timeline.

STEP 2: Include your current schedule for this semester. *(Hint: If you have transfer credits or previous college coursework, then your current semester will be listed in Semester 2 or later. If you have no transfer credits or previous coursework, then you will list your current schedule in Semester 1.)*

STEP 3: When planning your coursework for future semesters, include any developmental education or other pre-requisite and co-requisite coursework that you may need to complete.

STUDENT NOTES

Other helpful hints:

- List co-requisites in the same semester. For example, at many community colleges SPA 111 and SPA 181 are co-requisites and must be taken in the same semester.
- Credit hours are the number of hours that will be listed on your transcript and the number of hours that you will pay tuition for.
- Contact hours are the number of hours that you will spend in class, including class, clinical, and lab hours.

Sample Academic Timeline

This student used the Transfer Guide for Political Science Majors at UNC Greensboro to complete the Academic Timeline below. The student plans to graduate with the AA degree and then transfer to UNC Greensboro to study Political Science.

Semester 1 (Semester/Year: Spring 2025**)**

Courses	Credit Hours	Contact Hours
ACA 122	1	2
ENG 111	3	3
COM 231	3	3
MAT 143	3	4
Total	10	12

Semester 2 (Semester/Year: Summer 2025**)**

Courses	Credit Hours	Contact Hours
SPA 111	3	3
SPA 181	1	2
HUM 110	3	3
Total	7	8

Semester 3 (Semester/Year: Fall 2025**)**

Courses	Credit Hours	Contact Hours
MAT 152	4	5
SPA 112	3	3
SPA 182	1	2
ENG 112	3	3
ART 111	3	3
Total	14	16

STUDENT NOTES

Semester 4 (Semester/Year: Spring 2026**)**

Courses	Credit Hours	Contact Hours
BIO 111	4	6
SOC 210	3	3
ENG 232	3	3
SPA 212	3	3
Total	13	15

Semester 5 (Semester/Year: Summer 2026**)**

Courses	Credit Hours	Contact Hours
BIO 112	4	6
POL 120	3	3
Total	7	9

Semester 6 (Semester/Year: Fall 2026**)**

Courses	Credit Hours	Contact Hours
PSY 150	3	3
HIS 111	3	3
POL 210	3	3
PHI 240	3	3
Total	12	12

Roman Borodaev/Shutterstock.com

STUDENT NOTES

Remember from Chapter 5 that credit hours are the number of hours that will be listed on your transcript and the number of hours that you will pay tuition for. The credit hours are typically listed on all of the college's Plans of Study.

Contact hours are the number of hours that you will spend in class, including class, clinical, and lab hours. You may need to use your college's website to look up the contact hours associated with a specific course.

Your Academic Timeline

Use the tables below to record the classes you have already completed, the classes you are currently enrolled in, and—most importantly—the classes you plan to take in the future.

Your Program of Study: ______________________________

Your Credential: ______________________________

Semester 1 (Semester and Year: ____________)

Courses	Credit Hours	Contact Hours
Total		

Semester 2 (Semester and Year: ____________)

Courses	Credit Hours	Contact Hours
Total		

Semester 3 (Semester and Year: ___________)

Courses	Credit Hours	Contact Hours
Total		

STUDENT NOTES

Semester 4 (Semester and Year: ___________)

Courses	Credit Hours	Contact Hours
Total		

Stephen Coburn/Shutterstock.com

Semester 5 (Semester and Year: ___________)

Courses	Credit Hours	Contact Hours
Total		

STUDENT NOTES

Semester 6 (Semester and Year: ___________)

Courses	Credit Hours	Contact Hours
Total		

Semester 7 (Semester and Year: ___________)

Courses	Credit Hours	Contact Hours
Total		

Semester 8 (Semester and Year: ___________)

Courses	Credit Hours	Contact Hours
Total		

STUDENT NOTES

Semester 9 (Semester and Year: ___________)

Courses	Credit Hours	Contact Hours
Total		

Semester 10 (Semester and Year: ___________)

Courses	Credit Hours	Contact Hours
Total		

Conclusion

As you set your academic and career goals, keep in mind the important strategies from the beginning of this chapter. Most importantly, remember that the most effective goals are SMART goals. That is, they are Specific, Measurable, Attainable, Realistic, and Time-Bound. As you prepare to write your SMART goals, you should always consider what you know about your personality, interests, and values from various self-assessments. You should also take into consideration any academic and career research that you have conducted as part of your goal exploration. Goals that are informed by this level of self-assessment and exploration are that much more likely to be achieved. Keep track of your goals and share them with those who will help you achieve them (for example, family, friends, advisors) in order to ensure you stay on course and have the support you need to succeed.

Record your SMART academic and SMART professional goals on the tracking sheet on page 92 for easy reference in the future.

STUDENT NOTES

REVIEW QUESTIONS

Chapter 7
Goal Setting

These questions will help you monitor and evaluate your learning, two important parts of metacognition.

1. Read the goals listed below and put a check mark under S, M, A, R, and/or T if the goal is Specific, Measurable, Attainable, Realistic, and/or Time-bound. If any of the elements are missing, rewrite the goal to make it SMART. The first one is done for you.

	Goals	S	M	A	R	T
Vague Goal #1	I will improve my time management this semester.			✔	✔	✔
SMART Revision	I will use a weekly planner to keep up with assignments and activities this semester.	✔	✔	✔	✔	✔
Vague Goal #2	I will pass my final exams.					
SMART Revision						
Vague Goal #3	I will graduate with an associate degree in one year.					
SMART Revision						
Vague Goal #4	I will earn a cumulative GPA of 3.0 or higher.					
SMART Revision						

2. Write one academic goal and one professional goal in the table below. Put a check mark under S, M, A, R, and/or T if the goal is Specific, Measurable, Attainable, Realistic, and/or Time-bound. If any of the elements are missing, rewrite the goal to make it SMART.

	Goals	S	M	A	R	T
Academic Goal						
Professional Goal						

3. Re-read the Community College Goal Setting Action Plan on pages 178–180. Highlight or underline the steps that you will need to complete this semester or next. Also, identify three additional steps that you will need to complete to earn your credential at your community college.

   a. ____

   b. ____

   c. ____

Discussion Questions

What is a goal that you have set in the past that you did not accomplish or one that you have seen someone else set and not accomplish? What SMART elements was the goal lacking? How would you revise the goal based on these five criteria?

Unit 3

ESB Professional/Shutterstock.com

LEARNING STRATEGIES

Successful students know and apply a variety of learning strategies in college. Depending on your learning style preferences and the subjects you are studying, you may need to use a variety of learning strategies. You may also find that as you progress through your academic program, your classes get more and more challenging, and you need to use strategies that were previously unnecessary. This unit of *Success by Design* will address the following useful learning strategy topics:

CHAPTER 8: Time Management
Community college students are very busy people. Many students balance academics with work and family. Other students experience more flexibility and unscheduled time than ever before. Therefore, effective time management is critical to success in college.

CHAPTER 9: Reading Strategies
Reading textbooks and other academic materials takes a very different set of skills than reading a magazine or piece of fiction. Some college students are surprised by the amount of reading that they must complete; this chapter will help you make the most of all of those reading assignments.

CHAPTER 10: Note-Taking Strategies
Note taking is a critical step in the process of turning new information (through classroom instruction and reading assignments) into the knowledge base that will prepare you for future coursework and your career.

STUDENT NOTES

CHAPTER 11: Study Strategies

Successful college students do more than re-read the textbook and make flash cards to prepare for a test (not that there's anything wrong with flash cards!). This chapter will introduce study skills that will help you maintain your learning in a class as well as prepare for assessments.

CHAPTER 12: Test-Taking Strategies

Finally, tests give you the opportunity to demonstrate how much you have learned. In addition to fully understanding the course content, it is beneficial to know some techniques that will help you show your instructor the breadth and depth of your understanding.

Important Learning Outcomes for Unit 3

- Demonstrate time-management strategies, including identifying unproductive activities, listing ways to use time more effectively, and showing use of a weekly planner.
- Evaluate learning strategies, including note-taking, test-taking, information processing, time management, and memorization techniques, and identify strategies for improvement.

Unit 3: Learning Strategies Tracking Sheet

STUDENT NOTES

As you read Unit 3, record the individual elements of your personal learning strategies in the table below. This will be a helpful record to track your personalized preferences and plans.

Time-Management Goals	Reading Goals

Note-Taking Goals	Study Strategies Goals

Test-Taking Goals	Learning Strategies Strengths

STUDENT NOTES

UNIT 3

Chapter 8

Time Management

Before you read this chapter, reflect on the following:

1. *What time management strategies have you used?*
2. *Which ones have worked and which ones have not?*
3. *What do you want to learn from this chapter?*

These questions will help you plan your learning, an important part of metacognition.

One of the most significant differences between college and high school is the amount of work that college students complete outside of class. Successful college students manage their time effectively in order to take responsibility for their learning in a way that is unlike learning in high school. A full-time course load in college is typically only 12 to 16 credit hours because college instructors expect students to spend additional hours each week outside of class reading the textbook, working on assignments, meeting with study groups, and reviewing notes.

If you follow the 2:1 rule, where will you do most of your learning? On your own or in the classroom? Is this similar or different from the expectation in high school?

More specifically, college instructors expect students to spend two hours outside of class working on course content for every one credit hour assigned to the course. This is called the **2:1 rule**. For example, if you take a three-credit English class like ENG 111, your instructor most likely expects you are spending six hours per week outside of class learning course concepts or completing assignments. What exactly should you do during these six hours? Most students realize that they should complete assignments. What many struggling students don't

STUDENT NOTES

understand is that they should also use this time to complete maintenance studying (see pages 262–263 in Chapter 11 for more about the need to study and review notes regularly, not just before an exam) and to complete pieces of larger assignments (for more on breaking up large assignments into manageable tasks, see distributed practice on page 205).

Many students think of time management as a way to manage competing demands on their time. But good time management also allows you to live your values more fully. If you value your family, then you likely spend many hours each week caring for them and doing activities with them and for them. If you value your education, then you will have to manage your time so you can do the necessary activities that lead to your educational goal.

Finally, as you'll see later in this chapter, time management is directly related to stress management. One of the first steps that many college students take when they realize that they are experiencing stress is to manage their time more effectively by starting assignments earlier, minimizing time wasters, using a planner, or applying distributed practice.

Even if you're already adept at handling a full schedule, college will require you to apply these skills to a diverse range of new tasks. To help you with this transition, there are two tools you should know how to use effectively: to-do lists and weekly planners. These are the basic foundational tools of all time management, and successful students and professionals utilize them constantly. If you are just beginning with time management, these two are the place to start.

Anna Hoychuk/Shutterstock.com

To-Do Lists

A **to-do list** is a list of activities or tasks you need to complete, often during a specific period of time (for example, a day or a week) or for a specific project. Nearly everyone has made a to-do list at some point, but some to-do lists are better than others. Consider these two lists below. Why is Jay's list more effective?

Michael's list

Basketball
Study
Clean kitchen
Bank
Email pictures to Sean

Jay's list

1. Look over flash cards for Biology Chapter 3. Quiz tomorrow
2. Call Mom
3. Brainstorm thesis and outline for paper due next week
4. Grocery: milk, bananas, cereal
5. Call Melanie about party

Jay has included two things that Michael hasn't: detail and priority. First, Jay is more specific in his list, and that means his chances of completing his tasks are greater. For example, on Michael's list "study" is so vague that it would be easy for him to skip it. Conversely, imagine you're Jay. Seeing on your to-do list that you need to review your flash cards over Chapter 3 for the quiz tomorrow is so specific that you will more likely complete that task. And that's one of the most important things about a to-do list. Sure, it lists tasks for the day, but more importantly, a to-do list sets your intentions. The more specific you are with your intentions through your to-do list, the more apt you are to accomplish them once you've set this goal on paper.

Jay also ordered his list by **prioritizing** items, which means strategizing the order in which he'll complete tasks from his to-do list. It's important to ask yourself three questions in order to rank your tasks:

1. What is important?
2. What is urgent?
3. What is both important and urgent?

Important tasks are those that lead to achieving your goals. Urgent activities usually demand immediate attention, but these are often in response to other people's needs or requirements. Urgent and important items are tasks that are important to your goals and also timely.

To effectively prioritize your day's activities, use the following matrix that has been adapted from Stephen Covey's *The 7 Habits of Highly Effective People*. As you can see, you'll complete urgent and important activities first, then items on your to-do list you labeled important but not urgent. Finally, you'll complete urgent items and then those items that are neither urgent nor important.

STUDENT NOTES

One of the greatest values of a to-do list is setting your intentions for the day.

Based on the order of his list, what can you assume about Jay's call to Mom? Is it important, urgent, or both?

SG SHOT/Shutterstock.com

STUDENT NOTES

Which block of items do you currently prioritize on your list? When should you complete them, according to the chart?

Prioritization Matrix

Urgency

Urgent, Not Important COMPLETE 3RD	Urgent and Important COMPLETE 1ST
• Interruptions • Emails • Phone calls • Required daily tasks	• Deadlines • Some calls or emails • Commitments, such as meetings, classes, work shifts
Neither Urgent Nor Important COMPLETE LAST	**Important, Not Urgent COMPLETE 2ND**
• Distractions • Time wasters • Mindless activities, such as watching TV	• Preparation, planning, and decision-making • Time with friends and family • Critical conversations

Importance

This process ensures that you don't live your life only responding to the most pressing concerns or the ones that evoke the greatest stress. Instead, there's intentionality and design in your day. You control your schedule instead of your schedule controlling you. Strive to spend time on the things that matter most by checking to see that you've been intentional with your day, not just reactive. After you order your list in the method described, see if your to-do list reflects your goals in life.

In addition to the content and order of the list, the method you use for making your to-do list is important as well. Establishing a routine is best. Many people keep a to-do list in a pocket notebook that they use daily. There are several apps that organize your to-do list and many online calendars have a task list. When you think of something that needs to be done, get out the notebook and write it on the list or add it to your app. Important reminders and tasks are less likely to be lost using one of these methods. An added benefit is peace of mind, knowing that nothing important will be forgotten.

STUDENT NOTES

Also, you should develop a routine for when you'll create and prioritize your list. If you are a morning person, then get up a few minutes early and write out your to-do list before the hectic day begins. If you are a night person, then write your to-do list before you go to bed. If you find yourself having a difficult time falling asleep or feeling anxious at night, writing down your tasks for the next day may provide you relief from stress or anxiety. Many people find that having a place devoted to writing down pending tasks reduces their stress because it starts a plan for completing responsibilities.

In fact, a large component of stress management is effective time management. If you're feeling stressed, your to-do list can help you reduce the feeling of being overwhelmed. Writing things down reduces the mental energy required to keep track of your responsibilities, allows you to prioritize clearly (through the three questions), and also begins the process of accomplishing a goal rather than worrying about a stressor.

Planners

One of the most useful tools to any successful person is a daily, weekly, or monthly planner. A planner is not the same as a to-do list. A planner is much more specific than a to-do list because you select a precise time or date to complete the task on the to-do list. Consider the differences:

To-Do Lists	Planners
Often used for just one day or a specific event	Used continually, usually for a year at a time
Lists events by importance and urgency	Lists events by the date or time of day
Indicates the order in which you plan to accomplish the task; does not indicate at what time	Allows you to set aside a specific date or time to devote to an activity

Many different types of planners are available, but the most important distinction is the length of time you can view across two pages when open. The most common three types are monthly, weekly, and daily planners. Consider the advantages and disadvantages of the examples that follow. Specifically, notice the items listed for the 18th day of the month.

The **monthly planner** allows you to see upcoming events far in advance, which can allow you to see patterns in your activities and keep track of important dates, such as birthdays and due dates.

STUDENT NOTES

Sample Monthly Planner

S	M	T	W	Th	F	S
1	**2**	**3**	**4**	**5**	**6**	**7**
			Math study group 11–12			
8	**9**	**10**	**11**	**12**	**13**	**14**
			Math study group 11–12			
15	**16**	**17**	**18**	**19**	**20**	**21**
	Math Test Ch. 6–10		CIS 110 Project 2 due	ENG 111 1st Draft due		
22	**23**	**24**	**25**	**26**	**27**	**28**
		ACA Paper Due	Math study group 11–12		Trey's b'day party	

Notice that tasks are not written on the monthly planner. Now, consider this example of a weekly calendar that follows for the week of the 16th–22nd. With a **weekly planner**, not only are planned events noted, but they are also assigned to a specific date for completion. Therefore, while monthly planners allow you to "forecast" your life, weekly planners are more detailed by showing regular events such as class.

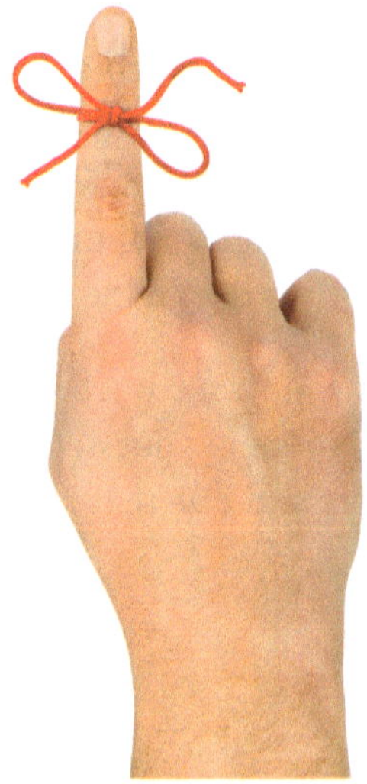

Tatiana Popova/Shutterstock.com

Sample Weekly Planner

STUDENT NOTES

SEPTEMBER 16–22	
16 Monday	**19 Thursday**
MAT 121 — Test Ch. 6–10	ENG 111 — 1st draft due
CIS 110	Work Study Job
17 Tuesday	**20 Friday**
Gym	MAT 121
ACA	Study on Campus
ENG 111	
Work Study Job	
18 Wednesday	**21 Saturday**
MAT 121	
Dr. appt. @ 11:00	
CIS 110—Project 2 due	
2–5 Study on Campus	**22 Sunday**

Compare the previous weekly planner example to a daily planner example that follows for Wednesday, the 18th. As you can see, the **daily planner** adds an even greater level of specificity. For this date, the monthly calendar didn't mention any tasks, and the weekly planner only mentions where the students needed to be at specific times. The daily planner, however, also includes specific tasks to accomplish. For example, "Make final edits to ENG 111 paper and print" from the daily planner is much more specific than the weekly calendar's "Study on Campus."

STUDENT NOTES

Sample Daily Planner

WEDNESDAY SEPTEMBER 18	
7 a.m.	
8 a.m.	MAT 121 8:00–10:10 Ask about project due next wk.
9 a.m.	
10 a.m.	
11 a.m.	Dr appointment
12 p.m.	Grab Lunch
1 p.m.	CIS 110 1:00–2:20—Project 2 Due
2 p.m.	Make final edits to ENG 111 paper & print
3 p.m.	
4 p.m.	Write interview questions and email contact for ACA portfolio
5 p.m.	Finish one set of math HW problems
6 p.m.	
7 p.m.	
8 p.m.	Watch game!

STUDENT NOTES

As you can probably now see, the monthly planner alone is not specific enough for use by college students. You need a planner that allows you to devote specific tasks to the hours of the day in order to make the most of your time. A weekly planner, or preferably a daily planner, is necessary for the demands of a college student.

While your planner's display is important, how you use your planner is what matters most. On monthly calendars, write anything that's significant at the date level, such as due dates or birthdays. For a weekly or daily planner, on the other hand, write anything that is significant at the hour level, such as appointments or specific goals for that time, for example, the number of chapters to review or the steps of a project you'll complete. Be as specific as the space allows.

Entry	Example	Monthly	Weekly	Daily
Appointments or one-time events	Study groups or doctor's appointments	✔	✔	✔
Important dates	Due dates or birthdays	✔	✔	✔
Recurring events	Class times		✔	✔
Routine tasks	Lunch or picking up the kids		✔	✔
Specific times for completing items on the to-do list	Completing ACA homework or going to the grocery store			✔

michaeljung/Shutterstock.com

In using a planner, skilled time managers will not only include what they need to accomplish and when but also how they plan to accomplish those goals. For example, look at Wednesday, the 18th on the weekly planner. This student plans to spend three hours studying from 2:00 to 5:00 p.m. The student knows what he'll do (study) and when (2:00–5:00), but he doesn't include how. He's left out a level of detail that's crucial to the completion of tasks. Compare this to the daily planner, which encourages you to be more precise about your time. This student has noted specifically how he will study from 2–5 and what he'll accomplish. Remember, the more specific you are about how you'll use the time, the more likely you are to actually complete the task rather than procrastinate or skip it. Detailed notes in your planner mean you're less likely to get distracted or skip the task. The likelihood of using time as intended increases with greater specificity listed in the planner.

Luckily, completing this crucial step of planning specific tasks is easier once you have your to-do list in hand. As you now know, a useful planner will have time increments on the side so that you can devote specific tasks to a particular time.

STUDENT NOTES

Once you've created your to-do list, you can assign the individual tasks to a specific time, a technique referred to as **time blocking** or time boxing. Remember to consider the rank of importance and urgency you gave a specific task before you settle on a day or time to devote to the task. For example, return to Jay's to-do list at the beginning of the chapter. Jay obviously consulted his monthly planner or flipped ahead in his weekly or daily planner before he wrote his to-do list because he's aware that he has a paper due next week.

You'll practice time blocking with the Time Management Self-Evaluation on pages 219–222.

Now, it's time for him to plan his day. If this were today's date in his planner, how would you use time blocking to arrange his to-do list on page 196 by time so he can accomplish the most during his day?

Jay's Planner

7 a.m.	
8 a.m.	
9 a.m.	Philosophy Class 9:20–10:40
10 a.m.	
11 a.m.	
12 p.m.	
1 p.m.	
2 p.m.	
3 p.m.	SGA meeting
4 p.m.	
5 p.m.	
6 p.m.	
7 p.m.	
8 p.m.	

In order to plan Jay's day, you likely had to ask yourself several questions, including how long each activity would take and when he completed his daily routines (eating, showering, packing lunches for the kids, etc.). To-do lists often don't include routine tasks such as these. Planners often do not either. However, you should consider these things when time blocking. Compare your time-blocked day for Jay with the following example. What did you forget to include? What other considerations might need to be noted when using your planner that to-do lists do not include?

Jay's Planner Example

7 a.m.	
8 a.m.	
9 a.m.	Philosophy Class 9:20–10:40
10 a.m.	
11 a.m.	Make flash cards for BIO
12 p.m.	Call Mom
1 p.m.	Paper: brainstorming thesis & outline
2 p.m.	
3 p.m.	SGA meeting
4 p.m.	Grocery
5 p.m.	Dinner
6 p.m.	Call Melanie—What should I bring?
7 p.m.	
8 p.m.	

STUDENT NOTES

For which class and project did Jay use distributed practice?

Another important aspect of using a planner effectively is dividing large assignments into smaller tasks, which are completed over a span of time rather than all at once. This is a form of **distributed practice**. Distributed practice is the opposite of cramming. It is an effective strategy for time management and for study. See pages 261–262 for an explanation of why cramming doesn't work over the long term in college.

To use distributed practice, find the test date or the due date for a project, paper, or significant assignment and back up two to three weeks. Ask yourself what individual steps you need to complete in order to have the task finished on time. Then, plot these steps on your planner, committing yourself to accomplishing bits of work over a span of time in order to improve your final product and limit your stress. Think of this approach in terms of an eating analogy: it's much easier, healthier, and more enjoyable to eat your meal in bites rather than gulp it down in its entirety in one swallow without chewing! Similarly, you want to allow yourself to "digest" a large project, paper, or assignment. It's unreasonable to expect quality work and learning if you don't allow yourself adequate time to complete the assignment.

STUDENT NOTES

JohnKwan/Shutterstock.com

Whether your planner has a kitten on the cover or is kept digitally on your smartphone, you must refer to your planner often for it to be useful to you. A planner is only effective if you make use of it. Mark down appointments and events as soon as you hear of them. For classes, this means that you should place test dates and deadlines for papers and projects into your planner as soon as you get the course syllabus. You can evaluate how well you're using your planner by completing the Time Management Self-Evaluation at the end of this chapter.

5 TIPS FOR USING A PLANNER

1. Put all due dates and tests in your planner as soon as you get the syllabus
2. Make a to-do list daily and prioritize it. Then assign tasks a specific time in your planner.
3. Look at it daily: in the morning to plan your day and throughout the day to stay on task or adjust plans if necessary. At night, look to see what tomorrow holds and everything you accomplished today.
4. Look ahead a week or two and use distributed practice for upcoming assignments or projects.
5. Realize when you're most productive. If you're a morning person, don't plan to work on big projects at night.

STUDENT NOTES

Where to Begin with Time Management

No matter where you're starting with time management, we can all improve. So where should *you* start? Use the Time-Management Pyramid below to help you strategize your next steps to improve your time management.

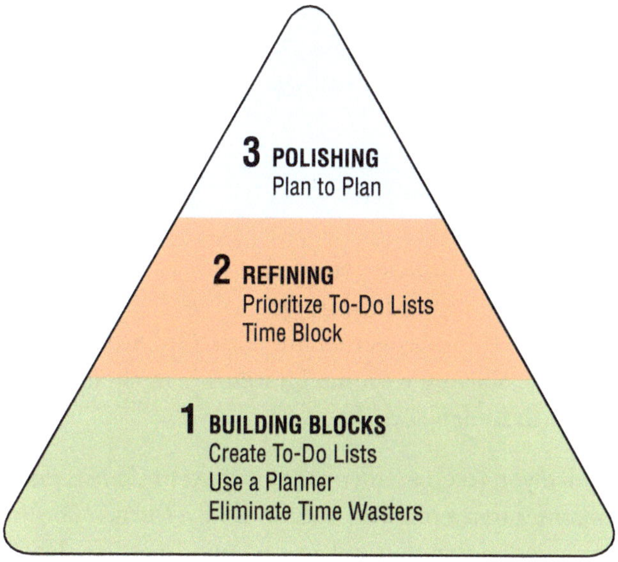

The Time-Management Pyramid is composed of three levels. Everyone should begin at the base. At each level, you assess the frequency with which you consistently utilize these strategies effectively. Only when you've met the goals for that level do you move up. If you haven't mastered the first three pieces and use them routinely, now is the time to do so. They're the foundation for all other time-management tools and succeeding in college will likely prove challenging without them.

Level One: The Basic Building Blocks

Create To-Do Lists: Make a daily to-do list and strive to make it specific. Your goal for this step is to create a new, specific list every day.

Use a Planner: Your goal for this step is to look at your planner daily to stay on track with what you need to accomplish and to update it daily with any changes to your schedule or due dates.

Eliminate Time Wasters: Time wasters are the activities we engage in when we have other, more pressing priorities. See the section on impulsivity and procrastination on pages 72–73 to review the connection between time wasters and priorities. Your goal for this step is to identify your time wasters and limit their distraction. Begin by asking yourself: What are some of my unproductive behaviors? What are some of the things I'm most

STUDENT NOTES

If you need additional help determining your time wasters, use the Time Management Self-Evaluation activity at the end of this chapter.

tempted to do when I should be studying or working on an assignment? To overcome these time wasters, turn them into rewards. If you work on your paper for one hour, allow yourself 15 minutes on TikTok. The trick is to be firm about the limits you give yourself—15 minutes—so that you'll come back to your task at hand if you have more work to do. Set a timer if you have to.

Once you've utilized all three strategies daily for several weeks and feel confident in your abilities to use these strategies, you're ready to move on to the next level.

Level Two: Refining

Prioritize To-Do Lists: Prioritize your daily to-do lists by labeling each task according to the Prioritization Matrix on page 198: U for urgent items, I for important items, and UI for items that are both. Order the list by numbering your to-do list's tasks, starting with the UI items first, then moving on to the I items, and finally those labeled U.

Time Block: Once you've created your prioritized to-do list, devote specific times in your planner to accomplish your to-do list's tasks. For this reason, it's highly recommended that you utilize a planner that has the times of day listed down the side. Begin the day with your highest priority items. Estimate how long it will take you to complete each activity, and then block out that time in your planner and label it with the task.

Once you've utilized these two strategies daily for several weeks and feel confident in your abilities to use these strategies effectively, you're ready to move on to the next level.

Level Three: Polishing

Plan to Plan: Take a half hour at the same time each week to plot out your next two or three weeks. We've mainly focused on time management as a daily activity, but it's also important to look further out, especially as you develop more responsibilities. By planning to plan, you move from being reactive to proactive, focusing not just on deadlines but also personal goals. First, use distributed practice to look ahead several weeks for big events, assignments, or responsibilities. In your planner, time block by making an appointment with yourself, setting aside times to complete each step toward these larger goals. Also use the half hour each week to plan, prepare, research, or communicate with others in order to advance your goals. These are often the things we want or need to do but never find the time for. For example, if your goal is a promotion at work, use this time to set up an informational interview with your boss or another contact.

STUDENT NOTES

Procrastination

Procrastination is postponing work you should be doing now until later. Nearly all of us have procrastinated on an academic assignment or project. While you may have had some short-term success with procrastination, you also caused yourself unnecessary stress, did not submit your best effort, or failed to acquire all the skills or knowledge the instructor intended the assignment to develop. You also set yourself up for some self-defeating assumptions; ask people why they procrastinate, and many will tell you it's because of a character flaw, such as laziness. In reality, the problem is poor planning and the inability to identify the true difficulty.

If you find yourself putting off tasks, you need to determine the reason you're procrastinating. Students procrastinate because they're overwhelmed by the size of the assignment, unclear about the expectations, unsure how to begin, or uninterested in the work. To determine why you're waiting until the last minute, ask yourself what you're avoiding by waiting to begin. Often, procrastination is merely a means of avoiding something we'd rather not deal with. To overcome your procrastination, ask yourself "What am I avoiding?" Realizing the answer to this question can actually empower you to complete the task.

Ground Picture/Shutterstock.com

Often the answer reveals something you didn't realize was affecting your behavior or coursework. For example, are you avoiding starting your English paper because you don't know how to begin researching the topic? Realizing this problem will allow you to find reasonable and achievable solutions, such as working with a reference librarian, talking to classmates for tips, or making an appointment to see your instructor during office hours.

The answer to the question "What am I avoiding?" will help you find the real reason you're not tackling your responsibilities as planned. Once you have the answer to this question, try these methods to help you start your project.

STUDENT NOTES

Strategies for Overcoming Procrastination

- **Ask yourself what advice you'd give to a classmate or friend facing the same problem.** Sometimes you're too close to the situation to see clear solutions. If you think about the reason you're avoiding the work from a more neutral perspective you may be more likely to think of several reasonable solutions.

- **Set up rewards for yourself.** Find an incentive that motivates you, and then determine what work you need to accomplish in order to receive your reward. Tell yourself that if you complete your outline, you'll treat yourself to a coffee or watch a half hour of TV. But you need to be firm about when you'll use these entertaining distractions, or you'll continually find yourself losing valuable time you need for something else. Grant yourself a precise amount of time to enjoy something fun and then get back to work.

- **Divide the task into smaller pieces so it won't seem as overwhelming.** For example, divide writing a paper into six parts: brainstorming, researching, planning, drafting, revising, and editing. Each individual part is completely manageable. The enormity of the task may be intimidating and preventing you from starting. See page 205 for more information on distributed practice.

- **Remind yourself of the task's purpose.** Ask yourself what you can get out of the assignment, so you don't see the project as an exercise you *have* to complete but as an opportunity. Reading and taking notes on two Anatomy and Physiology chapters not only will fulfill your homework assignment, but it will also make you more knowledgeable once you're a health care professional. You might not be interested in becoming a computer engineer, but learning how to create an Excel spreadsheet in your class could help you make a budget or add another skill to your résumé.

- **Use the Pomodoro Technique.** Your attention decreases the longer you spend focusing on a task; researchers call this the vigilance decrement. In an experiment that tested methods of combatting vigilance decrement by psychology researchers at the University of Illinois, participants' performance decreased significantly over the duration of an activity. However, a group that completed the same task but with two brief breaks stayed focused the entire duration and saw no decrease in performance. Small breaks work!

  Applying this proven strategy to your coursework can combat procrastination. The Pomodoro Technique helps you achieve more in less time by focusing your attention for a concentrated period of time after which you have a brief 5-minute break. Instead of open-ended or unlimited study time, you set a specific amount—usually 25 minutes—to accomplish a specific task. The finite amount of time helps you resist distractions and keep your attention on the task at hand. The result? You're more efficient and effective at completing your academic task.

STUDENT NOTES

Pomodoro Technique

- **Pick a task.** This technique works great for things you've been avoiding or putting off!
- **Set a timer for 25 minutes.**
- **Get to work!**
- **Remain focused.** Jot down things you need to return to later if they pop up, but keep your focus on your selected task.
- **Take 5.** Step away for 5 minutes to stretch or grab a snack.
- **Repeat.** After 5 minutes, start another focused 25-minute session. After your fourth round of this technique, take a longer break of 20–30 minutes.

As you try the Pomodoro Technique, experiment with different times for various activities to find what works best.

Time Management for Online Classes

Time management is especially important for students enrolled in online classes. Establishing a routine that helps you stay organized will ensure that you are devoting the time and effort necessary for success. In an online environment, students often set their own pace; this means that it is up to you to keep up with assignments, deadlines, and participation. Students taking online classes can create structure by setting up a dedicated study schedule that ensures they have time to absorb and engage fully with the material. Treating online classes as you would an in-person course, by showing up to your virtual workspace at the same time each day, can foster a sense of structure and routine.

As you consider your schedule for each online class, consider the pace of the course. When does new material become available? What work is due each week and when? How is your attendance determined? These will differ from class to class, so it is important to consult your syllabus for each online class. For example, your online English class might have weekly deadlines on Fridays at noon while your online Sociology class has weekly deadlines on Tuesdays at midnight. Put these weekly deadlines in your planner, so you don't confuse them.

Students often underestimate the importance of engagement with the course materials, classmates, and instructors in online classes. Online learning can feel a bit isolating. Active participation in discussion boards, contact

STUDENT NOTES

with your instructor, and participation in any synchronous meeting options will foster a sense of connection and offer important learning opportunities.

Having a reliable and comfortable workspace with the appropriate technology will help you work more efficiently in online classes. Make sure you have access to a stable internet connection. Also, to enhance your productivity, familiarize yourself with the college's learning management system (such as Canvas, Blackboard, or Moodle) as well as the course site layout anytime you begin a new online class. Finally, be prepared in case of technical problems. For example, save backup files for your assignments and make sure you know how to contact campus IT support. These strategies will help you meet deadlines in your online courses and successfully complete the courses with minimal stress.

Conclusion

Mastering effective time management is one of the greatest challenges in college. With the transition from high school to college, responsibility for learning largely shifts from the teacher to the student. Understandably, students struggle to adapt to new expectations—such as the 2:1 rule and more complicated schedules—while also trying to overcome ineffective past behaviors, such as procrastination.

However, with practice, the tools outlined in this chapter will help you make better use of your time. Utilizing distributed practice, prioritizing to-do lists, assigning tasks to specific times in your daily planner, and using the strategies for overcoming procrastination will all be worth the effort when you find balance for your competing priorities, experience less stress, learn more, and achieve better grades.

Record your goals for improving your time management habits on the tracking sheet on page 193 for easy reference in the future.

STUDENT NOTES

Time Management Troubleshooting

Problem	Solution
Waiting until the last minute to start papers or projects	• Ask yourself, "What am I avoiding?" • Recognize the stress you're causing yourself and others by putting off the work. • Use distributed practice by placing due dates in your planner as soon as you get your syllabus, backing up several weeks, dividing the paper or project into smaller steps, and then plotting those individual tasks in your planner.
Starting your homework 10 minutes before class	• Use a planner. Write assignments down after every class and then check your planner several times a day to make sure you're on track to complete everything. Adjust if you are not. • Do first the homework you least want to work on. • Realize your motivation for completing the class or college.
Feeling like there isn't enough time in the day	• Use a planner to time block by devoting a specific time to accomplishing your daily activities. • Prioritize by asking yourself what is urgent, what is important, and what is both urgent and important. Complete the tasks according to level of urgency and importance.
Wasting time	• Remind yourself of your goals for college or the course. • Use a planner to stay focused by plotting your daily to-do list and routinely checking your planner throughout the day to make sure you're on track to accomplish your goals. • Use fun activities as a reward for completing less-desirable tasks. Set limits for these reward activities and stick to them. • Utilize the Pomodoro Technique to focus your study time. • Complete the Time Management Self-Evaluation at the end of this chapter. Revise your schedule and activities if your priorities and actual activities don't align.
Not following your planner	• Keep your planner in a way that makes sense to you. If you're obsessed with your smartphone, keep your planner on it. • Create a to-do list and then plot it in your planner. Be specific in your entries. • Consider if your planner meets your needs. Are you using a monthly or weekly planner? Switch to a daily planner. • Complete the Time Management Self-Evaluation. Revise your schedule and activities if your priorities and actual activities don't align.
Not knowing where all your time goes	• Complete the Time Management Self-Evaluation. Revise your schedule and activities if your priorities and actual activities don't align.

STUDENT NOTES

REVIEW QUESTIONS

Chapter 8
Time Management

These questions will help you monitor and evaluate your learning, two important parts of metacognition.

1. Using the three questions to prioritize your to-do list, rank this student's to-do list. In the left column, write I for important and U for urgent. Remember, some items may be both urgent and important, so label them with both letters. Some items may be neither, so don't label them. Then, on the right, rank the items in the order the student should complete them, with 1 being the first task to complete.

Urgent? Important?	Task	Priority
	Read psychology homework (due in two days; won't be graded)	
	Study for math quiz (in four days; 2% of total math grade)	
	Interview for ACA portfolio (due in four weeks; 25% of total ACA grade)	
	Research financial aid options for next semester	
	Look at brother's vacation photos on Instagram	
	Return library books (due yesterday)	
	Go to the tutoring center for help with English paper (due in one week; 20% of total English grade)	

2. Create a to-do list of the things you need to accomplish this week. Then prioritize these tasks by asking yourself the three prioritization questions and using the matrix.

3. In your own words, what is distributed practice?

REVIEW QUESTIONS

4. Select a big project or paper you have due for a class. Apply the strategy of distributed practice by dividing this project into smaller individual tasks. List each step.

5. What are the differences between a planner and a to-do list?

6. What are the three planner types? Which planner type is best for you? Why?

7. What should you ask yourself when you realize you're procrastinating?

8. What are your two biggest time wasters? How will you manage them? Write two goals to help you overcome these time wasters.

9. Where do you need to begin within the Time Management Pyramid? Why?

10. Although Tina wants to be a successful student, she has a serious problem with procrastination. She is taking ENG 111 for the third time, and she has to pass the course this semester because the college's policies state that a student cannot enroll in the same course more than three times without special permission. She failed the course the first two times because she always read the assignments and wrote papers at the last minute. What specific strategies can you recommend that Tina use to stop procrastinating?

11. George has a 20-page research paper for his Abnormal Psychology class due at the end of the semester. The instructor asked that an annotated bibliography, an outline, and a rough draft be turned in at the same time as the final draft. George is feeling overwhelmed because he is taking three other courses and has many assignments to complete for the other courses as well. Help him map out a plan of action for his Abnormal Psychology research paper, so he can fulfill the requirements with minimal stress.

Discussion Questions

Reflect on how you currently manage your time and share one tool or strategy that works well for you. What is one area where you struggle? How might you address it going forward?

REVIEW QUESTIONS

Time Management Self-Evaluation

STUDENT NOTES

Even the most self-aware planners can find themselves having difficulty meeting all their obligations. These moments often occur when we face a new challenge. Times of transition, such as starting a new job, beginning college, or switching semesters can throw the best of planners off course. When your time management needs an adjustment, a time management self-evaluation can help.

The two tables on the following pages can help you identify your problem. Complete **Log 1: Planned Week** according to the instructions below. After finishing Log 1, record daily how you actually spent your time in **Log 2: Actual Week**, so you can see how well your actions matched your intentions. Then you can begin to problem solve to learn how you can use your time effectively.

Log 1: Plan Your Next Week

1. In the orange row at the top, write the days of the week, beginning with today. For example, if today is Wednesday, write W, TH, F, S, S, M, T across the top row.
2. Block out times for your specific commitments, such as class, work, meditation or religious activities, exercising, and family or social events. Also mark out the hours you sleep, which should be no less than 7–9 hours per day. You may want to color-code your schedule with highlighters.
3. Now, with your weekly to-do list in hand, write in the specific times when you'll accomplish this week's tasks, such as writing an essay or reading chapters. Don't forget to consider time you'll need to commute, prepare meals, shower, clean, work out, and complete other important routine tasks.
4. Be sure to include some personal downtime, which is necessary for physical and psychological health.
5. Next, devote specific time to study. Consider the time of day you learn best. Also, make sure you set aside enough time to learn. Remember the 2:1 rule as you schedule your study time. If you are taking 12 credit hours, then you should be studying 24 hours per week.

Is all of your time every day already allocated after step 2 of Log 1? If so, you need to reconsider your schedule because you're overcommitted. While you may think you're maximizing the little time you have, by depleting this resource you're not allowing yourself to be successful. The unexpected will happen, and you'll need time to deal with unplanned events, such as transportation problems or illness. You should not expect yourself to calmly and responsibly address unplanned events if you do not provide yourself the time to do so.

Log 2: Record Your Actual Week

1. Label the top row in the same way as Log 1.
2. Throughout the next week, account for all of your time by recording your activities in the second table at the end of each day.
3. Evaluate your results with the questions that follow the logs.

Log 1: Planned Week

6 a.m.							
6:30							
7:00							
7:30							
8:00							
8:30							
9:00							
9:30							
10:00							
10:30							
11:00							
11:30							
noon							
12:30							
1:00							
1:30							
2:00							
2:30							
3:00							
3:30							
4:00							
4:30							
5:00							
5:30							
6:00							
6:30							
7:00							
7:30							
8:00							
8:30							
9:00							
9:30							
10:00							
10:30							
11:00							
11:30							

Log 2: Actual Week

6 a.m.							
6:30							
7:00							
7:30							
8:00							
8:30							
9:00							
9:30							
10:00							
10:30							
11:00							
11:30							
noon							
12:30							
1:00							
1:30							
2:00							
2:30							
3:00							
3:30							
4:00							
4:30							
5:00							
5:30							
6:00							
6:30							
7:00							
7:30							
8:00							
8:30							
9:00							
9:30							
10:00							
10:30							
11:00							
11:30							

Self-Evaluation

At the end of the week, analyze your use of time by answering the following questions:

1. What surprised you most about your use of time?

2. What went well?

3. For what tasks did you not budget enough time?

4. What activities were most difficult to complete as intended? Why?

5. What time wasters prohibited you from staying on track?

6. What activities did you procrastinate starting? Why did you avoid completing them?

7. Did impulsivity play a part in getting you off track?

Reflection

Your honest answers to these questions can help you more effectively use your time and accomplish all of your weekly responsibilities. Don't get discouraged if your two logs look dramatically different. The goal isn't to stick to the planned week's schedule exactly. The goal is to learn how to create and follow a plan that will help you use your time most effectively so you can fulfill all of your responsibilities while also mitigating stress. Keep in mind that building good time-management habits takes time. Reference the Time-Management Pyramid on page 207 to determine targeted strategies that will help you the most.

Diego Cervo/Shutterstock.com

UNIT 3

Chapter 9

Reading Strategies

Before you read this chapter, reflect on the following:

1. *What do you usually do when you read? Where do you read? Do you underline? Highlight? Take notes in your book?*
2. *How has this been effective for you? How has it not?*
3. *Which of the techniques described below would help you the most now?*

These questions will help you plan your learning, an important part of metacognition.

Instructors often assign college students to read textbook chapters, articles, and online content. However, students sometimes fail to understand what an instructor means by "reading" an assignment. Moving your eyes from left to right down the page is not what instructors intend for you to do. When an instructor assigns reading, he or she actually means any number of the following activities:

- Learn the material on the assigned pages and be ready for a quiz.
- Make note of material on the assigned pages you don't understand and ask questions.
- Begin some foundation work on this concept, so you will be prepared for lecture or in-depth analysis of the concept in class.
- Comprehend what's on these pages and be prepared to contribute your critique to class discussion.
- Know this material well enough to apply it during an upcoming class activity.

STUDENT NOTES

It's helpful to consider the way reading expectations differ between high school and college. **Bloom's Taxonomy,** a hierarchical model that illustrates progressively complex learning objectives, can provide a visual framework for understanding college reading expectations. The illustration below, based on Bloom's Taxonomy, explains what you need to look for when reading and what you will be asked to do with the information at each level. High school reading expectations mainly focused on the lowest levels of learning: you were expected to read for facts and understand main ideas. You may have spent class time learning that basic information. Commonly in college, the expectation is that you have at least completed the bottom two levels on your own so that you can then be ready to apply, analyze, evaluate, or create during class or through an assignment. In some classes, the expectation may be that you are reading for one of the top levels of the taxonomy, such as standards and criteria. Determining your instructor's purpose for the reading assignment will help you focus your reading, which means it'll be easier and you'll be more prepared.

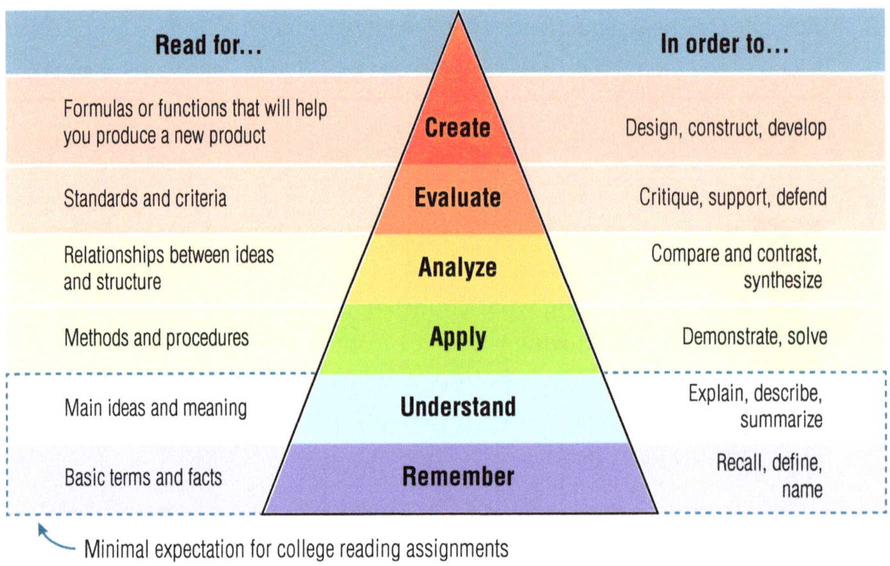

Text Genres

The expected depth of learning isn't the only thing that changes between reading in high school and college. The type of texts you read also change. You will encounter many academic genres in college, but the most common can be divided into three categories, and you will approach each differently. Knowing the purpose, intended audience, and typical structure of these genres will allow you to target your reading and more confidently and easily make sense of the material.

Academic Genre	Provides	Example	Structure	Purpose	How to Read It
Textbooks	Introductory overview of an academic discipline	*Success by Design*	Chronologically or conceptually organized into chapters with headings	Explain established knowledge	Use PSAR (see pages 228–235)
Scholarly Articles	Research studies, reviews, and critiques usually in peer-reviewed journals	"Comparison of Mortality Rates for Male vs. Female Medicare Patients"	Logically structured with required specific sections	Explain new ideas or research	Begin with the abstract (see page 226)
Literature	Entertainment through non-literal expression	*Things Fall Apart*	Follows the narrative arc (see page 227)	Entertain	Identify the narrative arc.

STUDENT NOTES

Textbooks provide an overview of a field for newcomers, presenting foundational principles as an introduction to the discipline, such as *Introduction to Sociology* or *Principles of Biology*. Textbooks are written in an expository style, meaning they intend to explain or inform by presenting the information logically in a clearly structured way, and are often accompanied by photographs, charts, or other images. Most textbooks do not include persuasive writing because they are not arguing for or against a position; they are more factual, which is why some students find them "dry." Textbooks usually share a common organization, dividing the information into units and then chapters with the format illustrated on page 226. Instructors usually assign entire chapters and may instruct students to complete chapter review questions or practice problems typically found at the end of the chapter. Because textbooks are the most commonly assigned course material for undergraduates, this chapter presents a strategy for reading textbooks, PSAR, on pages 228–235.

College disciplines are fields of study, such as Economics, Physics, or Business.

STUDENT NOTES

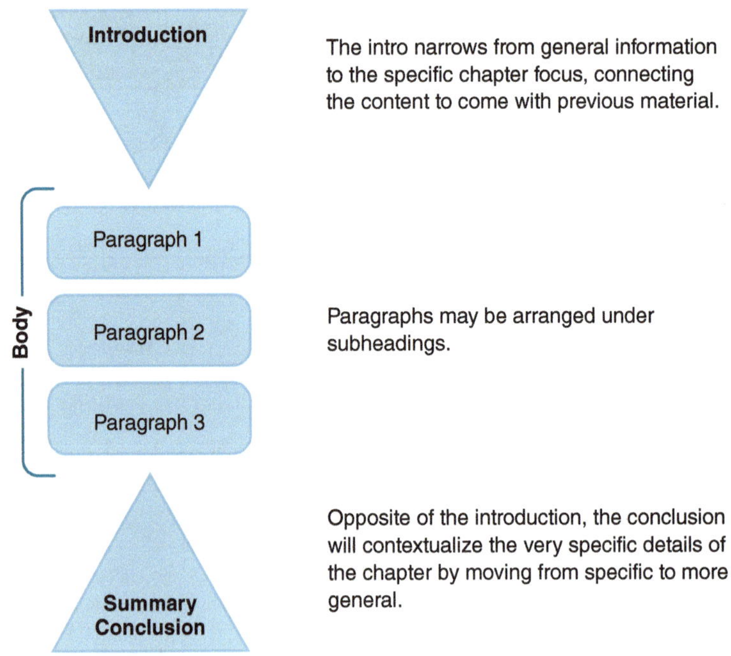

Scholarly articles present new information, usually beginning with the author presenting a new hypothesis or argument and then supporting or refining the claim with research or evidence. The non-fiction articles are found in peer-reviewed journals, written by experts in the field for other experts in the field. That's why journal articles go into great depth and can be very technical, which sometimes presents a challenge to students new to the field. And don't let the word "article" fool you; scholarly articles can be upwards of 10 pages. You'll most likely encounter journal articles when you are in advanced courses or when you are providing evidence for arguments in a research paper. Most often, scholarly articles are found through a library's database and include very detailed tables and graphs. As a new undergraduate, the best place to begin with journal articles is with the **abstract**, which is usually a single paragraph summary of the article that appears at the very beginning of the article. Then read the introduction and conclusion. The literature review section may also be helpful for background information on the topic, and the footnoted sources here may be worth looking into. Don't get too bogged down in the methods and results sections unless warranted.

STUDENT NOTES

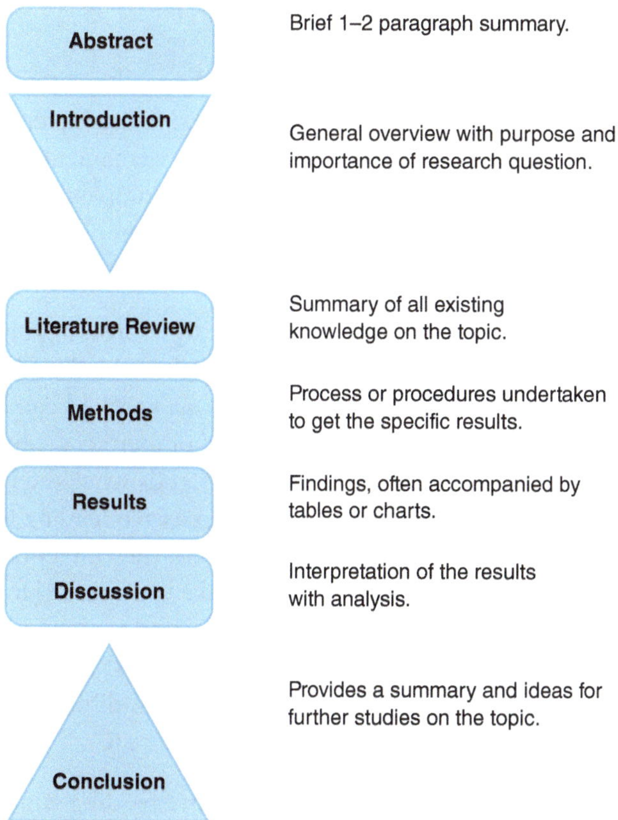

Literature is most often intended to entertain. You will read literature in college in order to understand perspectives, historical moments, or individuals' expressions. Although there are many literary genres, the most common forms in college include novels, short stories, poems, or plays that are usually limited to literature, composition, or drama courses. The text is usually presented in an artistic and sophisticated manner, using advanced language through non-literal or abstract writing to convey a story. Most do not contain images, graphs, headings, or summaries. Literature commonly follows a narrative arc, which consists of five elements. Searching for and identifying these elements will provide you with a task to complete while reading, keeping you focused and helping you make sense of complicated material.

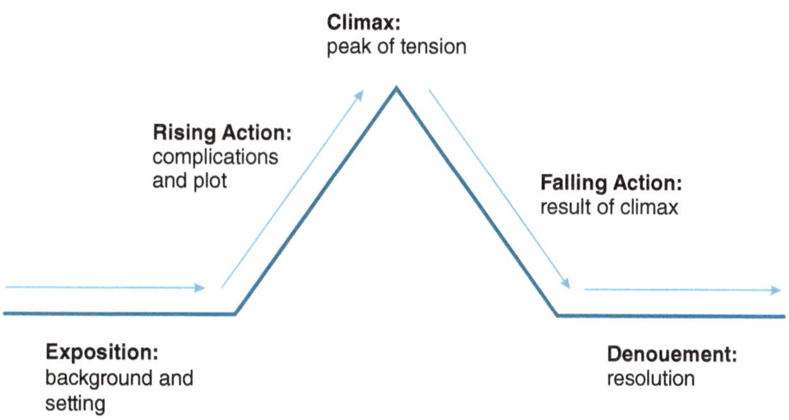

STUDENT NOTES

What do you do when you read? Compare your usual methods to the PSAR strategy presented on the next few pages.

Diego Cervo/Shutterstock.com

PSAR

Now that you understand more about what you'll be reading in college, it's helpful to understand how to read college textbooks. Some material is easy to comprehend. However, since college introduces you to many new ideas, how do you understand what you've read when topics are complex, foreign, or even uninteresting to you? The answer is actually very simple: Be active—not passive—when reading.

Many students *think* they're being active readers by using a highlighter or pen to underline important ideas. However, highlighting and underlining are actually passive techniques. Think about it: a six-year-old can be given a highlighter and manage to mark bold terms and numerous sentences in a college textbook. Does this mean that she understands what she has read? Absolutely not! Highlighting and underlining are passive reading techniques because they do not require you to do anything with the concepts; you're simply marking up your book. How does that make you think? How does that help you process or understand information? While you may have used highlighting and underlining with some success previously, as you move into higher-level college classes the material will increase in difficulty, and you'll need different skills to make sense of the material.

For this increased difficulty, you'll need to use active reading strategies. **Active reading** forces you to interact with the presented ideas through annotating, or taking notes while you read. During active reading, you write notes in your book or on a piece of paper. While you may already make a few notes here or there—such as when you encounter a new term—active reading is more than this. Active reading requires you to ask questions, compare new information with your past knowledge and experiences, note your reactions and judgments to what you've read, and consolidate ideas in brief summaries. There are many active reading methods you can research and use, but all of them have the following basic components, which can be remembered through the acronym **PSAR**:

Prepare,
Survey,
Annotate,
Review.

Prepare

Prepare Yourself

Before you read, make sure you're ready to learn and have set realistic expectations. At the end of a day, your body and mind don't have the necessary energy to tackle learning new material. Additionally, we often learn material in small chunks rather than in lengthy quantities. Waiting until the end of the day to read dozens of pages isn't reasonable; instead, divide your assignment into smaller sections to read at more optimal times of the day. For example, if you need to read two chapters for Thursday, read five pages at a time over four to five days by using your breaks between classes and time during lunch.

Set an intention. Be specific about how much you want to read in a certain amount of time. For example, if you have an hour between classes, it would be realistic to read and take notes on 15 pages. If you reach your goal, reward yourself. You could go for a walk later, meet a friend in the cafeteria for lunch, or watch your favorite TV show that night. These rewards provide a much-needed mental break to refresh your concentration and motivation. Reward yourself when you reach your goals, but also make sure you get back on track so you don't find yourself getting drawn into watching more TV than you intended or not finishing the rest of your reading.

Also, estimate your reading time effectively. College students often underestimate the amount of time actually required to read and understand a text. On average, students read about 200 words per minute when learning. College textbooks contain about 350–400 words per page; therefore, you can probably read about one page per two minutes. However, this estimate does not include time to make notes (see the A of PSAR) or time required to make sense of particularly dense material. Therefore, it's much more helpful to estimate between three and four minutes per page of reading. Use this guide to help you plan your time effectively. If you have a reading assignment that contains twenty pages, you'll need between an hour and an hour and twenty minutes to understand the material and complete your reading. Consider how much you need to read and provide yourself adequate time to complete the reading to ensure better comprehension.

This estimate also does not consider your familiarity with the material. If you are reviewing a topic you're familiar with, it's a good idea to **skim**. When you skim a textbook chapter, you usually read the following parts:

- the first paragraph of the chapter,
- the first two lines and last line of the other paragraphs, and
- the last paragraph of the chapter.

If you see any unknown terms, names, or dates, if there are illustrations or charts that don't immediately make sense, or if you are confused, you should stop skimming and instead read that information carefully. After you skim, you should be able to state the main idea and provide a general overview of the text. If you cannot, you should go back and fully read the sections you cannot summarize.

STUDENT NOTES

See pages 210–211 for the Pomodoro Technique, which is a structured way to focus tasks such as reading.

The estimate that you'll need three to four minutes per page of text is a generalization. What factors affect whether you can read the material at a faster pace? What factors would force you to slow down?

STUDENT NOTES

Finally, prepare yourself for reading by taking care of your body. Eat small, healthy meals throughout the day and make sure you're getting enough rest. Studying after a large fast-food meal isn't very productive. Also, avoid caffeinated or sugary drinks; although they may provide a quick energy boost, these short-lived periods of energy are followed by an energy slump. Prepare your body and mind to be alert. Review Chapter 3 for additional wellness strategies.

What are your biggest distractions when reading? What do you need to do in order to minimize those distractions?

Prepare Your Environment

Create a space that's conducive to learning new material. Sit upright at a desk or table; sitting in a recliner or on your bed doesn't signal that you're intending to get work done. Let your friends and family know that you're studying and can't be reached. Turn off your phone and put it out of sight. Go to the library or find a room with a door you can close. Avoid common areas where you might run into people you know or overhear conversations.

Survey

After you've prepared yourself, **survey** the text. Start by looking at the table of contents in the beginning of the book to see what you'll be learning and how it fits with other course information. Within the assigned chapter or section, look for chapter headings and subheadings and turn these into questions. Look at the metacognition questions at the beginning of Chapters 8–12 of *Success by Design* or examples of the kinds of questions to ask before you read a chapter. Think about what you already know about the material. Begin finding connections between the material and your personal life or previous academic experience. For example, if you looked at the table of contents for Chapter 12 of this book, you'd see the following list. Look at the comments to see how you could achieve some of the mentioned goals of surveying this chapter:

By surveying the text in this way, you'll have an easier time staying focused because you'll be more invested in discovering answers to your questions and seeing if your ideas are mentioned. You can also scan the chapter for bold or italicized words to see how much new vocabulary you'll be learning. Unlike skimming, which aims to improve your overall understanding of a chapter's main topic, **scanning** usually has the goal of locating specific information within the chapter. When scanning, you usually have a specific target in mind, such as finding bolded or italicized words. Scanning is particularly helpful during the R step of PSAR, reviewing. See the Review step for more on scanning.

STUDENT NOTES

Annotate

To actively read, you must have a pen or pencil in hand and you must annotate. **Annotating** is taking notes while you read. It's easiest to make notes in the textbook, but you can also annotate in a notebook.

Think of annotating as having a discussion with the text. No one likes a one-sided conversation, so interact with the text by annotating.

Why annotate? Because students' biggest problem with reading isn't that they can't comprehend the material, it's that they don't think enough about the content. Annotating forces students to interact with the material, which helps make sense of the ideas presented and allows readers to recall the information later. Annotating also makes reading less painful because it provides a specific task to accomplish when reading. In other words, annotating is a simple process that makes it easier to understand what you read.

For examples of methods you can use when taking notes in a notebook, see Chapter 10.

What kinds of things should be noted? How is annotating actually done? Consider this guide:

Note	Specifically	How to Annotate
Important Information	Definitions, terms, significant examples, helpful diagrams	Develop a consistent system. For example, box key terms, star significant examples, and circle helpful diagrams.
Questions	Questions you have as you read	If your question isn't answered by the time you finish the assigned material, ask your instructor in class.
Responses	Your reactions to the material	How do you feel about what's being discussed and the way the author presents it? Draw a smiley face if the concept is funny or seems like a great idea. If the topic seems confusing, draw a frowny face with a question mark above it.
Conclusions	Brief summaries	Write a few words or sentences per section to summarize the main ideas. You'll process the information and create a reference for when you need to study for the test.

wavebreakmedia/Shutterstock.com

STUDENT NOTES

One of the reasons this book has wide margins is to provide the space for you to annotate the material. Try annotating page 281 from Chapter 12 on test-taking strategies in your book. Then, look at the annotating example below to compare your annotations with the ones completed here.

Annotating Example of Page 281 in Chapter 12:

CHAPTE
Test-Tak

During the Test

As soon as you are allowed to begin, immediately write down formulas, mnemonic devices (see page 270 in Chapter 11), or specific dates or names you're afraid you'll forget. This method, called a **mind dump**, will allow you to concentrate on the test rather than on remembering.

Never heard of this. Is this OK with my instructor?

After you've written down this information, write your name on the test materials and then **survey** the test. Look over the exam to determine its length and which sections are worth the most points. Then, decide how you will budget your time effectively to get the most points. Will you begin with the essay on the last page? Should you start with the identifications in the middle of the test? Surveying the test and planning your test strategy should take no more than two to three minutes.

* Survey = strategize amt. of time and order of ?s by looking over text before beginning

* Great strategy for Chem tests *

Make sure you don't foolishly give away points by failing to read the directions. Students often skip the directions out of nervousness and haste. However, this can be a very costly mistake. When reading the directions, annotate them by marking verbs (for example, *match, consider, evaluate, circle, define, compare and contrast*) and any other words that stand out to you in the instructions. Make sure you know your task before you write in any answers. If your instructor has asked you to compare and contrast two events, discussing just the similarities will cause you to lose points. Sometimes

I do this!

Examine the annotations this student made. Of the four things to note when annotating (important information, questions, responses, and conclusions), which did this student include? Did she forget any?

Shutterstock.com

STUDENT NOTES

Review

After you read, **review** the material. Scan your textbook and notes for terms, examples, or ideas presented during class lecture. Remember, when you scan, you have a specific target in mind. Since you probably read the material before class lecture, it would be a good idea to scan your book for terms the instructor introduced, especially if you still have questions about a concept. Annotate these ideas if you did not previously. You may not have realized how important these ideas were when you first read the chapter.

Look over your annotations periodically. Taking five to ten minutes to review notes while they're fresh helps commit them to memory. You will fill in gaps more easily than if you wait until before the test to review your notes. This short review can save you time later when you're studying for a test or completing a project. In this way, your annotations are great reference tools, since they likely include the most important information from the chapter. Reviewing these annotations is more time-saving than re-skimming or re-reading the entire chapter.

You can also try reciting your notes. Shut your book and put away your notes. Speak aloud what you've learned. You can divide this up by heading or section. Check back in your book. What did you have a hard time explaining? What did you not remember? Make note of that information in your annotations. Reciting notes can be especially helpful to students with strong verbal learning style preferences (see Chapter 4 for descriptions of specific learning style preferences).

Don't forget that reviewing your notes can also help you get more out of your time in class. Review annotations and other notes right before class to prepare for the day's lessons, discussions, and activities.

Using PSAR Strategically to Overcome Common Reading Problems

When reading, students often have problems in one of two areas. Either they cannot remember specific points and facts they've read (supporting details), or they cannot identify overarching concepts (main ideas). Some of the problem may lie in students' learning style preferences and previous educational experiences. For example, sensing learners and students who have previously studied fact-based subjects and proven, systematic approaches to problem solving may more naturally focus on definitions and specific facts while ignoring abstractions or large concepts. On the other hand, intuitive learners and students who prefer abstract thinking over rote memorization may be drawn to large themes and relationships between ideas when they read, not paying as much attention to details. See Chapter 4 for more

STUDENT NOTES

Mnemonic devices are memory tools. Learn more about them on page 270 in Chapter 11.

information on learning style preferences, including tips for developing a more balanced approach to acquiring new knowledge.

When encountering such problems while reading, return to PSAR and use the mnemonic to improve your reading strategy. Here are two ways to tailor PSAR for common reading problems.

Difficulty Identifying Main Ideas

Prepare: Set your intentions on seeing the larger picture of what you read. Tell yourself that while you will not ignore details, you will not concentrate on them alone. Write the questions "How?" and "Why?" at the top of your notes, so you'll concentrate on these while reading and not the "What?," "Where?," "Who?," and "When?"—usually items of detail.

Survey: Look over the chapter and turn the headings and subheadings into questions. Examine questions at the end of the chapters, especially those that ask about relationships between ideas, such as essay questions. Keep all of these questions in mind as you read the chapter.

Annotate: As you read, summarize sections or paragraphs. Periodically return to your list of questions (from the Survey step) to see if you're able to answer any part of them. Continually try to answer the questions "How?" and "Why?" as you read.

Review: After you've read, try to answer the questions you've posed. Recite your answers aloud to make sure you really can explain what you've learned from the readings. If you cannot, return to the text and re-read. Keep in mind that introductions and conclusions often contextualize, connect, and summarize main ideas and key concepts.

Difficulty Remembering Supporting Details

See page 264 in Chapter 11 for tips on using flash cards effectively.

Prepare: Set out flash cards to write down specific information. Also have various highlighters on hand to categorize information: blue as definitions, yellow as important names, and pink as other specific information of note.

Survey: Look at how the author notes specific information. Are terms or names bolded? Are key terms listed at the beginning or end of the chapter? Write these items on the front of flash cards.

Annotate: As you read, write on the flash cards any other specific items you read, such as steps in a process or chronological order. Highlight the information in the text according to the color key you determined earlier.

Review: Test your knowledge in two ways. First, look at each flash card you created during the survey step and try to write your understanding of that term's significance on its backside. Double-check your answers with the information in the chapter or in the glossary if your book has one. Also, look at the headings and sub-headings for each section. Can you provide the answer aloud for each of these questions in each section: who, what, when, where, why, and how? If so, you have a great understanding of what you read. If not, go back and find the answers in the chapter.

STUDENT NOTES

Tish1/Shutterstock.com

Reading Strategies for Online Classes

Online classes require students to utilize effective reading strategies. Students taking online classes read not only the college textbook, but assignment guidelines, rubrics, lecture notes, and other course materials without the same guidance from the instructor that would be more readily available in a seated classroom environment. Therefore, it is especially necessary to turn to readings for identifying central ideas, understanding complex concepts, and carefully attending to course and assignment guidelines.

Utilizing the active reading techniques outlined in this chapter will help students recall important information and ensure comprehension for online forums, as well as exams and projects. The independent nature of online learning leaves room for students to engage with readings in ways that align well with specific learning style preferences. For example, a student with a preference for visual learning might draw graphs or diagrams that align with readings, while a student with a preference for verbal learning might read the material into a voice recorder for later listening while exercising or driving.

Even when your classes are online, you want to make sure to have a pencil and paper handy. Actively reading and annotating your text helps you stay alert and engage with complex material. It can be tempting to type notes

STUDENT NOTES

since you spend so much time at a computer for online classes, but research shows that varying your annotation methods, including handwriting your notes, improves retention and comprehension.

Record your goals for improving your reading strategies on the tracking sheet on page 193 for easy reference in the future.

Conclusion

Remember that reading requires adaptation. You'll read a wide variety of texts in college, and you shouldn't assume that just because you're a skilled reader in one subject that you'll be as proficient a reader in another area. Reading material varies, as does what your instructor or discipline expects you to take away from the reading. While you may read and understand specific and detailed information well—such as definitions and formulas in a math or science class—you may have a harder time in classes that focus on broader themes—such as theories in a philosophy class or cultural developments in a history class. When you find yourself struggling in a class, examine your reading style and adapt your focus within PSAR to those areas of greatest importance to the course.

Keep in mind, too, that reading is a skill that requires practice, and everyone can improve their reading. While completing the steps of PSAR may seem time-consuming, the more you practice them, the more ingrained they will become and the less effort you'll need to use them. You'll not only become faster, but you'll also understand more of what you read.

STUDENT NOTES

Reading Troubleshooting

Problem	Solution
Struggling to understand what you read because you encounter words you don't know	• Use the context surrounding the word to try to determine its meaning. • Divide the word into its parts (affixes) and use these to help you narrow the definition. • If you still don't know the word, look it up in the book's glossary or online dictionary. • Keep a log of new words and their meanings in the back of your notebook. Review these periodically.
Getting bored or distracted	• Consider the text's genre, and read with the goal of identifying the key parts shown in the diagrams on pages 226–227. • Revisit the P of PSAR. See pages 228–230 for tips on adequately preparing your environment. • Remember that reading doesn't just require your eyes. To read actively, you must have a pen in your hand, and you must be taking notes. • Make sure you're annotating well. Don't just mark new words, dates, and names. Challenge yourself to write a question, response, or conclusion for each paragraph. • Revisit the S of PSAR. Survey the chapter to ask questions. Turning chapter headings into questions will help you concentrate and read with the intent of finding their answers. Having a question in mind can invest you more in reading to find the answers. • Utilize the Pomodoro Technique to structure your reading and be more efficient and effective. See pages 210–211.
Having trouble remembering what you've read	• Focus on improving the A of PSAR. Annotating requires you to interact with the text, which is key to remembering the information. How could you annotate better? • Turn chapter headings into questions and quiz yourself by trying to answer the questions verbally. • Be strategic in your PSAR approach. See the two approaches on pages 233–235.

STUDENT NOTES

REVIEW QUESTIONS

Chapter 9

Reading Strategies

These questions will help you monitor and evaluate your learning, two important parts of metacognition.

1. Without looking back in the book, can you name the steps of PSAR? Can you explain aloud to yourself the meaning and importance of each step? If you've forgotten any of them, return to the chapter, scan for PSAR, and then reread that section.

2. What should you do before you read? Why?

3. Use the steps below to practice the S step of PSAR and survey Unit 3 of this book.

   a. Turn the title, headings, and subheadings into questions.

   b. What connections can you make between the material in Unit 3 and what you've already learned in this class?

   c. What connections can you make between the material in Unit 3 and your personal life?

   d. What connections can you make between the material in Unit 3 and your previous academic experiences?

4. Of the S and A steps of PSAR, which do you think you're most likely to forget to do? How will you make sure you do it?

5. Do you usually complete the R steps to reading? If not, how will using these suggestions pay off?

6. Examine your current use of annotating. Look at any two pages in Chapter 2, which you've already read. Use this checklist below to assess your annotating skills.

   Annotating checklist

   - ☐ The page is marked with multiple symbols and drawings so that I can locate important information quickly.
   - ☐ I've written questions in the margin.
   - ☐ I've written responses in the margin.
   - ☐ I've written conclusions in the margin.

   If you have not placed a check in any of these boxes, go back and review the information for that concept on pages 231–232.

7. Keisha is in her first semester of college and is taking 11 credit hours: ACA 122 (College Transfer Success), CIS 110 (Introduction to Computers), PSY 150 (General Psychology), and MAT 143 (Quantitative Literacy). She never tried very hard in high school but still managed to graduate with a 3.0 GPA. She's doing well in her classes, except for CIS 110 and PSY 150. Both regularly have multiple-chapter reading assignments. In PSY 150, she's failed her first test and all three of her quizzes. In CIS 110, she hasn't had a test yet, but she feels completely lost. She's frustrated with the classes. She blames her instructors for not teaching well and is thinking about dropping the classes. Based on this chapter, what advice would you give to Keisha to help her with her problems?

8. Natasha is almost ready to transfer to a four-year institution to pursue a degree in English. She's taking the last of her courses, including BIO 112 (General Biology II) and HIS 131 (American History I). Unfortunately, she's not doing well in either class. She finds that she can't remember the specific terms the instructors test. She does well on the essays and short-answer questions, but she fails the matching and fill-in-the-blank sections. She's embarrassed because she's done the reading assignments but still can't recall what she's read. Plus, she's even questioning her ability to pursue an English major because she is doubting that she can read and understand different texts. What two strategies from this chapter do you think would help Natasha most?

Discussion Questions

So far, what differences have you noticed in your college reading assignments compared with reading assignments in high school? How are the books similar or different? What about the ways in which the assigned readings are used?

REVIEW QUESTIONS

Eduard Stelmakh/Shutterstock.com

UNIT 3

Chapter 10

Note-Taking Strategies

Before you read this chapter, reflect on the following:

1. *For which classes do you take the best notes? Why is that?*
2. *For what classes or what kinds of material do you need a different approach?*
3. *Which of the following techniques can you begin using this semester to help you?*

These questions will help you plan your learning, an important part of metacognition.

In college, it is assumed you're taking notes over readings and activities during class because writing things down helps you remember them. College tests cover much more material (often three or more chapters) than exams in high school (often only one chapter or section). You cannot expect yourself to remember information from a class lecture that took place a month ago if you only listened. Another reason notes are so important in college: they are great reference tools. You can go back and review the recorded information from your notes, but if you just listen in class, you have nothing to refer to. Also, your notes will often contain information that will be necessary to know for a test, presentation, paper, or project. Finally, taking notes keeps you active during the class. You'll be more focused and engaged and less prone to distractions and a loss of concentration. Research shows that the better your notes, the better you do in the course. Taking notes is a surefire way to indicate to yourself that you want to pass a course.

Annotating, or taking notes while you read, is discussed specifically in Chapter 9.

STUDENT NOTES

When to Take Notes

While there are times you should be taking notes outside of class, most students think they know when to take notes during class: when the instructor writes on the board. However, passively copying only what the instructor writes on the board onto paper is not effective. Taking notes requires active thinking and listening. Besides, there are many other times throughout class when you should be writing down important information. Here are some additional times you should be taking notes.

Class Discussions

Note instructors' questions as they lead class discussions. Your classmates' responses and instructors' comments on those responses should also be written down. They'll likely appear on a quiz or test or will be expected to be addressed in an assigned essay.

Phovoir/Shutterstock.com

Student-Led Presentations

Instructors try various methods to present information to students. Sometimes they assign students to present the information to each other in order for students to practice communication skills and to meet learning goals for the course. Often during peer presentations, other students do not take notes because the information is not directly coming from the instructor. However, think like the instructor. Why is he devoting valuable class time to student presentations? What does he want you to learn from the activity? Consider these questions and use the answers to guide your note taking during peer-led presentations. Add to your notes anything the instructor asks the group or adds to their presentation.

Group or Paired Activities

As with student-led presentations, many students erroneously assume that group work or activities aren't note-worthy. If an instructor spends valuable class time to work in pairs or groups, you should include the information or experiences from these efforts in your notes. Don't just take notes to report back. Take notes as the activity is discussed or analyzed, too.

Explanations of Assignments

Often, you're presented with an assignment sheet for important projects or papers. While the instructor discusses the assignment, make notes in the margins of the assignment sheet, so you'll have additional guidance when you begin work. When discussing an assignment, instructors often provide important tips and explanations based on past students' performances, and this advice will be very helpful to you as you complete yours.

STUDENT NOTES

Demonstrations

Don't forget to have your notebook and pen ready for important information the instructor points out during demonstrations. Just because you're huddled around a lab table, car engine, or practice "dummy" doesn't mean you shouldn't bring along your note-taking supplies to write down questions, explanations, or tips.

What to Take Notes On

Always begin your notes by writing down the date, class, and topic. By writing these things down, you'll know when notes were presented. If your instructor puts an agenda on the board for each class, make sure you copy it down at the beginning of your notes for the day. Having the agenda within your class notes will be like having a table of contents for that day's notes. Also, you'll process the expectations of the class and be more focused on the class's progression by knowing what to anticipate next.

Most importantly, during class write down any information that **SOARS** above the rest. That's anything that is

Singled out,
On the board,
Asked,
Repeated, or
Stressed.

Singled Out

Your instructor will spend time addressing significant terms, processes, dates, events, or examples, which should signal to you that this information is important. When the instructor singles out information by devoting time to it as a topic, you should write it down. Conversely, when he or she mentions a word, name, or date in passing, that's usually the instructor's way of providing extra information, not core class content, so that information isn't always necessary to write down. However, if time is spent singling out an idea for discussion or elaboration, then it is note-worthy.

Information that's singled out often can be put on flash cards, so when you review your notes after class, go ahead and make your flash cards. See page 264 for tips on making and using flash cards.

On the Board

This category not only includes board work, but also information projected from the computer or overhead. When the instructor spends time and/or energy presenting terms, diagrams, outlines, or other information on the board or overhead, you should write this information in your notes. Try to use the same formatting as your instructor since it may be a form of a visual organizer that can help you understand relationships between concepts. (For additional tips about taking notes over PowerPoints, see page 254.)

STUDENT NOTES

Asked

Write down questions posed by the instructor, those asked by classmates, and any questions that pop into your head while listening. Write down the answers as well. Make sure to follow up on any unanswered questions after class. Often, the questions posed by the instructor appear on future quizzes and tests.

Repeated

Any terms or explanations repeated by the instructor should be noted. Listen for main ideas that are revisited as well. If time is spent reviewing a concept in class, this should signal its importance. Make note of what the instructor says about it.

Stressed

Instructors rarely literally say "This is important!" Instead, it's expected that you infer the significance through verbal and non-verbal cues. When the instructor pauses, changes her tone of voice, or varies her pace of words, she may be implying that the information is crucial. Also, watch for gestures she makes with her hands or arms, as well as any underlining or circling of items on the board. Make a note of the information the instructor is stressing and why.

Think like the instructor to write better notes. Instructors are charged with covering a large quantity of content in little time, so they must be efficient and clear. Consider how your instructor accomplishes this. What does she spend time and energy on? Making a handout? Creating a presentation? Defining important terms in class? Demonstrating a process? Get in the mind of your instructor by considering why she is presenting the information to realize what is most important and what should be included in notes.

Monkey Business Images/Shutterstock.com

How to Take Notes

STUDENT NOTES

Do you find yourself writing down too much information? Do you not refer back to notes you've taken? If so, the problem may be that you're not taking notes effectively. Follow these recommendations to make your notes more helpful.

Before Class

Separate your class notes either by committing one notebook for each class or by using a large binder and keeping notes for each class under separate tabs.

Prepare yourself mentally by ridding your mind of any outside thoughts or distractions. When you walk through the classroom door, tell yourself that you're leaving your emotional stressors outside the door until class is over so that you can concentrate.

Be physically prepared, as well. Get enough sleep the night before. Use the bathroom, have a small snack, or get a drink before class begins, so you won't be distracted. Eating during class means you're not concentrating fully on taking notes.

It's a good idea to review your notes from the previous class and annotations you took while reading your textbook. If you've marked questions from homework, reading, or review, read over them so you'll know what you need to ask your instructor to clarify.

Upon arriving to class, sit where you won't be distracted. Don't sit in lab near the guy who spends class time on YouTube. The temptation to watch what he is doing—rather than keep up with the instructor and your notes—will be too great. You need to not just hear, but to listen and think about presented material in order to take good notes. Make sure you have all your necessary supplies. Get them out before class begins and start writing down the class, date, topic, and agenda.

During Class

To take good notes, you need to avoid distractions. Put your phone on silent and place it in your bag. Only keep on your desk what you need for taking notes. To stay focused, notice when your mind wanders and come back to the activity by writing down the topic the instructor is discussing at that point. Put a question mark in the margin where you drifted so that you can fill in your notes later.

STUDENT NOTES

While taking notes, it is important not only to consider what SOARS but also the layout of your notes. Make sure you don't cover your entire notebook paper with writing. Instead, leave white space on your paper. About two inches of white space on the side or bottom of your notes will allow enough room for you to add additional information and questions when you review your notes. You can also put question marks in the unused white space when you don't understand something, so you will remember to ask the instructor after class. As you take notes on the presented material, don't forget to write down your own reactions or thoughts that arise as you listen. Were you surprised? Was something odd or funny? Did something remind you of a concept from another class or your real-world experience?

It's nearly impossible to write down everything that's said in a class period. It's also entirely ineffective. Writing down only the information that SOARS above the rest will allow you to capture just the important information, but you might still need to be faster in your note taking. Therefore, don't write concepts down word for word. Use short phrases instead of full sentences and paraphrase or summarize information.

Abbreviating common words or phrases also helps capture more information rapidly. You can use common abbreviations or you can try omitting all the vowels of longer words to speed your note taking. Incorporating new abbreviations into your note taking will take some practice, but they soon become ingrained. Most importantly, devise a method that you will understand and use, so that you can move from focusing on how to take notes (method) to the ideas presented (content). See the following table for some common abbreviations.

Mark the abbreviations you don't use but could begin using this semester.

Abbreviation	Longhand
ppl	people
info	information
gov't	government
natl	national
diff	different
thru	through
b/c	because
b/w	between
b4	before
w/	with
w/o	without
imp	important

Abbreviation	Longhand
aka	also known as, name changed
ex	example
@	at
+ or &	and
–	decrease or less
+	increase or more
=	equals, is, means
→	results in, leads to, caused
vs	against, as opposed to
♀	woman
♂	man
Δ	change, transform

STUDENT NOTES

In addition to regularly using abbreviations and developing your own shorthand, there are several note-taking methods that you can use to help organize your notes. The informal outline, two column, and Cornell methods model well-tested patterns for note taking. In the following examples, the students are taking notes on the same class lecture in a biology class. Compare the format and content of these notes to see if you can determine the characteristics of each style. Don't worry: you don't need to know anything about biology to be able to evaluate the notes.

Informal Outline

This **informal outline** method visually organizes the presented material by spacing information out on the page. Don't underestimate the importance of visually organized notes, especially if you have a visual or kinesthetic learning style preference (see Chapter 4 for information about learning styles). You can "see" relationships between items and infer them without thinking about them once you've taken notes in this form.

There are two advantages to notes taken in informal outline style. First, the method allows you to show relationships between ideas without spelling them out. How? Items of greater detail are placed underneath their larger group terms. Have a look at the note-taking example on the next page. You can tell that 1, 2, and 3 are all cell theories because they are all listed under the "CELL THEORY" heading. Also, the more to the right the item begins, the greater the level of specificity. While "TYPES OF CELLS" is a general term that lacks additional or detailed information, we can know that cells are divided by their functions, two of which are synthesis and reproduction, levels of details that are far from the left margin due to their level of specificity.

Further, items of similar importance are spaced at the same distance from the left margin. "Membranes" and "Organelles" are equidistant from the left margin. That equal positioning indicates that they are also of the same relative importance. In comparison, the fact that membranes function like a wall with holes in it is a detail that's not as important as knowing what organelles are and their basic functioning. Informal outlines convey these relationships succinctly without spelling them out in words.

The second characteristic of this note-taking method is the use of white space at the bottom of the page. Notes should be reviewed as soon as possible after class, and not more than 24 hours after the class ends. When reviewing notes, you need space to write down summaries, questions, and additional information you may have missed during class. You must leave space to allow for such reviews. Therefore, do not cover the entire page with information. As you take notes, leave the bottom third to quarter of the page blank for later comments and questions. Leaving space for review is critical, which is why all three methods discussed in this chapter require leaving white space.

Later in this chapter, you'll find strategies for what to do when reviewing your notes.

STUDENT NOTES

Of course, the challenge of this note-taking method is writing in outline form, especially for an instructor who does not present the information in such a linear, clear format. However, the more you practice this format, the easier it will become.

Informal Outline Example

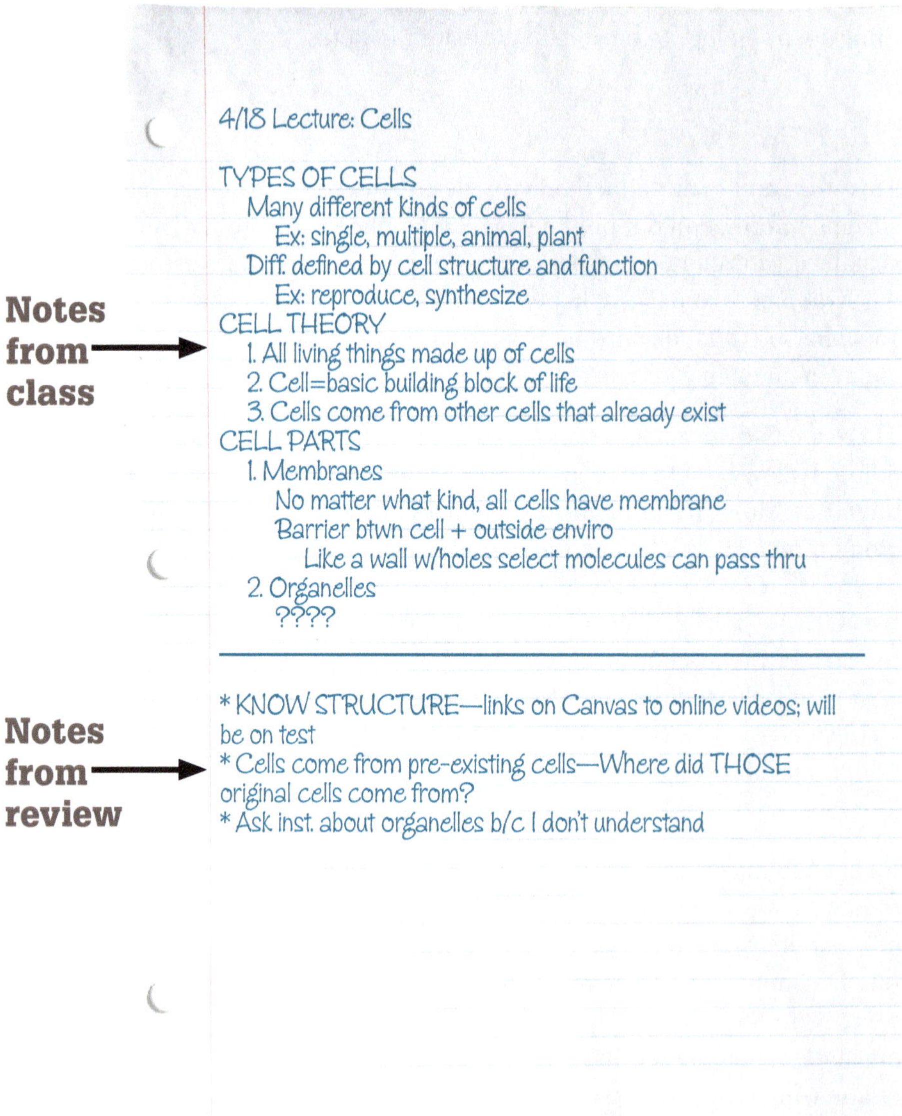

4/18 Lecture: Cells

TYPES OF CELLS
- Many different kinds of cells
  - Ex: single, multiple, animal, plant
- Diff. defined by cell structure and function
  - Ex: reproduce, synthesize

CELL THEORY
1. All living things made up of cells
2. Cell=basic building block of life
3. Cells come from other cells that already exist

CELL PARTS
1. Membranes
   - No matter what kind, all cells have membrane
   - Barrier btwn cell + outside enviro
     - Like a wall w/holes select molecules can pass thru
2. Organelles
   - ????

* KNOW STRUCTURE—links on Canvas to online videos; will be on test
* Cells come from pre-existing cells—Where did THOSE original cells come from?
* Ask inst. about organelles b/c I don't understand

STUDENT NOTES

Two Column

Another note-taking method is the **two column** design. Here, you fold the paper in half, making a crease down the center of the paper. You take notes only on the right side of the crease. When you review your notes, write a question on the blank left side that corresponds to the ideas on the right. In effect, you've created a self-test (page 265 in Chapter 11). You can easily quiz yourself by folding back the answers. Review the questions and when you need to check your responses, unfold the flap.

Two Column Example

Study questions written during review →

4/18 Lecture: Cells	
What are 4 types of cells?	TYPES OF CELLS Many different kinds of cells Ex: single, multiple, animal, plant Diff. defined by cell structure + function Ex: reproduce, synthesis
What are the 3 cell theories?	CELL THEORY 1. All living things made up of cells 2. Cell=basic build. block of life 3. Cells come from other cells that already exist
What are the cell parts?	CELL PARTS 1. Membranes No matter what kind, all cells have membrane Barrier btwn cell + outside Like wall w/holes select molecules can pass thru
What are organelles?	2. Organelles — ????

← **Notes from class**

STUDENT NOTES

Cornell Method

Unlike the informal outline method, the Cornell method of note taking does not use hanging indents or specific spacing to indicate relationships between concepts. However, the **Cornell method** does create sections designed for specific types of notes and reflection, as do the other two methods. The Cornell method of note taking, also called the **T method**, requires you to divide your note-taking paper into sections before you begin taking notes. To do this, draw a vertical line about two to three inches from the left-hand margin. Draw a horizontal line about three inches from the bottom of the page. Your paper should look something like the example below.

Cornell Method Example

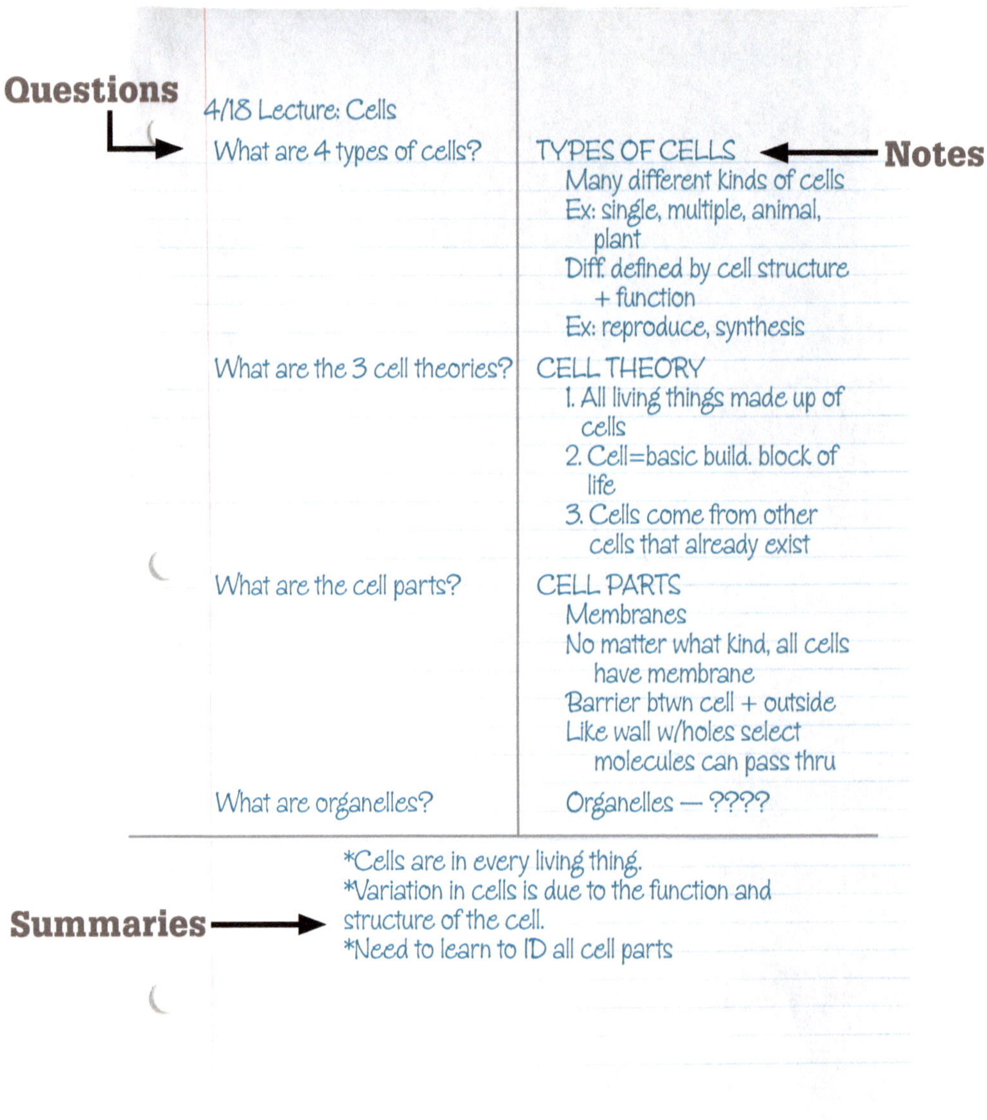

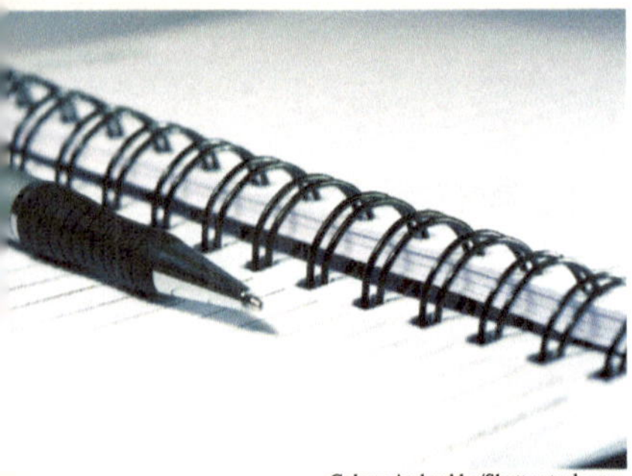
Galyna Andrushko/Shutterstock.com

Begin by writing your in-class notes in the larger right section (labeled "Notes" in the example). During and after class, write in the left quadrant any questions you have as you take notes or as you review them, such as ideas you don't understand, questions posed by the instructor, and possible test questions. At the bottom, write summaries of the information as you review it. The notes contain the same information as the informal outline method and the two column notes, so you can easily compare and contrast the three note-taking methods.

STUDENT NOTES

After Class

Don't just shove your notes in your bag at the end of class and forget about them. Before you rush out of the classroom door, consider doing the following:

- Look over your notes to see if you need to clarify any of your abbreviations or ask any questions. Fill in gaps or talk to your instructor before you pack up and leave.
- Write down the "muddiest point"—something you still don't understand and need clarification on. Try to find clarification in your book or notes. If you can't, ask your instructor.
- Write a one-minute summary. Spend just a minute writing down what you learned from the class.

Never allow a classmate to borrow your notebook! Go with the classmate to a photocopy machine or let him take pictures on his phone. Your notes are too valuable to risk losing.

After class, review notes immediately—and definitely within 24 hours—to commit the information to memory. Why should you look at your notes so soon after you've taken your notes? The information is still fresh in your mind but not exactly "learned" yet, so you have the opportunity to solidify that knowledge before you forget it by reviewing your notes within 24 hours. However, if you wait until before the test to study—which can be several days or weeks—those ideas will only be a fuzzy memory and will take much more work to learn.

Many students don't review their notes because they don't know how. Staring at what you've written isn't a good way to learn the information. Try these ideas instead.

- Color-code your notes by starring, highlighting, or underlining items of similar importance. For example, you may put dates in blue, processes in yellow, and key terms in a box. Items that might be on the test could get a star.
- Try to identify four to five main points. Do this in the white space you left on the pages of your notes.
- Share or compare notes with a classmate.

STUDENT NOTES

- Try to come up with two or three points or questions for class discussion.
- Follow up with the instructor if you have questions.
- Recite your notes or quiz yourself out loud.

I should be taking notes on notes? Really?

Yes, really! It will allow you to process the information better.

A Few Tips on Taking Notes When They Are Provided

Instructors sometimes provide students with copies of lecture notes, PowerPoint slides, or other material that's discussed in class. Some students make the mistake of equating these photocopies to their own set of notes. If you just rely on what's already copied for you, you're not gaining all of the benefits of active note taking, such as processing the information or remembering what you've written. Having a written record of class information is just one benefit of note taking.

If your instructor gives you the notes before class, write down explanations and points not written on the handouts. Try to identify the main points. Since the basic information is already written down for you, focus on understanding the relationships between the presented material and analyzing it. Also, focus on thinking critically. Ask, "How? Why? So what?" since the "Who?" and the "What?" are likely provided in the notes. Then, review these notes after class just as you would your own.

Note-Taking Strategies for Online Classes

Online classes require careful use of effective note-taking strategies. Taking notes while engaging with online material promotes both active listening and active reading; this, in turn, improves your understanding of course material and your ability to recall important concepts. Online classes often include video or audio recorded lectures, and you should engage with these lectures while note-taking, just as you would take notes while the instructor is teaching in a traditional classroom setting. Writing down key points aids in the learning process. And if your instructor provides lecture notes, highlight, annotate, and take your own notes on top of those provided notes to help you commit the information to memory.

Having a reliable system for taking notes can help you stay organized in online classes, where much of the structure is self-imposed. Notes that you take in your online class can also serve as helpful study tools when it is time for an exam. Well-organized notes can easily be used to create study guides and practice tests.

By developing effective note-taking habits, students are more likely to make connections among different concepts. Such connections lead to insights and deeper understanding. Strong note-taking skills will help you better manage the demands of online learning and enhance your overall academic success.

STUDENT NOTES

Conclusion

Learning to take good notes requires practice before it becomes habitual. Remember, the point of taking notes is not only to have an accurate record of information presented in class. The acts of selecting what information to include, deciding on a format, and actually writing the ideas on paper are important steps in learning the material and committing it to memory.

Record your goals for improving your note-taking strategies on the tracking sheet on page 193 for easy reference in the future.

To improve upon your current method, think of note taking as a three-step process: preparing to take notes, writing down what SOARS in one of the three note-taking formats, and then reviewing your notes after class. Just as mastering note taking itself requires some practice, so too does learning how to make the most of the notes you've taken. All too often students stuff their notes in their bags at the end of class, forgetting about them until it's time to add more information during the next class. However, reviewing your notes by writing questions, summaries, and comments in leftover white space within 24 hours of the class meeting is a critical step of the process. Begin practicing better note taking now so that you'll have mastered a successful and reliable method by the time you enter higher-level, more difficult courses.

STUDENT NOTES

Note-Taking Troubleshooting

Problem	Solution
Not knowing what to write down	• Review SOARS.
Writing longhand (in complete sentences)	• Use abbreviations. • Summarize ideas. • Paraphrase ideas.
Covering the entire page with writing	• Leave a blank space at the bottom or side of your notes for questions when you review your notes. • Skip lines. • Review the note-taking methods, such as informal outline, two column, and Cornell methods. Pick one to try.
Not being able to keep up with the instructor	• Put a star in your notes when you get behind and move on with the instructor. After class, either get notes from a classmate or ask the instructor what you did not write down about that concept. • Use abbreviations. • Practice taking notes in outline form.
Doodling in the margins or losing concentration	• Ask yourself why this material is important. If you don't know, ask your instructor (in a polite and sincere tone, of course) why this material is important or how it fits into other concepts you've studied.

fizkes/Shutterstock.com

Chapter 10

Note-Taking Strategies

These questions will help you monitor and evaluate your learning, two important parts of metacognition.

1. What are three reasons you should take notes?

2. Review the list of activities during which you should take notes (pages 244–245). During which of these activities do you usually fail to take notes?

3. What does SOARS mean? When should you use it?

4. What abbreviations—other than those listed on page 248—do you use? Swap lists with a classmate or two to add some new abbreviations to your note taking.

5. How soon after class should you review your notes?

6. Read these notes with abbreviations. What do they mean?

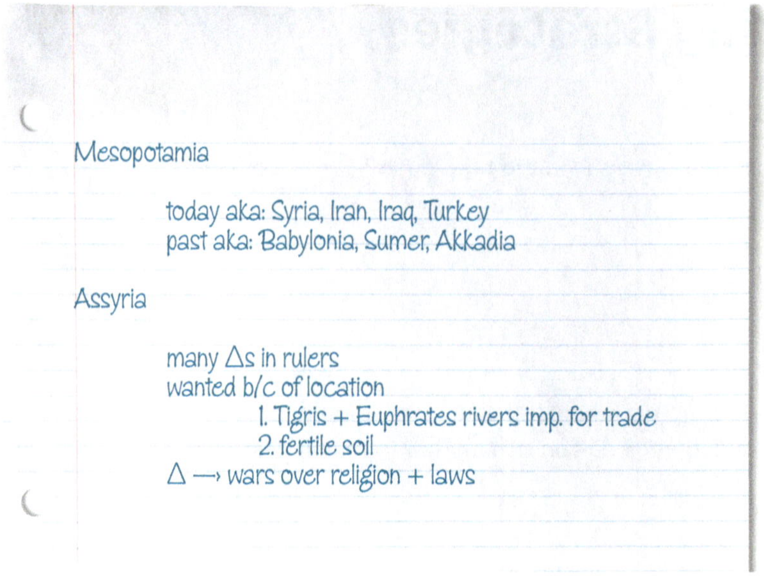

7. After examining the three methods of note taking—the informal outline, two column, and Cornell methods—name the advantages and disadvantages of each method. Is one method better suited to certain types of content? What do the methods have in common? Which do you prefer? Why?

8. Evaluate Jose's notes below. What three pieces of advice would you give him to improve his notes?

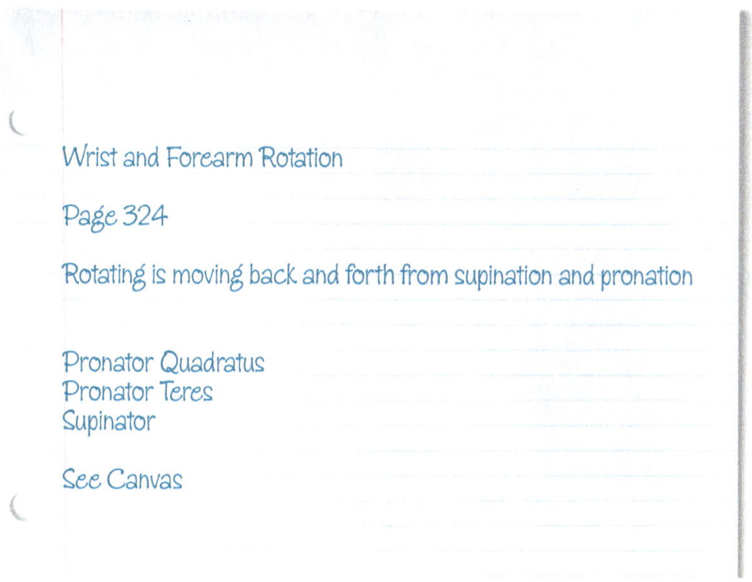
Wrist and Forearm Rotation

Page 324

Rotating is moving back and forth from supination and pronation

Pronator Quadratus
Pronator Teres
Supinator

See Canvas

9. Look back at your notes for the last two weeks for two of your classes. Rate yourself on how well you did the following. Use a scale of 1 (needs significant improvement) to 5 (consistently performed well).

	Class 1	Class 2
Noted specific details (who, what, when, where)		
Noted big picture ideas (how and why)		
Included white space		
Paraphrased		
Abbreviated		
Included all of SOARS		
Used a standard format (Cornell, Two Column, Informal Outline)		
Reviewed your notes (summaries, questions, color-coding)		

Discussion Questions

Reflect on your note-taking habits as they stand currently. What works well for you? Have you tried any specific techniques such as the Cornell method, informal outlining, concept mapping, or use of digital tools? If so, how did they help you? If not, what is a new approach you are open to trying?

Galina Barskaya/Shutterstock.com

UNIT 3

Chapter 11

Study Strategies

Before you read this chapter, reflect on the following:

1. *What study strategies have helped you the most? How do you think they helped?*
2. *Have you revised or improved these methods over time?*
3. *For what material or what classes do you need a better approach?*

These questions will help you plan your learning, an important part of metacognition.

Study is the first thing many students cut from their schedules because there's not an immediate repercussion for dropping it—no zero on an assignment, no public embarrassment from classmates, no disappointed looks from instructors. But dropping studying will affect you greatly in the long run, both in terms of your grades and in terms of your stress.

Besides making the time to study, another difficulty students encounter with studying is knowing how to study. You know you're supposed to study, but what are you supposed to do, exactly? Unfortunately, many of us were never taught helpful study methods. Instead, many of us just open the book and stare at the pages, hoping that somehow the information will just magically make sense to us and that we'll be able to remember it. Instead of hoping for a miracle, try some of the specific and proven study methods in this chapter when it's time to study.

Many college students also don't know when to study. Novice students will often wait until the last minute to study. This is called **cramming**, and while you may have had some short-term success with this method (in fact, you may have been

STUDENT NOTES

Shutterstock.com

Review notes within 24 hours of taking them.

For more information about distributed practice and using your planner, see Chapter 8.

able to pass a test or two), you won't be able to continue using this method. As you advance in your studies, the material and concepts you're expected to master will become more difficult, and cramming just doesn't work for a large volume of complex material. Secondly, college courses build upon concepts from previous courses, and you're expected to have understood and retained information from previous classes. Cramming doesn't allow for long-term recall. Finally, your future employers will expect you to remember information from your college courses. For example, do you really think your employer—or patient—will forgive you for forgetting important parts of the anatomy when you're a nurse?

When to Study

So when should a student begin studying? Think about dividing your purposes for studying into two categories: **maintenance**, which allows you to keep up with important information from class to class, and **preparation**, which is studying that prepares you for a specific task, such as a test, midterm, final, oral exam, or project.

Maintenance studying is the reviewing and reading you complete after each class to learn new material. Continual studying that allows you to learn new material must become habitual. Too many students skip this kind of studying altogether. One of the easiest ways to maximize what you discussed in class is to review your notes as soon as possible, and definitely within 24 hours of the class session. We don't naturally remember new ideas the first time we hear them, but if an idea is repeated or reinforced soon after it's introduced, the information will be solidified in our memory. You'll be amazed at how this simple technique can help you process ideas and remember them.

When most students think of studying, they envision **preparation studying**, which is targeted study that readies you for a specific application of your knowledge. Many students, unfortunately, wait until the last minute to begin this kind of studying. However, which of these sounds less stressful? Studying 20 minutes a day for eight days or studying six hours in one night? Luckily for us, the less stressful method is also the more effective method. Studying for shorter intervals (for example, 20 minutes) over a longer period of time (for example, eight days) is called **distributed practice**, and you should use this when preparing for tests. In your planner, you should have written the date of the test when you received your syllabus. Back up two to three weeks before that date, and write down when you'll study, the duration (for how long), and the specific method you'll use so that studying becomes a part of your to-do list for that day.

STUDENT NOTES

During both maintenance and preparation phases of study, you must eliminate distractions and create a work environment. On campus, go to the library and find a secluded spot. Sitting at a table in the middle of the library likely means you'll hear a lot of noise and may be interrupted by friends and classmates. Instead of sitting in plain view, find a spot downstairs out of view so that you'll be more likely to study uninterrupted. At home, set up a quiet spot away from family and the TV. Turn off your cell phone. Close the door if you can. Let others know that you need to be left alone for an hour. Sit at a desk or table. Lying on the bed or resting on the couch indicates relaxation and isn't a good way to signal to yourself or others that you're actively engaging in learning.

You should also have realistic expectations about learning the material. While some classes may seem easier than others, you will definitely encounter difficult classes in college. Don't set your expectations for college based on your easiest classes. Instead, expect that you'll need to do whatever it takes to learn. This means that you'll likely need to reread material, find and use resources (for example, instructors' office hours, tutoring, study groups, examples on the internet), employ multiple study strategies, and struggle. Expect that you'll need to invest many hours and much energy to master material rather than assume you'll comprehend everything the first time you encounter it.

One final note about studying: remember that the first time you do something, it takes more effort than it will in the future, and you will not likely maximize on the results the first time you try it. Keep refining your study methods, stick to the guidelines discussed above, and have patience as you find study strategies that work best for you.

How to Study

As mentioned earlier, most students don't know what they should actually do when they're studying. Listed here are some specific study methods with explanations and examples. Don't try to do all of these methods at once. Select the methods that best match the course material or your learning style preferences (see Chapter 4 for more information about learning styles).

Remember that as your activity increases, your learning increases. Avoid passive or surface-level studying and incorporate more cognitively active study methods.

Color-Code Your Notes

Develop a system in which different colors correspond to different types of notes, and when reviewing your day's notes, color-code the information. For example, you can highlight all definitions yellow, use pink to indicate an important example, and mark in blue important questions your instructor posed and then answered. You'll process your notes while "coloring" and in the meantime will make your notes easy to review later.

STUDENT NOTES

Make Flash Cards

Flash cards are helpful in two situations: when you have a large volume of very specific information to review, such as multiple definitions of key terms, numerous dates, or important vocabulary (see "Mitosis" example below); and when there are multiple pieces of information to remember for a single concept or idea, such as the steps to investigate a leak in a line or the three most common comma splice errors (see "Bay of Pigs" example below).

To use flash cards effectively, place the concept or word you need to know on one side, and the important information to remember on the other side. Use a rubber band or card case to carry your cards with you, so you can flip through them while waiting for the bus or when you have extra time between classes. This technique can be helpful for all types of learners and can be adapted. For example, you can draw on the cards instead of (or in addition to) writing the words if you find that helps you remember information.

You may also want to write the chapter number the material or terms came from in the corner of the card. This can help you easily determine which of your flash cards you need to study when it's time to review for a test over a specific chapter.

Flash Card Examples

front	back
Mitosis	Ch.2 process in which a single cell divides to produce 2 identical daughter cells

front	back
Outcome of Bay of Pigs Invasion	– Deaths of Cuban & Am. soldiers – Tarnished Kennedy's presidency – CIA officials forced to resign – Castro gained Cubans' support – Castro turned to U.S.S.R. out of fear of future U.S. attack—beg. of Cold War

Create Self-Tests

STUDENT NOTES

You often know what material will be on a test before your instructor hands it to you, so why not create your own version of the test as practice beforehand? There are several ways you can come up with the questions. You can use the questions the instructor posed in class. The questions at the beginning or end of the sections, chapters, or units in your textbook are also usually important. As well, you can turn the review at the end of chapters into questions, turn section headings from the book into questions, or use questions you had while taking or reviewing your notes. Make sure you can answer these questions by jotting down a response and then looking up the information to check, correct, or refine your answer.

You and a classmate could also create two different self-tests and give them to each other; each partner could check the other's answers. If you create the self-test early enough, you can ask your instructor to help you with the questions you did not understand. You can also search for practice tests online. A sample self-test for CIS 110 is below.

Brocreative/Shutterstock.com

Self-Test Examples

Chapter 1: Intro to Computers Self-Test

______ 1. Hardware
______ 2. Software
______ 3. RAM
______ 4. CPU
______ 5. ROM
______ 6. BIOS

a. programs that tell the computer what to do
b. permanent memory
c. working memory
d. the "worker"—carries out the instructions
e. the interface that boots up your computer
f. the physical components of a computer

7. What are the differences between input and output devices?

8. What part of the computer is considered the "brain" and why?

STUDENT NOTES

Complete the Practice in the Book

In classes such as chemistry, math, and foreign languages, the textbook likely contains practice or problem sets. Although you may complete some of these as assignments from the instructor, you could also complete those not assigned if the material has been covered in the class. Some books even have answers to these questions in the back. When completing the practice, make sure that you don't just do the first ones, as the level of difficulty often increases with the question number. Try a selection of the easy, medium, and difficult questions and then check your answers. Ask your instructor if you have questions.

Review Graded Homework, Tests, Projects, or Papers

If you missed points on an assignment, it most likely means you didn't understand a concept. It also means you'll likely miss similar questions in the future if you don't spend time analyzing your mistakes and learning from them. Spend time with your instructors' feedback and ask questions if you don't understand.

Form a Study Group

For many people, studying in a group is an effective way to learn material because group members can pool their collective knowledge and also benefit from others' perspectives. However, keep in mind that students only reap the benefits from study groups when expectations have been clearly communicated. Follow these guidelines to ensure the effectiveness of your study group:

- Set up a specific time and location to meet that is free from distractions. Make sure you include both a start time and end time so that the conversation stays on topic. Keep in mind that it's better to meet multiple times for shorter periods rather than for one long session.
- Assign specific content to every member so that each person has a responsibility. This not only keeps each participant active in the group, but also is a time-saving way to cover a lot of material. This method, called a **jigsaw**, requires each member to be responsible for teaching a specific chapter or concept to the rest of the group. Once each person contributes his "piece," the entire puzzle (for example, test or chapter) has been reviewed by the group.
- Clearly indicate what's expected of each participant. Will she provide a handout? Go over specific examples or problems? How long should each part take?

STUDENT NOTES

- Select members for the study group by evaluating classmates' dependability, attitude, communication skills, and study behaviors. You don't want to ask someone to be in a study group if he doesn't turn in his work, arrives late, seems unapproachable, or doesn't take notes.
- Keep the group small—between three and five members. Make sure everyone shares email addresses and phone numbers with all the other members of the group.
- Remember that you don't have to meet in person every time. Email practice questions to each other or exchange lists of important terms to work on before you meet in person.

Google Docs, Sheets, and Slides are a great way to share information with a study group since they allow everyone to access and even edit the same document remotely.

Create a Visual Organizer

Arranging information into charts or diagrams gives you something to do while studying, and in the process, you come to understand, assimilate, and therefore learn the material. Here are three well-known visual organizers and examples of each.

Venn diagrams are useful to compare and contrast two to three items. For example, if you are asked to write an essay on the similarities and differences of two civil rights leaders, a Venn diagram would be a great place to start.

Venn Diagram Example

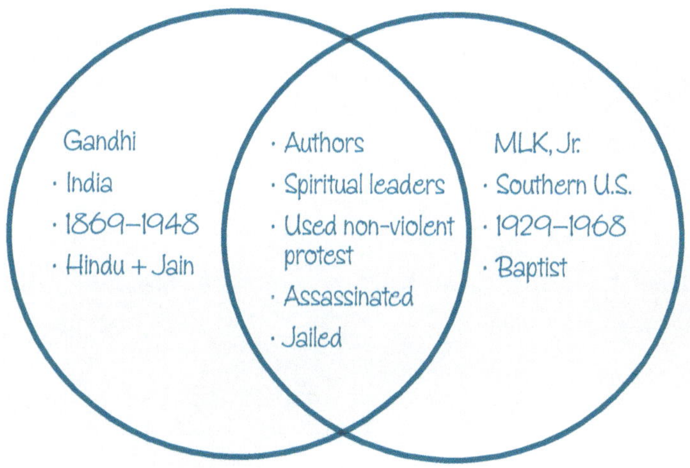

Notice that there are two circles that overlap. In the non-overlapping part of the left circle, all the information pertains only to Gandhi. Similarly, in the non-overlapping part of the right circle, information only pertaining to Martin Luther King, Jr. is written. You can see that Gandhi lived from 1869–1948 while Martin Luther King, Jr. lived only in the twentieth century.

STUDENT NOTES

Items in the non-overlapping areas indicate how the two civil rights leaders contrast. Similarities are written in the overlapping parts of the circles. Both Gandhi and Martin Luther King, Jr. were authors and used non-violent protest, for example. Venn diagrams allow for a visual representation of similarities and differences. Placing information into a Venn diagram while studying is a great way to prepare for essay test questions.

The **informal outline** is another visual organizer that allows you to visualize quickly the detail and importance of items. Creating an informal outline serves three purposes. First, important terms and people are identified. You should be able to define them all. Second, the informal outline succinctly sums up the most important ideas of the chapter or topic. It's a summary and you should know each part. Finally, it's an excellent visual representation of relationships between ideas. The more to the left an item is placed on the paper, the more general the concept. Items further to the right are more specific and give details and examples. In the following example, there are two modern philosophies and characteristics of each. If you find a concept further to the right, such as "tabula rasa," the term represents a more specific idea.

Informal Outline Example

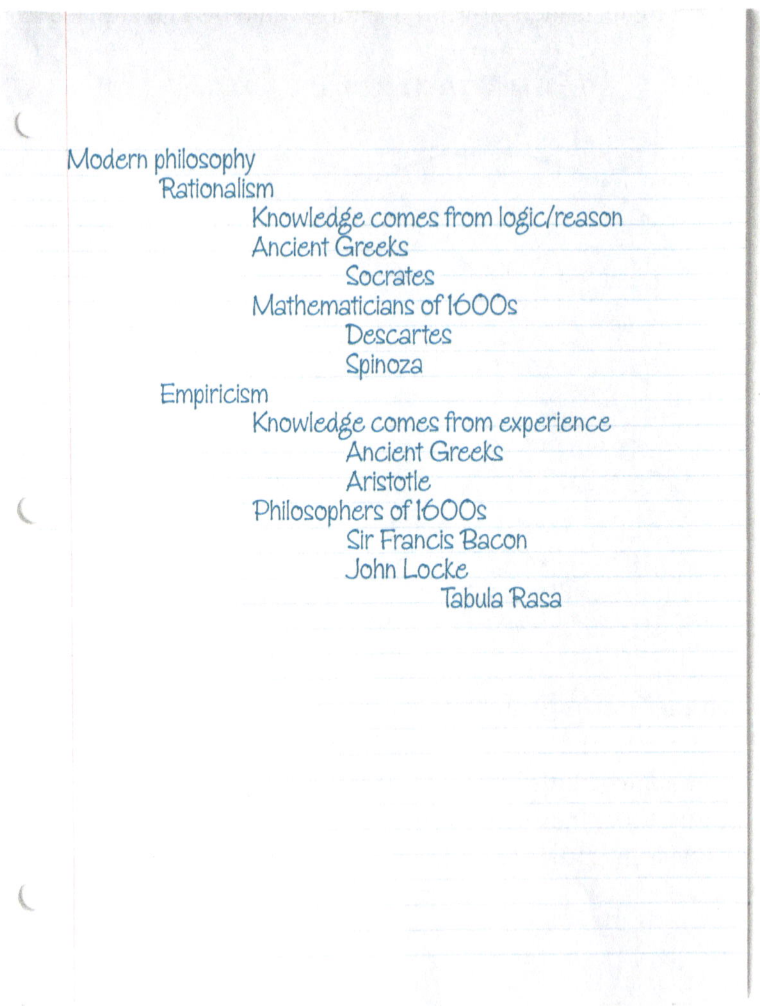

STUDENT NOTES

The order in which items appear emphasizes relationships between concepts. If items appear equally spaced from the left margin, they have the same level of importance (such as Rationalism and Empiricism in the previous example). Information that appears underneath an item but further to the right (such as Socrates) explains, provides details, or gives an example of the concept above it. While many of us learned formal outlines at some point, informal outlines are often just as helpful when studying, so don't worry if you've forgotten the order of numerals and letters that formal outlines require.

Based on this example, you can infer a wealth of information. Take Descartes and Spinoza, for example. With minimal writing, you can see that Descartes and Spinoza are mathematicians of the 1600s who follow the philosophy of rationalism, which holds that knowledge comes from logic and reason, not from experience. You can also see that they are not Ancient Greeks or empiricists.

Like Venn diagrams, you can also find commonalities between ideas. For example, since empiricism and rationalism are the same distance from the left margin and both are under the heading "Modern philosophy," you can infer from the outline that both empiricism and rationalism are modern philosophies.

Much like outlines, **concept maps** are helpful when there's a lot of material of varying importance or specificity to process. A concept map allows you to see connections between ideas. Begin with the most central idea and place it in a circle in the middle of your page. Next, place related ideas, such as examples or divisions, in circles and connect them to the main idea with lines. Keep creating circles, labeling them with definitions, examples, or divisions, and connecting them to larger ideas with lines. It's a good idea to make concept maps in pencil as you will likely need to erase because you're processing the information as you decide which circles to connect and at what level to include information. You might also experiment with Smart Art features in Microsoft Word or investigate various apps that allow you to easily generate a concept map.

Amir Ridhwan/Shutterstock.com

Much like the informal outline, the concept map allows for a very quick visual reference. By tracing lines to their connections, you can infer a lot of relationships and facts. For example, when you look closely at the following concept map, you see that John Locke and Sir Francis Bacon both connect to "Philosophers of 1600s." You can conclude that both Locke and Bacon are not only philosophers who lived during the seventeenth century, but also by tracing the line connecting "Philosophers of 1600s," you can conclude they are also empiricists and not rationalists or followers of Eastern philosophy.

STUDENT NOTES

With all visual organizers, the important thing to remember is that creating these is the learning process. When completed, you'll have a great visual reference, but it's the act of making one—deciding what goes where—that allows an exercise through which you can assimilate, comprehend, and remember information.

Concept Map Example

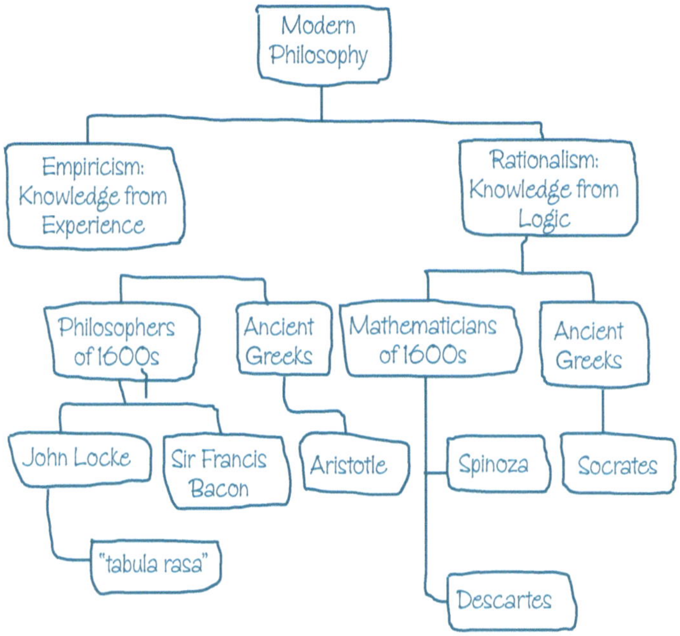

Use a Mnemonic Device

Mnemonic devices are memory tools that allow you to recall a large amount of specific information by creating a memorable word, sentence, or rhyme. Have you ever had to memorize the steps to a process or important details but found that it was difficult to remember everything? Generally, our brains cannot remember more than five to seven items at a time. Also, recalling the order of items is often difficult when the sequence matters. Organizing large amounts of information into a memorable word or sentence allows us to remember more details and their arrangement. In fact, acronyms, acrostic sentences, and rhymes can help you remember that information for a test and even for years after.

One of the most common types of mnemonic devices is the acronym. An **acronym** is a word that helps you remember information and the order of items. In an acronym, each letter represents a different word or set of words. You probably have used these before to remember information. Do you remember PEMDAS or FANBOYS?

STUDENT NOTES

Parenthesis	**F**or
Exponents	**A**nd
Multiplication	**N**or
Division	**B**ut
Addition	**O**r
Subtraction	**Y**et
	So

Thousands, perhaps millions, of students have learned the order of operations and coordinating conjunctions using these acronyms, and many can still recall the correct steps to solving mathematical equations and can connect independent clauses years later because they learned these acronyms.

Sometimes, the information you need to learn doesn't form a clear word. In that case, a different mnemonic device—an acrostic sentence—might be more useful. An **acrostic sentence** allows you to remember the order of steps or events as well. You actually probably already know a few. Does this sound familiar: My Very Elegant Mother Just Sat Upon Nine Porcupines? Or, My Very Eager Mother Just Served Us Nine Pies? Many students learned the order of the planets, starting with the one closest to the sun, through one of these sentences. The sentence is interesting enough to recall, and students can remember all the planet names in the correct order by using the first letter of each word. This acrostic sentence is much easier to remember than an ordered list of planet names.

My	Mercury
Very	Venus
Elegant	Earth
Mother	Mars
Just	Jupiter
Sat	Saturn
Upon	Uranus
Nine	Neptune
Porcupines	Pluto

How do you remember the number of days in a month? You might recite the well-known verse below:

Thirty days hath September,
April, June, and November;
All the rest have thirty-one
Excepting February alone:
Which has twenty-eight, that's fine,
Till leap year gives it twenty-nine.

STUDENT NOTES

Many of us use this **rhyme** and others to remember very detailed information, such as the last dates of the 12 months. You can create your own rhymes for information you're struggling to commit to memory. The rhythmic, repetitive sounds will help recall the next line of information.

Often, you don't have to invent your own acronym, acrostic sentence, or rhyme. Google your topic and the word "acronym," "acrostic," "rhyme," or "mnemonic" to see if you can find some existing helpful mnemonic devices. There are also YouTube videos of performed songs or rhymes on numerous topics that you can view to help you remember a long list of items.

Martin Allinger/Shutterstock.com

Create a Cheat Sheet

Create a **cheat sheet** for every test, exam, or quiz. Of course, do not actually use it unless your instructor allows you to do so. The act of making the cheat sheet will cause you to recognize which information you haven't mastered and then consolidate and review important information. In fact, once you make your cheat sheet, you often wouldn't even need it if you could use the cheat sheet. To create your own cheat sheet, divide an index card into sections by drawing lines. Organize information into these sections in a way that makes sense. Perhaps formulas go in one section, important definitions you have trouble remembering in another, and steps to an important process in the last. Organizing the information in these ways equates to making a type of visual organizer and will help you remember the information.

STUDENT NOTES

Cheat Sheet Example

Formulas:

Standard Form	Slope Intercept Form	Slope
$ax + by = c$	$y = mx + b$	$\frac{y_2 - y_1}{x_2 - x_1}$
$-a/b$ = slope	m = slope	
c/b = y intercept	b = y intercept	
c/a = x intercept		

Tricky:

- slope of perpendicular line = negative reciprocal
- slope of parallel line = same

Negative slope   Positive slope   Zero slope

Visualize

Like visual organizers, the practice of visualizing concepts appeals to many of us. Seeing the material, especially in motion, will allow you to absorb the information and remember it better.

Try to imagine the process in your head. In your mind's eye, can you see the process or ideas being described in the reading or notes? You don't have to rely only on your own imagination. You can Google the term and review the results under "Images" and "Video," or you can search for the term on YouTube or well-respected, free sites such as Khan Academy. There are many interactive sites with demonstrations, models, and graphics that bring to life the information discussed in your textbook or class lecture. For example, gear ratios can make a lot more sense if you see the concept explained as someone takes apart a transmission and points out the gear teeth rather than if you just read the definition in your book.

Use KWL

KWL is a technique to focus your studying so that you're aware of your strengths and improve on weak areas. To use KWL, begin by writing everything you know or think you know (K) about the topic. Then, draw a line on your paper to separate these ideas from the next step. Now, write down what you want to learn (W) or need to learn about the topic. You can use your notes, questions asked by your instructor or other students in class, or your test review to help you with this step. Next, you need to find some answers. You can consult your notes, your textbook, classmates, returned

STUDENT NOTES

Remember, between the W and L stages, you must do some research to find the answers to your questions and to confirm what you think you know about the topic (K category).

What myth did this student debunk for himself by using KWL?

assignments, or your instructor. Finally, draw a line to create the last section and write down what you learned (L). You may find that you thought you knew something when you wrote it down under the K category, only to find out that you were wrong. Write out what you learned. By using this technique, you confirm previous knowledge, clarify concepts, and gain new insight.

KWL Example

K: What do I know about organizing a paper?

- Need a thesis, which is the main point you're making
- Start with introduction
- Each ¶ needs a topic sentence
- Must have three body paragraphs

W: What do I want or need to know about organizing a paper?

- What's a good way to start the paper (intro)?
- What's the relationship between the topic sentence and the thesis?
  (instructor asked this in class)

L: What did I learn about organizing a paper?

- Intro should grab reader's attention. Try using a story, interesting statistic or fact, hypothetical situation, or quote.
- Actually, don't have to have 3 body paragraphs. Just make sure body ¶ order makes sense logically & that you have enough body ¶ to support your thesis.
- Topic Sentences support the thesis. Group similar ideas and find their common element to write TS.
- Don't forget transitions between ¶

Study Strategies for Online Classes

Effective study strategies are essential in online courses. Studying well combines strong time management, reading strategies, and effective note-taking. As mentioned, online learning requires an ability to manage a significant amount of material rather independently.

STUDENT NOTES

A dedicated study schedule will help students establish a routine that builds consistency and avoid overwhelm. Digital tools such as planners and study apps can help you stay organized. Taking time to review upcoming tasks and deadlines at the start of each week will help you determine a realistic study schedule for the week ahead.

Annotating your textbook readings and taking comprehensive and well-organized notes on the material in your online class will help you better engage with and retain course information. There are digital tools like Notion and Evernote that allow you to organize your notes in a searchable format, but keep in mind the importance of handwritten note-taking methods, as well. Figure out a system that works well for you; develop a personalized note-taking method that aligns with your preferred manner of processing information.

When studying, use active learning techniques like self-testing and explaining course content to a willing listener, such as a roommate or family member. You can also use websites like Quizlet to create interactive flash cards and practice tests. Consider forming a study group with other students in your online class and meeting synchronously online at a designated day and time every week. This can help you make connections with other students and make studying more interactive and engaging. The more you engage with the material, the more likely it is that you will feel confident in your online classes.

Conclusion

Students have many misconceptions when it comes to studying. They often assume studying means to sit passively staring at the book open in front of them. However, just like you learned about reading in Chapter 9, you must be active when studying if you are to engage enough with the ideas to understand them and commit them to memory. Color-coding your notes, making flash cards, creating Venn diagrams, writing a creative mnemonic device, drawing a concept map, working sample problems, creating a practice test, reviewing returned work, writing an informal outline, creating a cheat sheet, presenting to your study group, and using KWL are all study actions that lead to a better understanding of material. Finding the most effective studying strategies requires you to consider your learning preferences and the type of material presented. It will also require some time and patience, as well as the realization that studying is an ongoing process throughout the semester, not just in the few days or hours leading up to a test.

Record your goals for incorporating specific study strategies into your study routines on the tracking sheet on page 193 for easy reference in the future.

STUDENT NOTES

Study Strategies Troubleshooting

Problem	Solution
Not remembering specific, detailed information	• Complete problem sets or practice in the book. • Make flash cards for specific terms, dates, formulas, or processes. Use the mitosis example on page 264 to help. • Make an acrostic sentence or mnemonic.
Not remembering major themes or overarching ideas	• Form a study group. By identifying the main concepts to be divided amongst the group, you'll know the key areas and concepts to keep in mind. • Create a practice test, specifically focusing on possible essay choices. • Review the questions at the end of chapters, especially short answer or essay questions that include the terms "why" or "how." • Create flash cards similar to the Bay of Pigs example on page 264.
Losing focus or getting bored when studying	• Utilize the study strategies that are well-matched for visual or kinesthetic learners, such as making flash cards, color-coding your notes, or creating visual diagrams. • Look for videos of class concepts on YouTube. You'll be shocked at what is available. Just remember to consider the reliability of the source in selecting your video.
Cramming at the last minute	• Don't forget to complete maintenance studying. • Use your planner to devote specific times to complete particular study tasks. For example, between your two Monday morning classes, will you run through your computer science class flash cards twice or will you create a Venn diagram for history class? See Chapter 8 for more time-management strategies.
Not knowing how to prepare for a test or exam	• Look at the learning outcomes as well as the outline of instruction in the syllabus for topics to study. • Work with a study group to identify important material or themes.

REVIEW QUESTIONS

Chapter 11
Study Strategies

These questions will help you monitor and evaluate your learning, two important parts of metacognition.

1. What three things cause students to not study effectively?

2. List the 11 study methods on pages 263–274 and then label them as either Maintenance or Preparation. Compare your answers to a classmate's.

3. Examine the differences between the Venn diagram, outline, and concept map. Which of these do you find most helpful? In what ways do they help you?

4. Both PEMDAS and Please Excuse My Dear Aunt Sally help people remember the order of operations in math class.

   a. Which of these is an acronym?

   b. Which one is an acrostic sentence?

   c. Which helps you the most?

5. Now that Pluto has been stripped of its status as a planet, a new acrostic sentence needs to be created to help students remember the order of the planets. Create a suggestion.

6. Which of the study strategies do you currently use well? Which could you use better or have never used before? Write a SMART goal for how you will improve your studying for the rest of this semester.

7. Ryan passed all of his high school classes without opening a book. Now, he is in his first semester and is taking four classes: MAT 152 (Statistics), ENG 111 (Writing and Inquiry), COM 231 (Public Speaking), and BIO 111 (General Biology). He doesn't know how to even begin to study for his classes because he did not have to study in high school. What advice can you give him for studying effectively for those subjects? Identify at least one unique maintenance strategy for each subject.

8. Roger is an older student who has been out of the classroom for almost a decade. He is currently taking CHM 151 (General Chemistry I). In his Chemistry class, the instructor does not give quizzes, homework assignments, or lab grades. Instead, students take only two tests and a final exam. Roger is extremely nervous about the upcoming first test of the semester. He has joined a study group, but the other students get distracted easily and just make Roger more nervous. In fact, Roger is thinking about dropping the course and taking another science next semester. What advice can you give him for preparing for his upcoming test? Identify at least three strategies.

Discussion Questions

What experiences have you had so far studying in groups? Do you find it helpful or distracting to work with peers to study? What is one advantage and one disadvantage of study groups?

UNIT 3

Chapter 12

Test-Taking Strategies

Noah Strycker/Shutterstock.com

Before you read this chapter, reflect on the following:

1. *What are your preferred types of testing? Why do you like these types of tests more than others?*
2. *Have you ever felt you've done well on a test but then received a poor grade? Which of these tips could have helped you?*
3. *What goes through your mind before a test? During the test?*

These questions will help you plan your learning, an important part of metacognition.

The first step in doing well on a test is mastering the content. The previous chapters in this unit described many effective ways of doing this: reading strategically, studying with effective methods, managing your time to ensure you allow yourself the time to learn, and taking good notes. Using these methods should be your priority in preparing for a test. However, there are some additional important strategies to keep in mind for the test itself, categorized by time and the type of test.

Before the Test

Nip test anxiety in the bud before the day of the test by using effective study methods. Many students say they are bad test takers when their difficulties are actually a result of ineffective studying. Their text anxiety comes from knowing they are unprepared for the test or from feeling woefully unprepared as they read and attempt to answer the test questions. Consider if this describes your experiences in test taking. If so, review the study strategies in Chapter 11. It might be a good idea to create a short-term SMART goal for your test anxiety to see if using studying methods can help you overcome your test anxiety. Preparing adequately for your tests and setting goals to

STUDENT NOTES

minimize your anxiety should help you overcome test anxiety. However, if test anxiety continues to distract you, consult with a counselor in your college's counseling office to learn of other strategies to help you.

If necessary, change your behaviors in order to avoid the Nervous Nellies. Keep your distance from these students who tend to get worked up before the test and feed off each others' nervous energy. This group of students often ends up psyching each other out or building their anxiety levels by complaining about the test, discussing what will be on the test at the last minute (when there's not enough time to study if they did forget something), and otherwise causing negative anticipation for the test. Keep your distance by waiting down the hall before the test.

wavebreakmedia/Shutterstock.com

Make sure you clarify the testing method with the instructor several days in advance. It would be devastating to prepare for a multiple choice test, only to receive the test and find it is mostly short answer and essays. It's also a good idea to talk about time expectations. Will the test take the entire class period? Will the test be timed?

When studying specifically for a test, make sure you review your notes for any questions the instructor posed during class. These will likely appear on the test. Prepare yourself for the exam by sketching out possible answers to short answer or essay questions the instructor will likely repeat on the test.

If there are still a couple of concepts you're not completely confident about, you may want to write final reminders on an index card to review one or two more times on test day. In effect, you're creating a cheat sheet, which is one of the study methods discussed in Chapter 11. Of course, you won't use this card during the test, but creating the card will help you remember this tough material and also ease your nerves because you know exactly what to review one last time.

Also, try to reduce the potential for last-minute panicking. Make sure you have all your materials before the test, so you won't be scrambling for a pencil or calculator. It's a good idea to check your bag the night before the test to make sure you have the supplies you need to perform well.

On test day, plan to arrive to campus early. The last thing you want is to add to your normal stress levels by panicking about the time or becoming frustrated with traffic. Set your alarm for an earlier time and take the earlier bus or leave home 15 minutes early.

Further prepare yourself for the test by planning your behaviors on test day. Create a mantra, or positive statement, to repeat to yourself when you begin to experience anxiety. For example, when you feel yourself becoming nervous, you could inhale deeply and say to yourself, "I've prepared for this test. I will do well. I will be fine." Exhale slowly and repeat until you feel more at ease.

STUDENT NOTES

Also plan to sit away from others, even if this means you do not sit in your regular seat. If you are usually distracted when others get up to turn in their tests or leave early, make sure you sit far away from the door or the place where students submit tests. This will minimize the extent of the distractions.

During the Test

As soon as you are allowed to begin, immediately write down formulas, mnemonic devices (see page 270 in Chapter 11), or specific dates or names you're afraid you'll forget. This method, called a **mind dump**, will allow you to concentrate on the test rather than on remembering.

After you've written down this information, write your name on the test materials and then **survey** the test. Look over the exam to determine its length and which sections are worth the most points. Then, decide how you will budget your time effectively to get the most points. Will you begin with the essay on the last page? Should you start with the identifications in the middle of the test? Surveying the test and planning your test strategy should take no more than two to three minutes.

Make sure you don't foolishly give away points by failing to read the directions. Students often skip the directions out of nervousness and haste. However, this can be a very costly mistake. When reading the directions, annotate them by marking verbs (for example, *match*, *consider*, *evaluate, circle, define, compare and contrast*) and any other words that stand out to you in the instructions. Make sure you know your task before you write in any answers. If your instructor has asked you to compare and contrast two events, discussing just the similarities will cause you to lose points. Sometimes questions can have multiple answers or contain important words such as *except*, *not*, or *without*. Underline these important stipulations or risk losing points.

Shutterstock.com

As you move through the test, consider the type of question you're answering. You'll approach a multiple-choice question much differently than you will an essay prompt or a true/false question. Be mindful of the types of answers expected for specific question types as well as common mistakes students make. Read the "Types of Test Questions" section on pages 283–291 for specific information about question types.

You should also be careful to clearly mark your answers. Do not assume the instructor will know what your answer should be. Mark your answers as indicated in the instructions. If you erase, do so thoroughly and rewrite your answer so that it is clear and not difficult to read. When writing in your answers for multiple choice and true/false questions, make sure your letters are clear. Instructors will not assume what you meant by the dreaded

STUDENT NOTES

T/F hybrid answer (a T that also has the lowest bar of the F, shown below). It's best to be overly clear rather than to lose points because your answer is ambiguous or illegible. Erase your previous answer and consider writing out the word "true" or "false" if your answer is still not clear. Be obvious or risk losing points.

You will encounter some difficulties when proceeding through the test but don't be thrown off course. If you find yourself feeling anxious, focus on the positive. For example, take a moment to acknowledge the number of questions you did know or the areas of the test for which you feel very confident. Realize that you're feeling stress, which is often a result of doubt. To counteract this negative feeling, state the opposite to yourself through your mantra: "I've prepared for this test. I am doing well. I will be fine." Exhale slowly and repeat until you feel more peaceful.

If you're feeling stuck because you do not know an answer, fall back on the **two-pass method**, which is a strategy to ensure you're earning the most points by concentrating on the questions you'll most likely get credit for (the ones you know) and not wasting time on questions you'll likely get wrong (the ones you don't know). On the first pass, you work straight through the test, from the beginning of the test through to the last questions. When you encounter a question you don't know, quickly put an answer for the question (if it's essay or short answer, jot down some quick notes) just in case you run out of time on the test. But make sure you also mark that question by circling the number. Before you turn in your test or before time is called, take a second pass through the test and look at the questions you marked as uncertain answers. Did you remember anything during the rest of the test that can help you recall the answer? Did anything on the latter part of the test provide you with the answer? Change your response if necessary.

Two-Pass Method
1st pass: Answer only the questions you know. If you don't know an answer, quickly mark an answer, circle the question, and move on.
2nd pass: Return to the difficult questions you skipped.

While taking the test, also be mindful of the time. Being mindful is not the same as worrying. Mindfulness means that you periodically check the classroom clock or your watch to ensure your plan for completing the test is on track.

Remember, certain sections of the test are often worth more points than other sections. Usually high-point value areas are short-answer questions, advanced problems, or essays, which tend to appear toward the end of the test. You don't want to run out of time before you get to the big points, so make sure you keep track of time by knowing the end time of the test and watching the classroom clock. You can also complete these questions first, if you'd like.

Finally, check over your test before you submit it. Never leave questions blank. For true/false questions, you have a 50% chance of getting the answer right, so take a guess. For multiple-choice and matching questions, your odds are also favorable. Make an educated guess and move on. For essay or short-answer questions, aim for partial points by writing down what you do know. If pressed for time, still leave one to two minutes at the end of the test before time is called to mark answers to true/false or multiple-choice questions that you haven't gotten to yet.

After the Test

If you studied effectively and did your best, you should reward yourself by doing something that brings you joy. For example, you could go see the movie you've been putting off because you were studying or you could take your lunch outside for a picnic.

After you've treated yourself, evaluate your studying and test-taking strategies. How well did your methods work? In what ways were you well prepared? What could you do differently next time in order to perform better on the test? It's very important that you attend the class meeting during which your instructor will return the test, which is often the next class, so that you'll have the opportunity to review your work. When the instructor returns your test, don't just look at your grade or what you missed. Also consider how your studying or test-taking methods helped or hurt your score. Examine your test to learn from your mistakes.

Types of Test Questions

In addition to considering how you'll proceed through testing, you should think strategically about the tasks you'll be presented with during the test. Your approach and considerations should differ based on the question type.

Multiple Choice

Multiple-choice questions present a question and several possible answers. Your task is to select the best possible answer from the list, which is usually represented by a letter. Most often, there is only one response or letter that correctly answers the question. Following is an example.

STUDENT NOTES

Review Chapter 5 for the answer to this question.

1. Students desiring to take classes at a community college and then transfer to a four-year institution have how many options?
   a. None
   b. One
   c. Three
   d. Four
   e. Unlimited

Multiple-choice questions are common on college tests, although they rarely comprise the entire test. Many students erroneously believe multiple-choice questions to be the easiest section of the test. While it is true that your chances of selecting the correct answer are usually 1 in 4 or 1 in 5, it's doubtful that most students would be content with a 20% or 25% on the test! You should not shirk preparation studying just because a test is mainly multiple choice.

If you regularly miss multiple-choice questions, consider if your preparation (reading or studying) is part of the problem. If not, the likely culprit is the method you use to answer multiple-choice questions. The main problem that students encounter with multiple-choice tests is that they do not come up with their own answer to the question before looking at the answer choices. Unfortunately, once you read the answer choices, you cannot get those options or their wording out of your head. The test author's words may confuse you even when you know the answer, so make sure you use the following four-step process to avoid the common pitfalls of multiple choice tests. You're less likely to be influenced by false answers if you use this four-step technique.

Four-Step Process to Answering Multiple-Choice Questions	
1.	First, cover up the answer choices so you won't be swayed by them. You can use your hand, the answer sheet, or scrap paper if it's allowed.
2.	Then, read the question. Annotate its important parts, including words such as *not, without, only,* or *except.* Students often miss these words when reading the question.
3.	Next, formulate your own answer to the test question. Without the distraction of answers that "sound" good, you're more likely to be able to find the correct answer.
4.	Finally, uncover the answer choices and use the process of elimination, or POE. To do this, don't read the answer choices looking for the answer that most nearly matches yours from step 3. Instead, look for the wrong answers to eliminate. If the answers provided don't match your own answer, mark them out. The one that's left must be the right answer. Evaluate if it is indeed the one that most closely matches your own answer (keep in mind it might not be an exact match). Select this answer.

STUDENT NOTES

Consider the following example and the chemistry student's process for answering the question.

1. Before reading this question, the student covered up answer choices **a** through **d**.
2. She then read the question and considered what she knew about inert gases and their most important characteristics.
3. She then jotted down a few notes in the margin.
4. Finally, she uncovered the answer choices and eliminated any options that did not match her notes or that contradicted her list.

After this process, the only choice left is answer c, which has to be the best answer. The student may not remember what "valence" means, but she knows the other answers are incorrect.

Inert means doesn't move or react
Nitrogen is in experiments b/c it doesn't react and can be controlled

2. Which of the following is an important or defining characteristic of inert gases?
   - ~~a. Inert gases oxidize.~~
   - ~~b. Inert gases react strongly to chemicals.~~
   - c. The valence of inert gases is complete.
   - ~~d. Inert gases cannot be controlled in experiments.~~

Another reason students often miss multiple-choice questions is that they do not look at all the answer choices. Make sure you evaluate all answer choices, even if answer choice **a** seems to be correct. Remember, you're not looking for the right answer; you're looking for wrong answers to eliminate. By evaluating all the answer choices, you'll also avoid a common error, which is marking answer **a** when the answer is not only **a**. See the example below to understand.

3. Which of the following is true?
   - a. An infinitive contains the word "to" and the unconjugated verb
   - b. Verbs only need to agree in tense with the rest of the sentence
   - c. Verbs should match their subjects in numbers (plural verbs with multiple subjects; singular verbs with single subjects)
   - d. All of the above
   - e. Both a and c

STUDENT NOTES

While answer choice **a** is a factual statement, so is answer choice **c**. You must read through all of the answer choices to see that answer choice **e** is the correct answer for this item because it includes statements **a** and **c**.

While nothing beats knowing the content of the test, when you're confused on a multiple-choice question, consider the following strategies:

- **Look for answer choices that are opposites of each other.** One of these is likely the correct answer.

4. Which of the following is true of the larynx?
   a. It is open during swallowing.
   b. It is 4–5 inches long.
   c. It is closed during swallowing.
   d. It extends from the soft palate to the epiglottis.

Answer choices **a** and **c** are opposites: either the larynx is open or it is closed during swallowing. Therefore, the answer is likely either **a** or **c**.

- **Avoid picking the correct answer to the wrong question.** Just because an answer choice is a true statement doesn't mean that it correctly answers the question asked. Make sure your answer choice is not only true but actually responds to the posed prompt.

5. Why did the pilgrims come to America?
   a. To avoid religious persecution in their native country.
   b. King James succeeded Queen Elizabeth.
   c. The pilgrims founded New England.
   d. Because they wanted to eat a Thanksgiving meal.

Answers **a**, **b**, and **c** are factually correct. However, only **a** answers the question and is a historically valid reason why the pilgrims came to the Americas.

- **Avoid picking answers with absolutes.** Answers with the extreme words *every*, *all*, *totally*, *completely*, *only*, *none*, *never*, and *always* do not allow for exceptions, and in reality there are exceptions to nearly every rule. Therefore, answers containing these words are rarely correct. Instead, if you're stuck between two answers, look for the one that contains qualifiers, such as *usually*, *most*, *some*, *rarely*, *nearly*, *almost*, and *often* since these words allow for exceptions to the rules.

STUDENT NOTES

6. Pavlov's theory on classical conditioning can be best described as a theory that...
   a. Only applies to experiments with dogs.
   b. Always applies to food responses.
   c. Usually describes a behavior learned through the simultaneous presence of conditioned and unconditioned stimuli.
   d. Is supported by behaviorists, such as Bandura.

Surprisingly, you don't need to know anything about Pavlov or classical conditioning to narrow down the answer choices. Eliminate answer choices with extreme answers and then consider the answers with qualifiers. Answer choices **a** and **b** have extreme words (*only* and *always*), so mark them out. Now you're left with **c** and **d**. If you knew nothing else of Pavlov's theory and the answer choices, you should mark answer choice **c** as correct since it contains conditional language (*usually*).

True/False

True/False questions usually present a statement that the test taker must evaluate and mark as being a factual statement (true) or an inaccurate statement (false). Many students dread true/false questions because they become confused or find the questions tricky. Use the following two strategies to help you overcome the feeling that the questions were intended to mislead you.

Remember that if part of the answer is false, then the entire answer is false. Divide the sentence into phrases and place check marks above what is true and an X over any part that is untrue. If you place an X over any part of the sentence, then the answer cannot be true. Mark it false.

7. Shakespeare, a well-known ✓ poet ✓ and playwright, ✓ is often thought of as the greatest ✓ American ✗ author. ✓

Should statement 7 be marked as true or false?

STUDENT NOTES

Also, as with multiple-choice entries, avoid marking statements containing absolutes as true—or consider absolutes very carefully. Since most things in life do have exceptions, answer choices without conditions will often be false. The word *always* in item 8 below should make you wary of marking this answer as true.

> 8. **The law of demand states that the quantity and price demanded in a given market are always in an inverse relationship.**

Matching

Matching questions are usually presented in two columns. The test taker is to match the terms (usually in the left column) to the definition or characteristics presented (usually in the right column). These question types can be deceptively hard or time consuming. To avoid common matching errors, make sure you've read the directions. Sometimes answers can match more than one term or question.

Also, examine the columns presented for matching. Do you understand the task at hand? Find a systematic way to go about answering the questions. Often it is easiest to work your way through the right-hand column (usually the explanations for the terms in the left column) and find corresponding terms on the left rather than vice versa. Do not draw lines to match items. This is confusing and wastes time. Pair items mentally and then write the corresponding letter or number next to the question or term.

Don't forget to use the process of elimination (POE). Match the ones you know most certainly first and mark off the answers you've used. Then concentrate on the remaining choices.

1. ___ benefactor	a.	a kind or generous act
2. ___ benediction	b.	something advantageous or good
3. ___ benefit	c.	a person who donates time or money
4. ___ benevolent	d.	a blessing
5. ___ beneficial	e.	helpful

Rather than read through the terms in the left column to find the answer in the right column, begin with reading **a** in the right column and then find its answer on the left. Using this method requires less reading and is less time-consuming than the traditional method.

STUDENT NOTES

Fill in the Blank

Fill-in-the-blank questions provide a sentence in which one or more words are replaced with a space for the test taker to insert the term or phrase that will complete the statement or make it true. Usually, the instructor intends for you to provide a specific term, list of steps, date, or number when answering a fill-in-the-blank question.

9. The __________ connects the end of the ulna to the end of the radius and helps the pronator teres rotate the arm inside.

To answer these question types, think back to bolded words in the book, terms the instructor wrote on the board (the O of SOARS in Chapter 10), or terms your instructor repeated in class (the R or S of SOARS in Chapter 10). By visualizing the list of words, dates, or steps, you may be more likely to recall them, especially if your learning style relies heavily on visual stimuli to learn (see Chapter 4 for more information about learning styles). Look at the answer choices to other questions, especially multiple choice if they are on the test. However, be forewarned that fill-in-the-blank questions are the hardest to use strategy to solve if you don't know the answer. If you don't know the answer, you'll likely not receive credit since the instructor probably wants a particular term or date. Nevertheless, you can write an explanation of the term in the blank or write what you do know. You may receive some partial credit.

Short Answer

Short-answer questions require a brief written response. The length expectation can vary from one word to a phrase to several concise sentences, so make sure you read the directions and consult with your instructor if you're unclear how much to write. You don't want to spend excessive time on short-answer questions if your instructor only expected a few brief phrases. Here's an example of a short-answer question.

10. Define and explain the following terms by describing important features, contributions, or legacies. Write no more than four sentences for each.
    - Federalist Party
    - War of 1812
    - John Marshall

Short-answer questions tend to worry many students. To get the most points possible, do your best to be exact and concise with your answers. If the short answer requires an identification (like the example above), make sure

STUDENT NOTES

you include all relevant points by writing an answer that addresses all of the question words: *who, what, when, where, how,* and *why*. You don't want to risk not getting points when you knew the information but didn't write it down. Before you move on, ask yourself if you answered all of the question words related to the topic.

If you can't recall the correct answer, don't dwell on this. Instead of concentrating on what you don't know, concentrate on what you do know. Write down this information in the space for the answer. Partial credit is better than no credit at all.

Essay

Essay questions usually provide a prompt or question that students answer in one or more paragraphs. Essay questions require not only knowledge of the content, but also a clear understanding of the question, effective organization, and succinct writing. To lessen the stress associated with essay questions, read the question carefully and circle any verbs in the essay so that you'll understand your assigned task. For example, are you to explain, compare and contrast, analyze, or describe? Also, you should make sure you know exactly what topics you are to cover. You may want to underline these. Are you to discuss a person, her achievements, or her legacy? You should be clear about your job before you begin or risk losing significant points. Always annotate the prompt. The following prompt has been annotated to clarify the assignment and the student's responsibilities before he begins brainstorming.

11. Describe at least three significant causes of the War of 1812 and explain how each contributed to the U.S. decision to go to war.

After you annotate an essay prompt to gain a clear understanding of what's being asked, you should then recall all of your knowledge that could help you answer the questions. Write down what you know on the topic, so you can focus on what you do know rather than stressing about what you don't know. In other words, brainstorm in the margin or on scrap paper. If you get stuck, you may be able to flip through other parts of the test to refresh your memory.

After gathering your ideas, sketch an outline. If you don't have a plan for your essay, you'll likely stray off-topic. Also, you don't have time or space to revise your essay significantly. Taking a few minutes to write down a rough outline and thesis will pay off with more points in the end. It's a step well worth your time.

STUDENT NOTES

With your outline in hand, begin writing. Incorporate relevant specific points, names, dates, and terms to demonstrate your knowledge. Refer to the brainstormed list of what you do know for ideas. Periodically check back with the prompt as you're writing. Again, make sure you are answering the question that's being asked.

Scantrons or Bubble Sheets

Many students make errors on Scantron or bubble sheets, giving away points when they know the correct answers to the questions because they incorrectly mark their answers or do not thoroughly erase. You may not even realize that this is a problem for you since many Scantrons are used for final exams and often you do not have the opportunity to review your Scantron sheet for errors since the class is over.

To avoid losing points because of incomplete erasures—a common problem—write your answers on the test and only bubble in your selected answer either after you finish an entire page of the test or at the end of the test. This will prevent erasures due to changing your mind on an answer (because you won't bubble in answers until you're finished with the test itself) and will also prevent getting off a line when going back and forth after every question. Students give away points unnecessarily by accidentally skipping lines when going back and forth between the test and the answer sheet and also lose valuable time. To solve these problems, use the suggested method, so you're only moving back and forth from the test to the answer sheet at the end of the test page or at the end of the test. Also bubble answers in sets of three. It's less confusing and also time-saving to remember and bubble A-C-A and then D-B-A rather than to go back and forth for each answer (A, bubble, back to test, C, bubble, back to test, A, bubble back to test, etc.).

Test-Taking Strategies for Online Classes

Preparing for the unique qualities of an online test environment will be critical to your success. In addition to many of the strategies already mentioned, these tips for online test can also help you do your best.

Before the exam, know the details, such as whether the test will be synchronous (*taken* on a specific date at a specific time) or asynchronous (*due* by a specific date and specific time), how much time you have to complete the test once you begin, and where you can access the test. In most cases, tests are delivered through the college's learning management system (such as Canvas, Blackboard, or Moodle) although proctoring facilities or video monitoring tools may be utilized. It is important to consult your syllabus to find important details about testing in your online classes. Carefully read all guidelines and watch any videos the instructor may provide about what to expect for testing.

STUDENT NOTES

Also make sure you understand technical requirements, such as the recommended internet browser to use and whether a lockdown browser, a web camera, or proctoring software is required. Some instructors use online test proctoring software like Proctorio or Respondus to monitor students while they are taking tests. These software platforms often require students to have their webcams turned on for the duration of the test. You may need to download materials or software before the test. You'll also want to clarify questions about the format, such as whether you'll be allowed to skip around and whether the test is open-book or open-note. Finally, you should make a plan for your test-taking environment. Designate a space to take the exam that will minimize distractions and provide consistent internet access.

During the test, keep in mind that you should not leave the test page. If the test requires you to search for information, open a new tab in the browser and be careful when closing out windows. Often online tests only allow one attempt, and you don't want to accidentally end your exam before you've completed it or had a chance to review. Also make sure that you monitor your time periodically to ensure you'll be able to finish the exam within the time provided. If you encounter a technical problem, take a screenshot. Contact your instructor immediately to explain the challenge and ask how best to proceed.

After the test, don't forget to click submit. Some online tests require multiple clicks to submit, so make sure you receive a confirmation screen before leaving the test page. Then reflect on your online test-taking plan and what you would change for your next online test.

Conclusion

Record your personal test-taking goals on the tracking sheet on page 193 for easy reference in the future.

Students often remark that they're either good or bad test takers, as if one's performance on a test is a matter of an inherent trait that you're either born with or without. However, test taking is a skill that can be improved, and this fact may be perhaps the most important thing to remember about test taking. All test takers can improve their performances on tests with attention to their approach and knowledge of tests themselves.

Remember that instructors utilize tests in order to gauge how well students have mastered important course content. Since tests are designed to measure how well you know the material, the first steps of quality test preparation begin with good reading and study habits (see Chapters 9 and 11). Beyond knowing the content, you'll also need to prepare for the specific testing method. Remember, various types of test questions will require different kinds of preparation studying (see Chapter 11), so knowing the format and length of each test is critical to being able to show your knowledge.

STUDENT NOTES

When you have an important test coming up, decide on a three-part strategy: what you'll do before the test, during the test, and after the test. Will you utilize the two-pass method? What items will you write down as a mind dump? How will you keep track of and manage your time? How will you keep in mind the expectations of the question type to make sure you're including the kinds of information necessary to receive the most points? Finally, how will you learn from your mistakes to become a better test taker in the future? When it comes to successful test taking, preparing for the test itself is just as important as learning the material. Without either, you will not be able to demonstrate the full extent of your knowledge or abilities.

Test-Taking Troubleshooting

Problems	Solutions
Freezing on a test due to anxiety or your mind going blank	• Look at the rest of the test. Other content can trigger your memory. • Repeat your mantra. • Resolve to study better next time. Review Chapter 11 and adopt two or three new study strategies for the next test. • Change your test day game plan. Don't interact with Nervous Nellies, and sit away from distractions.
Running out of time on a test	• Sit where you can see the clock or wear a watch. Survey the test and then budget time for each section. • Prioritize points. If you cannot finish the test, go to the questions worth the most points and concentrate on answering those well. • A minute or two before the end of the test, turn to T/F or matching questions you have not completed and guess. • Use the two-pass method so you don't get hung up and use time unproductively. Concentrate on getting all the points you can by answering the ones you know first. Star or circle questions you don't know. Go back to them after you've finished answering the ones you know.
Missing questions when you know the answer	• Read questions carefully. Make sure you underline important terms such as *except*, *not*, and *least*. • Make sure you are marking your Scantron correctly. • Consider the question types and the tips for responding to each. • Pace yourself so that you have time to complete the test.

STUDENT NOTES

REVIEW QUESTIONS

Chapter 12
Test-Taking Strategies

These questions will help you monitor and evaluate your learning, two important parts of metacognition.

1. Look at the list of things you should do before you take a test. Which of these do you usually do? Which could you do better? Which ones do you need to add to your routine?

2. Which test format (multiple choice, true/false, fill-in-the-blank, short answer, essay) causes you the most anxiety? What will you do to improve your test taking for these types of questions?

3. Annotate this sample essay question prompt as you should when you take an exam. Mark the most important terms to keep in mind when responding to the prompt.

> In a three-paragraph essay, identify three causes of the American Civil War and explain how each led to secession.

4. Use the strategies discussed in this chapter to practice your test-taking skills on the practice test below. Don't worry, you don't need to know anything about the topics to be able to answer the questions. The answers follow.

Practice Test

Directions: Circle your answer.

1. True or False: Marsupials are only found in Australia.

2. True or False: Most diesel engines use a two-way catalytic converter.

3. True or False: Electrons are always lighter in mass than protons.

4. Which of the following is a city in Ghana?
   a. Sunyani
   b. Chapel Hill
   c. Durham
   d. Raleigh

5. Which of the following songs was not recorded by Michael Jackson?
   a. "Thriller"
   b. "Hey Jude"
   c. "Billie Jean"
   d. Both A and C

5. Sofia is new to the college, new to North Carolina, and new to the United States. She has a college degree from her native country, but has enrolled in a program at her local community college to pursue a new career. In her country, the only tests that students take are essay exams and oral exams. Before Sofia came to the U.S., she had never taken a multiple-choice or true/false test. So far this semester, Sofia has not made good grades on her tests even though she felt like she knew the material that the tests covered. What advice can you offer Sofia to help her succeed with these particular testing formats?

6. Kathy hasn't been in school for almost twenty years, and in her first semester back she's very concerned about taking quizzes, tests, and exams since it's been so long since she has taken one. In her PSY 150 (General Psychology) class, 20% of her grade comes from quizzes and 40% from the three unit tests. She's taken two quizzes so far, failing one and barely passing the other. Her first unit test is coming up in two weeks, and Kathy thinks that if she doesn't do well, she might drop the class. What three things from this chapter would you share with Kathy if she turned to you for help as a classmate?

Practice Test Answers:

1. False. Remember that the use of extreme words such as "only" often indicates that the question is false.
2. True. Words like "most"—instead of extreme words like "all" or "every"—often indicate a correct answer.
3. True. Yes, sometimes extreme words can be used in a true/false statement and the answer is still true. Remember, nothing should replace first knowing the course content!
4. This question illustrates that looking for the wrong answers to eliminate—instead of searching for the right answer—will help you on multiple-choice tests. While you may have never heard of the city of Sunyani, it was reasonable for you to assume that our local town names would not be names of cities in a country whose official languages do not include English.
5. You need to know a little bit about pop culture to get the answer to this one correct. If you marked A, C, or D, was it because you did not read the question carefully enough to see the word "not"? If so, make sure you read and annotate your questions before answering.

Discussion Questions

What advice would you give to someone who struggles with test anxiety? What strategies would be helpful in alleviating these feelings?

Shutterstock.com

Conclusion: Putting It All Together

As you near the end of your college success class, consider how you will synthesize everything you've learned to help you prepare for the end of the semester and the beginning of the next semester. The end of the semester is an excellent time to assess how well this semester went. For example, did you manage your time effectively to meet your goals and deadlines? Did you take an appropriate number of classes? Did you make use of the resources available to you at optimal times of the semester? To help with this assessment, consider the following information as you put all the pieces together.

Registration for Next Semester

Register as early as possible for the coming semester, so you can increase your chances of taking the classes you want in the instructional delivery format you want them (for example, online or 8-week classes). Registering early also gives you more choices in class schedules (for example, day, evening, or weekend classes). If you haven't yet met with your advisor this semester, you should make an appointment with them as soon as possible. Then register for next semester's classes as soon as you are eligible to.

As you prepare to meet with an advisor and to select a schedule for the next semester, reflect on how well you managed your course load this semester. If you were a full-time student, how well did you balance your schoolwork and your other responsibilities like family and work? Should you take one (or two) fewer classes next semester to avoid burnout? If you were a

STUDENT NOTES

part-time student, could you take more classes next semester to move more quickly through your Plan of Study? Or have you set a pace that will allow you to complete your credential with relatively little stress?

Remember, too, the impact of each course grade on your cumulative GPA. It may be a good idea to take fewer classes, so you can earn higher grades, and maintain (or improve upon) the GPA you will earn this semester.

When you meet with your advisor, take your completed Academic Timeline with you (see page 181). Your advisor is an excellent source of information about pre-requisites and co-requisites. Also, your advisor can give you more information about when your program classes are offered (for example, only in the fall semester or only in the summer term).

New Resources

If this is your first semester at your college, then you may have participated in a new student orientation before you registered for classes. Now that you are a returning student, you will not need to participate in another orientation. Instead, you will meet with your assigned advisor, take advantage of your college's advising and registration center, or meet with a campus transfer counselor. You may also consider seeking the advice of your instructors, who can be excellent advising resources if you have a quick question before or after class. For in-depth questions that involve your personal progress through your program or any analysis of your transcript, always go to your assigned advisor first.

Experimenting with New Learning Strategies

Success by Design and your college success course introduced you to dozens of new learning strategies, such as time-management techniques, note-taking strategies, and study strategies. Most likely, you have not had the opportunity to try all of these strategies this semester. Consider keeping this textbook even after the class ends and referring back to the strategies that you haven't yet tried out.

You may have had the experience of taking fairly easy classes this semester in which you didn't need to use any learning strategies other than those that were already familiar to you. In future semesters, as you take more and more difficult classes, you may want to be able to remember the individual strategies described in this book. Or your first semester of college may have been so difficult and overwhelming that you found two or three techniques that worked for you and then used them over and over. Remember that successful students have a whole repertoire of learning strategies that they can

STUDENT NOTES

apply in different classes and for different purposes. Even after this class ends, you should continue to develop your personal repertoire of effective learning strategies.

Preparing for Transfer and Professional Success

Success by Design and your college success class also introduced you to multiple options for transfer and helped you develop a plan for seamless transfer to a senior institution. As you learned in Chapter 7, community college students should complete a variety of tasks every semester that will prepare them for graduation and transfer. As you near the end of your first semester of community college, now is the time to finalize your decision making about which universities you plan to apply to and what major (and possibly minor) you will pursue. Your Academic Timeline is informed by these decisions and is a document that you can continue to refer to as you progress through your community college credential.

Now that you have made these decisions (or possibly confirmed that the academic and professional goals that you entered the college success class with are, in fact, the ones you want to pursue), prioritize the following tasks for your next semester of enrollment:

- Research what additional credentials you will need to succeed in your career.
- Revise your Academic Timeline (see page 181) based on any new understanding of course availability/scheduling or input from your advisor.
- Look for scholarship information on your community college's website. Many scholarships require that applicants be enrolled in a specific program.
- Meet with your advisor to select your classes for the next semester and to ask any questions you have about completing your credential.
- Research universities that offer your intended major if you plan to transfer. Watch for university recruiters to visit your community college, and visit university campuses during "open houses."
- Keep a list of classes you have completed or review your unofficial transcript.
- Look for extracurricular activities that support your goals.
- Monitor your GPA and notice the impact your grades in a single semester can make on your cumulative GPA.

STUDENT NOTES

Review the Community College Goal Setting Action Plan in Chapter 7 for additional strategies for future semesters.

And if you haven't yet decided on a major or senior institution or future career, prioritize these decisions. As you know from Chapter 5, the degree requirements and articulation agreements vary across the many community college credentials available to you. If you want to matriculate through your community college and university programs close to the traditional four-year timeline, then you need to be strategic about the classes that you take from the start.

If you plan to enter the workforce rather than transfer to a senior institution immediately after graduation, you can also support your professional goals by attending job fairs and researching internship opportunities. Most employers are looking for job applicants who have both education/training as well as work experience. Internships (as well as work-based learning experiences described in Chapter 2) provide students with the work experience that will set them apart from other job seekers.

Reflections on Personal Experiences

Finally, evaluate your experiences this semester by reviewing the following table of characteristics of successful and struggling students. To assess yourself, read the table and highlight or check the characteristics of successful students that you identify with. Then use a different color to highlight or check the characteristics of struggling students that you identify with. Hopefully, at this point in the semester, you identify with more of the characteristics of successful students. As you continue to develop as a student, keep in mind the areas you can improve. Remember, too, that even after this class ends, you will have access to many campus resources to continue developing a growth mindset and successful attitudes and characteristics.

STUDENT NOTES

Successful Students	Struggling Students
❏ Have a clear motivation that guides their goals and provides incentive for their day-to-day work	❏ Don't clearly see the meaning in their actions or current paths ❏ Don't have clear goals and don't know the specific steps to get where they want to go
❏ Know a wide variety of strategies to use and are flexible in selecting the best method for a situation	❏ Have few strategies at their disposal and often feel stuck or discouraged if their methods do not work
❏ Manage their day-to-day tasks while also keeping an eye on the future, prioritizing items by urgency and importance	❏ Respond to the task that elicits the most stress ❏ React rather than plan and manage
❏ Take initiative to complete tasks	❏ Wait to be told to do something
❏ Divide tasks into smaller pieces and establish a plan to accomplish the individual items on time	❏ Feel overwhelmed by the size of the task ❏ Wait until the last minute to start large projects, thereby causing themselves more stress and harming their results
❏ Expect the unexpected to arise	❏ Are derailed by unwanted or unplanned events
❏ Consider new information and other points of view in order to understand	❏ See opposing ideas or different methods as an attack or challenge to their beliefs and preferences ❏ Resist new ideas or methods
❏ Seek support and resources ❏ See assistance as a helpful and valuable tool	❏ Do not seek support ❏ See services as an indication of a personal weakness
❏ Evaluate their learning by thinking about how they learn best ❏ Personalize their learning according to their specific needs, such as selecting their study methods according to their learning style preferences	❏ Do not think about how they learn ❏ Blame the instructor or textbook if they do not do well ❏ Feel their learning is mostly the instructors' responsibility ❏ Assume there's only one way to learn
❏ Expect that they must supplement classroom instruction to learn	❏ Assume that learning occurs only during class

STUDENT NOTES

Successful Students	Struggling Students
❑ Believe they can accomplish their goals	❑ Make self-defeating assumptions, such as feeling inadequate or unworthy ❑ Repeat negative self-statements, such as "I'm a bad tester" or "I can't learn math"
❑ See setbacks, lack of success, or struggles as a challenge that can be overcome	❑ Assume problems cannot be solved ❑ Attribute problems to a personal flaw
❑ Can leave personal situations, emotional stress, or other difficulties at the classroom door in order to focus on learning	❑ Feel controlled by their emotions ❑ Allow their emotions to interfere with their learning
❑ See learning as a life-long adventure ❑ Have a natural curiosity that creates a desire to learn ❑ Find something interesting in nearly everything they encounter	❑ See learning only as a means to an end ❑ Do not value mental play, critical thinking, or other less immediate—but still important—benefits of education
❑ Find a way to connect personally to material	❑ Fail to see connections between the material and daily life

Monkey Business Images/Shutterstock.com

Index

STUDENT NOTES

STUDENT NOTES

STUDENT NOTES

About the Authors

STUDENT NOTES

Gabby McCutchen is the Provost for Arts and Sciences and the Scott Northern Wake Campus at Wake Technical Community College. She previously led the curriculum development for ACA 085, ACA 111, and ACA 122 at Durham Technical Community College. She has taught over 130 sections of ACA since 2006, and has trained over 200 college faculty and staff to teach ACA. Her favorite chapter in *Success by Design* is Chapter 7 Goal Setting.

Erin Riney has taught over 100 sections of ACA and has guided hundreds of students as their academic advisor since 2008. At Durham Technical Community College, Erin led the development of the campus food pantry, student basic needs supports, and Center for College and Community Service. She served as Durham Tech's first Director of Student Engagement and now leads a local nonprofit as Executive Director. Her favorite chapter in *Success by Design* is Chapter 8 Time Management.

STUDENT NOTES